PRESCRIPTION FOR SUCCESS

PRESCRIPTION *for* SUCCESS

The Rexall Showcase International Story and What It Means to You

PRIMA PUBLISHING

PRIMA PUBLISHING and colophon are registered trademarks of Prima Communications, Inc.

The stories discussed herein should not be construed as any guarantee or warranty of financial success or performance. Financial investments and business ventures are inherently risky. Therefore, while the author and publisher hope readers enjoy this book, they cannot be responsible for any liability, loss or risk, direct or indirect, resulting from the use or application of any of the contents of this book.

Library of Congress Cataloging-in-Publication Data

Robinson, James W.
    Prescription for success: The Rexall Showcase International story and what it means to you / James W. Robinson.
      p.   cm.
    Includes index.
    ISBN 0-7615-1981-5
    1. Rexall Sundown—History.   2. Drugstores—United States—History.
3. Pharmaceutical industry—United States—History.   4. Businessmen—United
States—Biography.   I. Title.
HD9666.9.R43R63   1999
381'.456151'0973—dc21   98-56030
                                                          CIP

99 00 01 02 HH 10 9 8 7 6 5 4 3 2 1
Printed in the United States of America

How to Order
Single copies may be ordered from Prima Publishing, P.O. Box 1260BK, Rocklin, CA 95677; telephone (916) 632-4400. Quantity discounts are also available. On your letterhead, include information concerning the intended use of the books and the number of books you wish to purchase.

Visit us online at www.primalife.com

Contents

Foreword

ANYONE THAT SPENDS any time around the executives or the distributor leaders of Rexall Showcase International quickly comes to understand that one commodity we never seem to be short of is our passion and commitment to the business. We've made some mistakes since the founding of this, the network marketing division of Rexall Sundown some nine years ago—and undoubtedly we'll make a few more. But our belief in the products and the business opportunity we offer is so strong that we are absolutely convinced that Rexall Showcase International's future will be defined by rapid global growth and it is our objective to touch thousands, even millions, of lives with our products and business opportunities.

When veteran author Jim Robinson visited us at our Boca Raton, Florida, headquarters in the Fall of 1998 and told us that he wanted to write an entire book about our company and the societal trends we're tapping into, it marked a gratifying and important milestone we had not expected to achieve so soon. After all, many network marketing companies are bigger and have been around longer. Some are well-established in dozens of countries and have, over time, accumulated a larger treasure chest of dramatic distributor stories.

But as Jim notes early on, what is really significant about Rexall Showcase International is not how big it is today but how big it has the potential to be.

America's population is aging, leading many to seek natural health products and remedies in order to maintain a fit, healthy lifestyle well into their golden years.

America's economy is strong, but changes in the corporate sector and its past tradition of secure lifetime employment are leading many to low-cost forms of entrepreneurship and the development of alternative streams of income.

And in the face of an aging population and a shrinking workforce, government's ability to maintain the social safety net of programs like Social Security and Medicare has been called into serious question. Particularly among the boomer generation, this concern has intensified interest in healthier lifestyles and more secure finances.

Finally, while conventional medical science has produced virtually miraculous improvements in health and longevity during this century, its limitations due to both cost and science are becoming increasingly apparent. Consumers and a growing number of medical professionals are looking for products and protocols that give much greater prominence to the role of prevention in health care.

These trends are more than just national developments, they are global phenomena—and Rexall Showcase International is positioned to address, propel, and benefit from every single one of them.

That's why we are so confident that Rexall Showcase International, backed by a strong, publicly traded parent company and an outstanding distributor force, will enjoy a bright and prosperous future.

Jim Robinson is the ideal person to tell this story, having written two previous successful books on the network marketing industry as well as several others on business, politics, and communications. His words and views are his own. This is an independently published book, and there is no business relationship between our company, Prima Publishing, or the author himself.

Most important of all, Jim has recognized that it is our distributor leaders who really define the quality and character of our company. At its essence, this is a book about people, not about products or a corporation. We are so pleased and proud that many of the individual men and women who have poured their heart and soul into RSI have received in this book the recognition they richly deserve.

Our vision is to build a global company that makes a positive difference in the health and finances of millions of people all around the world. In *Prescription for Success,* you will discover how we are doing that and how you can be a part of this exciting adventure.

—DAMON DeSANTIS, President,
Rexall Sundown

—DAVID SCHOFIELD, President,
Rexall Showcase International

Introduction

PRESCRIPTION FOR SUCCESS is the third book I have written focusing on the interesting, controversial, and somewhat mysterious industry called network (or multilevel) marketing. My 1996 book on Amway, *Empire of Freedom*, attempted to update and refresh a story told many times. I was particularly intrigued by the fact that in the 1990s Amway was seeing most of its growth come from outside the United States. Some comfortable and complacent Americans tended to disparage the idea of selling and to dismiss the fervent enthusiasm of Amway practitioners. But the fall of the Communist empire and the fresh embrace of market principles throughout the Third World unleashed an explosion of budding entrepreneurship that has reshaped Amway even while being shaped by Amway. Today, like McDonald's and other such quintessentially American companies, Amway has found that revenues from its international operations exceed domestic revenues.

The globalization of network marketing companies like Amway has not been without bumps. In early 1998, the Chinese government suddenly announced it was shutting down multilevel marketing companies in China, despite the hundreds of millions of investment dollars poured into the country by Amway and others. Officials cited the excesses and corruption of some practitioners. No doubt the freewheeling Chinese economic climate did give rise to some unscrupulous domestic operators—but to paint reputable U.S. companies with the same brush was grossly unfair. The U.S. Chamber of Commerce, the Direct Selling Association, and the United States Trade Representative all pushed the Chinese hard on this point. By the summer of 1998, companies such as Amway and

Avon had resumed operations, although sharp restrictions on the ability to attract new distributors remained.

In June 1998, I attended a number of high-level government meetings in Hong Kong with Amway President, Steve Van Andel. Hong Kong is a big market for the company and is now, of course, firmly part of China once again. As I watched this second-generation Amway leader press the case for the company in such high-powered sophisticated settings, I was struck by the new demands and realities of what is in its heart and soul an entrepreneurial, people-oriented business. Network marketing is not just about rallies and speeches or sales presentations to neighbors and relatives. In order to provide the average person with a successful, low-cost mom-and-pop business opportunity, the leaders of these companies must be highly sophisticated businesspeople, moving smoothly in the world of international capitals, financial markets, and government leadership.

In 1997, I followed *Empire of Freedom* with *The Excel Phenomenon,* the story of an upstart Dallas-based long-distance reseller that set the telecommunications industry on its ear by cracking a fiercely competitive market without advertising or an in-house sales force. Whereas in the Amway story, I saw the internationalization of American network marketing as a major trend, with Excel, my goal was to document the industry's serious foray into the world of services. After all, we are developing into a service economy. The deregulation of basic services such as telecommunications and electricity and the loosening of the rules of engagement in the legal, accounting, and financial-service arenas have spawned a frantic contest to retain and gain customers. Smart companies, old and new, are coming to realize that relationship selling must be an important component of their marketing strategy.

That's why, in 1998, the Canadian communications giant, Teleglobe, merged with Excel in a deal that permits Excel to retain its unique identity and corporate structure but nonetheless marries it to a major international player. Some Excel distributors understandably questioned what the move meant to them. The smart ones will come to see the clear-eyed strategy behind it: The reason a company like Teleglobe would pay such a handsome sum for Excel has nothing to do with the buildings, the switches, or even the quality management. Teleglobe bought Excel to gain access to Excel's highly motivated distributor force and the loyal customer base these distributors have acquired. They are not about to "kill the goose that laid the golden egg." For founder Kenny Troutt and Excel distributors, the merger gives them a chance to jump-start their way into the lucrative international telecommunications market. As the world market follows the U.S. lead in deregulating and privatizing phone companies, that is where the action is going to be.

For months following the success of *The Excel Phenomenon,* my publisher Ben Dominitz and I had many discussions about which company we might want to feature next. None jumped out at us. Having written about the "grand old lady" of network marketing, Amway, and then about Excel—a company that had already blasted off into the big time with revenues over $1 billion when we started and over $2 billion today—we hoped to spot a young company whose glory days were all ahead of it. Was there such a company in the network marketing field, we wondered, whose products and business opportunity were so in tune with emerging trends in our society and economy that it would be destined for huge growth and success? After all, if we could find it, we'd look pretty smart writing about it now.

Soon after these conversations, I was exchanging e-mail messages with an old friend, Jon Kaji, who runs California's Trade and Investment Office in Tokyo—an office I helped establish in the mid-1980s when I worked for former governor George Deukmejian. Jon told me that in the midst of Japan's growing economic crisis, a number of U.S.-based network marketing companies had targeted the world's second largest economy as a prime area of opportunity. As the traditional lifetime employment pact Japanese workers had enjoyed with the nation's big companies crumbled, the

Japanese penchant for relationship selling and tendency to "follow the pack" attracted these companies, he said. One making a particularly big splash, even though it had yet to even announce its plans to open operations in Japan, was Rexall Showcase International.

"Rexall®?" I asked. "You mean those old drug stores? What do drug stores have to do with network marketing?" Jon then explained that the familiar and trusted Rexall brand name had now metamorphosed into a highly entrepreneurial network marketing arm of a bigger company that sold preventative health care products and natural remedies directly to consumers through multilevel marketing. Understanding that such approaches to health maintenance are firmly rooted and highly respected in Asian cultures, Jon said, "Believe me, this company is going to be really big in Japan and especially with all the Asian Americans in the United States. If you're looking for the subject of your next book, this is it."

Understand that I first met John Kaji when he came to me in the governor's office in Sacramento fourteen years ago as a plucky Japanese-American entrepreneur with a harebrained scheme to sell California rice to the Japanese. Never mind that at the time the Japanese government had totally banned rice imports to protect their domestic crop. Jon nonetheless had figured out a way to attractively package boxes of "gift" rice from California and sell them in airport duty-free shops; the rice could then be legally brought into Japan as "souvenirs." The gift boxes were a hit. So when Jon gives me a business assessment like the one he offered about Rexall Showcase International, I tend to listen carefully.

Still knowing nothing of substance about the company, I was particularly impressed by the buzz that Rexall Showcase International had already created in Japan. When people start talking about a new book, movie, product, or business before it is even an official part of the market, that says something. Clearly, many Japanese Americans had already shared the news about the Rexall Showcase International products and business opportunities with family and friends in Japan and had talked up a possible opening of operations there months before the company announced it. (Rexall Showcase International's Japan operations will officially commence in Spring 1999.) Several unauthorized books had even appeared and were being eagerly devoured by the voracious Japanese reading public. Please forgive me, but as a writer hearing *that* news, I began to get *really* interested.

So that I could learn more, Jon put me in touch with a successful Rexall Showcase International distributor from Garden Grove, California, who had introduced him to the business. Her persistence, enthusiasm, and selling skills pushed me forward to learn more. She arranged a private meeting during Rexall Showcase International's August 1998 annual convention in Long Beach with Todd Smith, one of the top three distributor leaders in the business. Anyone who knows Todd—and everyone involved in the Rexall Showcase International business does—will understand what I mean when I say that once he was through with me, there wasn't any question that my new book would be about Rexall Showcase International.

But first, just like many serious business professionals have done before starting their Rexall Showcase International distributorships, I did my "due diligence." I checked the company out. I visited the corporate headquarters, met with senior management, reviewed independent analyses of the company and its products, and talked to many experts in and out of the direct selling industry.

What I found in the sun-kissed coastal community of Boca Raton, Florida, an hour north of Miami, was a team of entrepreneurs who has reached into the past and future to build a company that is turning traditional approaches to business and health on their head. The company is called Rexall Sundown, and its network marketing arm is called Rexall Showcase International (RSI).

Founded in 1976 by a restless drug store manager named Carl DeSantis, the enterprise began inauspiciously enough. With the aid of a pharmacist friend, DeSantis developed and sold a cheaper alternative to expensive suntan and sunburn-relief lotions in his Miami

Beach drug store to fair-skinned "snowbirds" from up north. Soon after, he spotted the growing interest in vitamins and sold his own through mail order—propelled by ads in the *National Enquirer*. In 1986, DeSantis acquired the revered Rexall name and blended together an old-fashioned brand—one that had come to symbolize quality and trustworthiness for generations of Americans—with pioneering products in preventative health care and a business approach that is dramatically transforming the way we buy and sell—network marketing.

Twenty-two years later, Rexall Sundown had become a market pacesetter—developing, manufacturing, marketing, and selling vitamins, herbals, nutritional supplements, and consumer products through retailers, mail order, and a strong and growing team of independent representatives who market specially branded products and convince others to do the same.

I liked what I heard and learned about Rexall Showcase International; and the result, you will find, is a positive portrayal of a business opportunity and a company that I believe is poised for dramatic and profitable growth.

I want to emphasize that point because, despite the commercial success of my previous books in this field, some journalistic reviewers don't like my approach. They equate a positive book with a whitewash. Let me explain that I have no desire to be a muckraking journalist. Some go looking for a scandal to write about and don't start writing until they find it. There's certainly a place for that kind of exposé. We need people to blow the whistle on the scams and the boondoggles afflicting many of society's institutions.

My approach is in fact the mirror-opposite of theirs. I go looking for something positive to write about and don't start writing until I *find* it. My goal is to bring you word of a new and different kind of health and business opportunity, inform you about how others have capitalized on that opportunity, and let you judge whether it is one you wish to personally pursue.

No company is perfect—and that includes Rexall Showcase International. Every company makes mistakes—and that includes Rexall Showcase International. All companies are in it for the money—and that includes Rexall Showcase International. But only a few companies offer the right products at the perfect time in the ideal market and sell them through the most powerful distribution system ever devised—and Rexall Showcase International is one of those companies.

I have formed this judgment independently. I am not part of the Rexall Showcase International business. I don't distribute products or own stock in the company. Neither Prima Publishing nor I have received any compensation from the company for producing *Prescription for Success.*

Yet we have received helpful cooperation from the company's executives, staff, and leading distributors. Many gave me their time, insights, and guidance as I tried to capture the qualities that are making Rexall Showcase International a successful company, especially: Rexall Sundown founder and Chairman Carl DeSantis; Damon DeSantis, President of Rexall Sundown; Dave Schofield, President of Rexall Showcase International; and Rexall Showcase International's 10-member Presidential Board of Advisors, the company's leading distributors.

At Prima, which has published all of my work to date, I am truly grateful to Susan Silva, Andrew Mitchell, Linda Weidemann, and Joan Pendleton for their tremendous efforts to produce this work under such tight time constraints. Tom Rajaratnam provided thorough and accurate research support. Prima founder and president Ben Dominitz has been a supportive friend and a great teacher, and each time he puts his faith in me, I realize anew that I will never be able to repay all he has done for me. Tom Donohue, my boss and mentor, who heads the United States Chamber of Commerce, has been extremely supportive and patient—and I thank him for that. My Chamber colleagues Rita Bond and Suzie Matthews have been particularly helpful. Speaking of the Chamber, I must point out that the views expressed or represented in this book are my own and not necessarily those of the Chamber or its members. Finally, my friend Duc Huu Nguyen has kept me on deadline and in reasonably sane spirits throughout the agony and ecstasy known as writing with his steady support and loyal friendship.

A word about the term used to describe Rexall Showcase International is in order at the outset. The company and its participants refer to themselves as a *network marketing company* and so do I. This description is often used interchangeably with the term *multilevel marketing (MLM)* and indicates a business approach that uses independent distributors not only to sell a company's products and services directly to consumers, but also to recruit and help others do the same. Participants derive income from both their own sales and the sales of those they recruit.

Network marketing is the preferred term today because it more accurately describes the nature of this activity in the information age and the world economy, where the global breadth of a distributor organization becomes as important as the depth. And because the term *multilevel marketing* has taken on negative connotations in many quarters, particularly among higher-educated, upscale professionals, *network marketing* is seen as a more positive moniker. After all, the white-collar baby-boomer generation brought the whole concept of "networking" into vogue.

Whether it is called network or multilevel marketing, this business sector is part of a broader and highly significant industry known as direct selling. Direct selling companies move products from the manufacturer directly to the consumer, bypassing intermediaries such as retail outlets and often skipping expensive marketing steps such as big advertising campaigns. A direct selling company is not necessarily a network marketing company. In many direct selling businesses, independent salespeople put all their effort into and make all their profit from buying product at wholesale and selling it at retail; in network marketing, entrepreneurs divide their time between product sales and recruiting distributors.

Finally, let me address at the very beginning one of many reasons why Rexall Showcase International is stirring such interest and even passion in the business and medical worlds. In short, its core products directly impact the area of our lives that is so personal, so important, and so central to everything we do, hope for, and plan—our health. Tom Donohue is right when he points out that no topic produces such intense emotion and debate as the whole subject of health care. We heap on to the health care system incredible expectations and, ultimately, impossible demands. As Tom says, "None of us want to get sick and none of us want to die, but seven out of seven of us will!"

So touchy and emotional is the subject of health and the manner in which we care for ourselves and our families that we bombard the system with contradictory complaints, demands, pleas, and expectations.

Most of us like to say, "Nothing is more important than health." Under the circumstances, you would think we'd be willing to pay for it or at least be willing to abide by a set of rules and procedures to keep the cost of health care down and access to it high. Instead, we blame politicians or health care plans that make us pay even marginal deductibles or premium increases or who come up with commonsense restrictions to avoid waste.

Have you ever felt the way I have when I leave the doctor's or dentist's office bad-mouthing my health care plan because it wouldn't let me leave without paying a twenty-dollar co-payment? Did I curse the movie theater or restaurant with equal gusto when I dropped twenty dollars or more there? Wait a second, isn't good health supposed to be more important than money, movies, or restaurants?

We complain, often with justification, about health care that has grown increasingly impersonal, treating doctors like assembly-line workers and patients like the next widget coming down the conveyor belt. Yet this flawed system has come about in large measure as a response to the flawed behavior of both patients and doctors. Equipped with generous, no-questions-asked point-of-service health insurance, many of us started running off to the doctor at the onset of the slightest sniffle. Many doctors got the joke too. We've all seen it—doctors triple-booking appointments, depositing patients in multiple examining rooms, shuttling to and fro and then billing our insurance companies a king's ransom for each "visit." It's an assembly line too, but with a difference—in that case the doctor got to keep most of the money.

We complain that the system is not keeping us well and is too expensive. Yet how many of us drive up those expenses by failing to take care of ourselves? Look around you the next time you're standing in a public place anywhere in America. How many people are overweight? How many obviously don't exercise at all? Are you one of them? How many of us keep putting off our physical and dental exams? How many avoid self-testing for lumps, refuse prostate exams and pap smears, fail to get our blood pressure and cholesterol checked, or ignore symptoms in the hope that "what we don't know won't hurt us"? Are you one of them?

The bottom line is that we spend a greater share of our national wealth on health care than does any other advanced country in the world. We probably have more unhappy patients than does any other country in the world. And we have more uninsured people than does any other industrialized modern society in the world. No one can agree on how to fix the problem or even whose fault it is.

Most of us also look at the health care system through the highly personal lens of our own good and bad experiences with it. Many of us harbor secret resentments toward a doctor, a hospital, an insurance company, or a pharmaceutical manufacturer for not taking that one action that could have saved a loved one's life. Fair or unfair—probably mostly unfair—we all make those judgments, and they are locked in our minds forever. Yet at the same time, many can recall a singular act of skill or courage, a moment of kindness, or new medical discoveries that helped a loved one or us get well.

I have had both experiences in my life. Viscerally, and admittedly without evidence or insight, I blame the health care system for the untimely death of my mother from cancer at age 45. But I also credit that same system for astonishing breakthroughs that have helped a close friend beat incredible odds in his fight against a serious illness. I marvel at a system that can accomplish such a feat.

So rattling around in my own head are an incompatible collection of health care heroes and villains. Maybe the same is true for you. It's important to understand that—as we discuss in this book—a new movement is rapidly emerging, an approach to care that focuses on prevention before we get sick rather than on intervention after we get sick.

Some are turning to preventative care because they are genuinely excited by it; others because they want to have as little contact as possible with the conventional health care system they are unhappy with and want to avoid. Rexall Showcase International is sitting right at the center of what is and will be a profound and growing movement toward preventative care and total lifestyle management. In sharing this enthusiastic approach to health with you, I do not intend to demean the need for and the incredible contributions of traditional health care. It is fashionable today to trash the HMOs, the insurance companies, and the drug companies. With all their flaws, they still all play an important role in delivering care and cures, while trying to operate in an environment of intense emotion and high expectation that has come to define the subject of health.

The bottom line is simple: Any society that in the course of a single century can increase average life expectancy thirty years, as we have done in this country, must be doing something right. But the economic and health care system that jointly delivered that miracle is changing. That's because we are changing and the world is changing. The new millennium calls for new approaches to business and entrepreneurship and to lifestyle and health care. That's what *Prescription for Success: The Rexall Showcase International Story and What It Means to You* is all about.

PRESCRIPTION FOR SUCCESS

CHAPTER ONE

Rx for Success

The market forces propelling the Rexall group of companies forward can be simply explained: nearly one-seventh of the United States of America's $12 trillion economy is consumed by health care. This share can only grow as our life spans lengthen and as care and cures become more sophisticated and more expensive.

In fact, in no other industry can analysts look forward and see such unlimited demand and unmatched capacity for growth. The question facing entrepreneurs seeking the opportunities of the future is this: Do you want to be one of the overwhelming majority of users and consumers who pay ever greater shares of their wealth into the health care system?

Or do you want to become a beneficiary of that system, capitalizing on this exploding sector and helping yourselves and others in the process to better health and better finances?

That's the proposition put forward by Rexall Sundown and what Todd Smith calls its entrepreneurial arm, Rexall Showcase International—and in just eight years, tens of thousands of active

1

independent distributors from all around the world have already embraced that proposition. With minimal up-front cost and an initial time investment of a few hours a week, they are building their own home-based businesses with a growing line of innovative health care products that can't be purchased in stores and that address our most profound health and lifestyle concerns: high cholesterol, cardiovascular health, breast and prostate cancer, weight management, and the aging process.

The example set by Todd Smith is highly illustrative of the mark this relatively young company is making on America's professional and entrepreneurial ranks.

Todd is one of Rexall Showcase International's top three performing independent distributors, along with Randy Schroeder and Stewart Hughes. We will hear from these three often and draw upon their experiences throughout this book, for together, they are credited by both the corporation and the distributor force for sparking much of the growth and momentum Rexall Showcase International enjoys today. They are looked upon as inspirational role models by many fledgling distributors in and out of their own organizations—although they consider themselves simply representative of the kind of successful but dissatisfied professional who finds Rexall Showcase International an attractive way to generate and diversify income while freeing up quality time to spend with family.

In Todd Smith's case, this native of Elgin, Illinois plunged right into the working world upon graduating from high school and soon found himself earning a degree from the "School of Hard Knocks."

"In the summer of 1981, I got a job digging ditches and laying cable for the local cable TV company," Todd recalls. "I got laid off on my birthday! Then at Christmas time I got a temporary job with UPS to help handle the holiday rush. Guess what happened to me after Christmas?"

Laid off from two jobs in six months, Todd decided that entrepreneurship—being his own boss—had to be his ticket to success.

He moved to Chicago at the urging of his older brother and started a silkscreen printing business that sold designer T-shirts, caps, and other items. "We started with a $3,000 investment and within four and a half years, we did a million dollars' worth of business and employed twenty-five people," explains Todd. It was an important learning experience for a young man still in his early twenties. "Sure I was my own boss," he points out, "but I was working ninety hours a week and pulling just $35,000 a year in personal income out of the business."

So at age twenty-three, Todd started selling real estate. And he wasn't just a success, he was a spectacular success, becoming the second-highest-producing real estate agent in Illinois with an annual income of more than $400,000 in his peak year by the end of the 1980s.

But with a young and growing family—Todd and his wife Joy today have four young children from the ages of three to twelve—the super motivator found himself questioning the meaning of success. "I just got burned out," Todd explains. "I couldn't take my wife out on a date on a Friday night without the pager going off ten times. I'd come out of church on Sunday and there'd be fifteen messages on my answering service. In the meantime, real estate was changing. Commissions went down a point, then another point, then down again.

"I finally reached a point where I made a decision. This was not what I wanted to do for the rest of my life. I wanted something different."

Although Todd Smith's formal education does not include college, he has always been a sharp student of the times and the trends, continually soaking up information from all sources on business opportunities and economic conditions. "I was very methodical about my search for a new venture," he reports. "I took out a yellow legal pad and listed everything I learned and everything I wanted from a business.

"I wanted something I could start part-time, something that could be built while maintaining my real estate income. I wanted to be in business for myself but be backed by strong products and a strong infrastructure. Where was this ideal business? I knew I would find it somewhere."

One day Todd saw an ad in *Business Opportunities* magazine that intrigued him. "It hit all the hot buttons," he remembers. But when he found out it was to start a network marketing distributorship for Nu Skin Enterprises, Inc., Todd was skeptical and disappointed. While he was on his way to meet his potential sponsor he popped a cassette he had been meaning to listen to into the car's tape player. "It was Brian Tracy's 'How to Get Rich in America,'" Todd recalls. "And it was such a fortuitous coincidence because on that tape, Brian Tracy said that 85 percent of what anyone needs to know about running a successful, profitable business in America, they could learn from network marketing.

"That caused me to be a lot more open-minded about network marketing and it helped me to understand the power of generating a leveraged income, that it could be done part-time, and that I could use all my contacts in real estate to full advantage. And I learned it was a portable business which was vitally important because we had already decided we wanted to move to Florida and focus on our family's quality of life."

Todd began his Nu Skin distributorship in May 1990 and within four months built an organization of more than 1,600 distributors and generated $200,000 in sales volume. His first check after four months of part-time effort was for $31,600.

What Todd and other Rexall Showcase International "stars" like Randy Schroeder and Stewart Hughes, who also began their network marketing careers with Nu Skin, did not and probably could not foresee was how a spate of bad publicity and a poor compensation plan could impact a distributor network, which after all is built on volunteerism. That's what happened to Nu Skin as the national media and a state attorney general teamed up to use the company as exhibit A in a new broadside against multilevel marketing. The bad publicity caused Todd and others to lose many of the distributors they had enlisted. Although they still have kind words for the company and its products, Todd for one believes that success in network marketing has to be built around the success of the part-time distributor. At the time, he didn't see this quality in Nu Skin. "Otherwise the company collapses from the bottom up," Todd says.

Nu Skin was not the only company whose network marketing plan was hitting bumps in the road. Around the same time, in 1990, Rexall Sundown couldn't even get into first gear with its new network marketing division called Rexall Showcase International. "There is in this industry a kind of roving band of distributors—the network marketing junkies we call them—who move from company to company, product to product, looking for a fast buck. At the beginning, Rexall Showcase International attracted some of these folks and ran into some serious problems," Todd explains. "After a year in operation the company was selling less than $200,000 a month in product through network marketing."

That figure changed fast when Todd, Randy Schroeder, and Stewart Hughes made the transition from Nu Skin to Rexall Showcase International in 1991. In just his second month as a single Rexall Showcase International distributor, Todd Smith matched and then exceeded what had been the entire division's monthly sales volume.

Rexall Showcase International President Dave Schofield pulls no punches: "Todd, Randy, and Stewart were the key leaders who came to the company in our time of need. It was their leadership that turned around Rexall Showcase International's initial poor performance."

Flash forward to 1998. Todd earned more than $2.3 million from Rexall Showcase International that year—a total of $9.8 million in seven years. "I did that by personally recruiting just forty-four people—that averages less than one a month for those seven years," Todd emphasizes. "But those forty-four people multiplied themselves into an organization consisting of thousands of distributors in fifty states and several countries. They work in a legitimate network marketing business backed by a solid parent company. They don't have to do large sales presentations or accumulate large inventories of product.

"As for myself, I have zero stress. My commute to work is however many steps it takes to walk from the bedroom to the office in my home. And the way I look at it, I'm really in two businesses. One is transforming the health, longevity, and vitality of people through unique products that work. And the other is transforming the finances and lifestyles of ambitious people through a unique business opportunity."

Indeed, the company's management team working in tandem with distributor leaders such as Todd have strategically positioned the company at the intersection of the defining economic, health, demographic, social, and technological problems and trends of our time:

- Longer life spans and a decline in birthrates in the United States, Japan, and Western Europe have created tremendous strains on these societies. There are fewer and fewer workers to support each retiree. In the United States, by the year 2020, the ratio of workers to retirees will be down to less than 2 to 1.

  As people live longer, their focus has shifted from the length of life to the quality of life. This changing focus has manifested itself in many ways, from booming fitness, leisure, and wellness industries to right-to-die and physician-assisted suicide movements in many states.

  Alternative health care is already an $18 billion business in the United States—Rexall Showcase International stands at the center of that movement.

- Traditional medical science, which seems to be able to deliver just about everything *except* what people really want— eternal life—is also subject to severe strain and serious ethical questions. How far and to what expense should it go to keep the aged alive those extra months or years? To what extent should genetic engineering be employed to wipe away all health defects? Will those advances lead to human cloning and "designer babies"? How much longer will we allow class-action lawsuits and fear of liability to impede developments and discoveries?

The same strains are testing the health care delivery system. Health care already consumes 15 percent of the U.S. economy, yet millions don't even have basic health care coverage, and the caregivers are increasingly being turned into accountants and time-clock punchers. Class-action lawsuits and the fear of liability keep lifesaving drugs off the marketplace and drive doctors from the profession.

The deadening of the soul of today's health-care system has led many respected health-care professionals out of traditional medical careers to Rexall Showcase International, where they find they can become caregivers once again.

• On the economic front, the very tools and principles of business organization that have made modern societies so productive help feed a sense of alienation and lack of individual control over one's financial destiny. The global economic meltdown, spreading like a contagion to three continents so far, triggers layoffs, shutdowns, and loss of investments in the United States, underscoring the individual's loss of economic control. A bank goes bust in Indonesia, and within months, workers are laid off in a microchip plant in California. The rise of flextime, consulting, and telecommuting, made possible by information technology, works very well for some individuals but also cuts people off from a sense of community, plunging many into a stultifying suburban isolation.

As a result of the economic situation, highly successful professionals, hitherto underrepresented in network marketing,

*seize the business opportunity offered by Rexall Showcase
International—not just for income security, but also for personal growth and the fulfillment that comes from becoming
part of something larger than themselves.*

Certainly one of the most noteworthy achievements in the
twentieth century has been the extraordinary expansion of life for
the average American—from just forty-eight years in 1900 to
nearly seventy-eight years today. Much of the credit has to go to
traditional medical science and the triumph of an economic system
that, fueled by breathtaking developments in technology, transportation, management, and communications, raised living standards almost everywhere around the globe.

A company tracing its roots back to 1903 was part and parcel
of that progress. A young man named Louis Liggett, who by age
twenty-six had already organized a powerful national association of
America's druggists, was riding on a train to Seattle when he first
dreamed of the idea of Rexall drug stores. A forerunner to franchising, Rexall gave hard-working families a chance to own their own
business but at the same time be part of a larger organization with a
respected name. In thousands of communities, it gave Americans a
trusted corner drug store and even a place to socialize.

But, as we begin the twenty-first century, the demographic,
economic, technological, and workplace trends we've looked at are
dramatically reshaping our society and our individual lives. A company positioned to shape and steer these trends, rather than simply
surrender to them, stands to be highly profitable in this complex
environment. While most people, especially those we elect to public office, have buried their heads in the sand, content to pass the
effects of a changing society on to future generations, others are
changing their focus from an approach to health that simply seeks
to extend life to an approach that improves the quality of life. Still
others are looking for new forms of entrepreneurship that take full
advantage of technology while restoring a sense of family and com-

munity—entrepreneurship that is spurred by rapid change and a sense of adventure, but nonetheless delivers secure ongoing streams of income no longer found in the traditional business world. The leaders and independent distributors of Rexall Showcase International count themselves among these embracers of change.

By staying in touch with—even ahead of—these trends, Rexall Sundown and Rexall Showcase International have, in a short period of time, established impressive growth trendlines. The company ended the 1998 fiscal year with sales of $530.7 million, up 83 percent from 1996 sales of $290.6 million. Rexall Sundown's Chief Executive Officer, Chris Nast, observes: "We continue to achieve a substantially higher sales growth rate compared to the overall nutritional industry. I think it's due to our continued success at gaining new distribution, broadening distribution within our existing accounts, expanding our direct-sales distributor base, and introducing new science-based products." This performance led *Fortune* magazine in September 1998 to name Rexall Sundown one of the "100 Fastest Growing Companies in America"—the twenty-eighth fastest-growing company nationwide and number two in Florida.

Equally impressive is the growth registered by Rexall Showcase International as well as its rapidly expanding reach around the globe. From a mere $1 million in sales in its first year (1990), the network marketing division reached $160 million in 1998, a 51 percent increase over the prior year. In addition to the United States, Rexall Showcase International operates in Hong Kong, Korea, Mexico, and Taiwan, and will enter the lucrative Japanese market in Spring 1999.

Many companies—in and out of the health and network marketing fields—are bigger. A few are even growing faster. I have chosen to write about Rexall Showcase International not because of how big it is, but because of how big I believe it is going to be. Based on my research, I have delineated twelve key reasons why Rexall Showcase International will experience rapid growth and its participants enjoy substantial profits beginning now and for the foreseeable future:

Reason One—The Preventative Health Care Boom: As baby boomers age and retire and as standard medical practices become increasingly overburdened with cost and liability, the demand for alternatives focusing on fitness, wellness, and prevention will explode. Americans already spend anywhere from $18 to $27 billion annually on alternative medicine, $8 to $10 billion on vitamins (including herbals), and billions more on diet and fitness programs. Preventative health care will be the buzzword of the first decade of the new century—and Rexall Showcase International is positioned to be a market leader.

Reason Two—Proven Products: Any network marketing company's long-term prospects for success depend on a product line that both distributors and customers trust and are excited about. The company offers more than 100 exclusive products which are offered only through the independent distributors, including natural health and traditional remedies as well as nutritional products and homeopathic medicines. All of the products provided by Rexall Showcase International are exclusively formulated and some, like Bios Life®, are protected by U.S. patents for their proven ability to lower cholesterol and are endorsed and used by thousands of doctors nationwide.

Reason Three—A Great Brand Name: Rexall is one of the most recognized brand names to Americans, middle-aged or older, and has come to symbolize trustworthiness and quality for generations. Many successful Rexall Showcase International distributors report that it was the Rexall name that helped them overcome their initial skepticism about joining a network marketing company. And it makes it far easier to introduce the products and business to others.

Reason Four—A Strong Parent Company: Rexall Sundown is a publicly held corporation that is financially strong with no long-term debt and a focus on global growth. Its Boca Raton headquarters includes a 20-acre corporate campus with over 700,000-square feet dedicated to manufacturing, packaging, and distribution, producing over 500 million tablets, capsules, and softgels per month. The company has over 1,200 employees and over 1,000 products that it sells in more than 50 countries. Among the products are Sundown Vitamins®, the largest-selling vitamin brand in the United States.

Reason Five—A Lucrative Business Opportunity: Many direct selling companies claim they have the best marketing plan for distributors. Rexall Showcase International executives believe the proof is in the percentage of each sales dollar that ends up in the hands of the distributor. Rexall Showcase International ranks very high in this regard and offers several different ways to derive income—including stock options and stock purchases in the parent company.

Reason Six—The Quality and Caliber of the Distributor Force: The company's tens of thousands of active distributors shatter the stereotype of the direct selling industry as a whole. Most are highly educated, high-income professionals. Close to 30 percent come from the health care field.

Reason Seven—An Online, Global Vision: Rexall Showcase International is implementing an aggressive international expansion plan, which will be highlighted by its opening in Japan in the Spring of 1999—thereby positioning itself to capitalize on the huge growth of direct selling businesses around the globe. The company is also embracing technology as a means to ease recruiting as well as ordering and delivery of products. A distributor's customers can use the telephone or the Internet to place orders directly with the company 24 hours each day, seven days per week, and distributors are automatically credited.

Reason Eight—Meets the Needs of an Aging Population: Fifty thousand of the 76 million baby boomers turn 50 every day. By the year 2020, the percentage of the U.S. population aged 55–64 will double. Similar trends are changing Japanese and European societies as well. Rexall Showcase International and its products are ideally positioned to capture a substantial share of these health- and wellness-oriented consumers.

Reason Nine—Offers an Appealing Health Care Alternative for Doctors and Patients: Today's health care delivery system has grown cold and impersonal. Patients feel as if they are getting assembly-line care, and many doctors feel more like accountants and employees than they do caregivers. Rexall Showcase International has attracted tens of thousands of doctors to the business, giving them and their patients a range of products and procedures that focus on what is supposed to be the first task of medicine—keeping people well.

Reason Ten—Answers Economic Uncertainty with Opportunity and Security: The global economic crisis has reminded many that, even in good times, the individual who is tied to the fortunes of a single company, industry, or salary is perpetually at risk. Rexall Showcase International addresses this concern by offering busy professionals an opportunity to maintain their current career while developing significant alternative streams of long-term income.

Reason Eleven—Addresses the Needs of Families and Time-Strapped Professionals: Even those who succeed economically are finding that this success comes at a heavy cost. More time is spent on business travel and commuting and less with family and community. Companies like Rexall Showcase International that offer participants a chance to build successful home-based businesses are finding that they can attract top-caliber and highly motivated professionals to their ranks.

Reason Twelve—Embraces the New Economy, Network Marketing: The way we buy and sell things is changing quickly. Companies are establishing multiple distribution channels to reach consumers. Rexall Sundown spotted this trend eight years ago and established the Rexall Showcase International network marketing division, which moves products from the manufacturer directly to the consumer by inviting individuals to set up their own independent distributorships under the company rubric and convince others to do the same. An estimated thirty-six million people worldwide now participate in this kind of business and the numbers in the coming years will explode. Companies who ignore this method of attracting loyal customers and sales agents do so at great risk to their long-term profitability.

In the ensuing chapters, I touch upon each of the twelve reasons why I believe Rexall Showcase International and the family of companies it represents in the network marketing world are prepared and positioned for phenomenal growth. Specifically, Chapters 2–4 will reveal how this interesting company got its start; explain how it changed dramatically over the years; portray the family, the leaders, and the vision behind Rexall Showcase International; and describe the products and the business plan that are capturing the allegiance of health care professionals and consumers across America and, now, throughout Asia.

In Chapters 5–7, I'll discuss three profound sea changes that are reshaping our society and our economy and explain how a company like Rexall Showcase International is showing us a way to navigate through those sea changes in positive and profitable ways. The last two chapters preview new Rexall Showcase International products and markets and attempt to address the doubts many prospective network marketers have when considering joining a company like Rexall Showcase International. And throughout the book, but especially in Chapters 8–11, I'll introduce you to some of the most interesting and successful leaders in the business, people from all walks of life who have seized upon what distributor leader Jim Moyles calls "a gift of health—a gift of finance."

CHAPTER TWO

Back to the Future

With the introductions made and the pleasantries dispensed with, Carl DeSantis reaches into the lower-right drawer of his finely polished desk and pulls out a slick color catalogue called "The DeSantis Collection."

"This is my latest venture," he informs me. "I started in the mail-order business. It's great to be back in it. Nothing beats it. You're making money even while you're asleep because people keep placing orders!"

The DeSantis Collection—custom-made shirts, high-end neckwear, and other fashion items for men—sold $7 million worth of products this year, and the fifty-nine-year-old businessman seems more excited by this achievement than he is about being one of south Florida's largest employers and chairman of a $530 million company.

"I've got an art gallery too, and a restaurant. And a couple of other businesses," says Carl.

Once an entrepreneur, always an entrepreneur!

Now taking several steps back from the daily management decisions of his growing Rexall Sundown empire and turning the reins over to son Damon and a corporate management team, Carl is clearly nostalgic for the glory days of entrepreneurship. Doing it yourself. Acting almost instinctively to decide what products will sell and which consumers will buy them. Yes, flying just a bit by the seat of the pants.

"The most fun is that time leading up to when you take a company public," explains Carl, who in 1993 took his company public. It was one of the most successful new public offerings of that year. In fact, of the many thousands of Initial Public Offerings (IPO) during the 1990s, Rexall Sundown is among the twenty most successful as ranked by *Investors Business Daily.*

But Carl stresses the excitement of building a business before it is public: "When you're private, you compete against your competitors. You try to come up with the best ideas, the best products, and the best marketing strategies. You work hard. You reach milestones, and you celebrate with your team around you.

"When you're public, you compete against yourself. The Wall Street analysts say, for example, that if you did $500 million in sales this year, you ought to do $700 million next year—so you compete against the expectations set for you by others. Now, if I'm still private and we go from $500 to $600 million, I'm going to throw a party. As a public company, instead of celebrating, we'd spend our time explaining. It's a different game."

But this man knows many games when it comes to business—especially how to spot consumer trends and respond to them and how to find good people and motivate them. "I think one of my strengths is I'm a good judge of people, what they need, what they want, what they're all about. When it comes to hiring, I've usually been able to sense whether the fit is right and whether I'll be able to motivate them to their full potential."

Almost on cue, I get a firsthand look at one of Carl DeSantis's highly motivated protégés. A human tornado named Nickolas

Palin bursts into the office holding an unlit cigar. Neatly attired (perhaps in items from the DeSantis Collection), he bounds over to Carl, extends his hand, and shakes the founder's hand enthusiastically. "Thank you, sir, for making me a rich man," Nick exclaims. It was a bit of tongue-in-cheek stage acting to impress the visiting author.

Nick is senior executive vice president and a director of Rexall Sundown—and a former undercover officer for the New York City police department. An ex-cop playing a leading role in a $500 million preventative health and wellness company?

"He's a people person," Carl explains. "His marketing skills are responsible for a great deal of the sales of this company. He can sell anything!"

Nick Palin proved that to Carl DeSantis for the first of many times when they met at Carl's breakfast table at a crowded Miami Beach deli fifteen years ago. "The place was packed, so I asked Carl if I could share his table. A few minutes later I asked him if he needed anyone in his business," Nick recalls.

"I'm retired and I need a job," he explained at the time. "Retired? You look like you aren't even 40 yet," Carl replied.

"I'm not. I'm 35. I'm an ex-cop who served his time—and they let me out early! So whaddya say?" Carl gave Nick a shot in telemarketing. Nick advanced through the company's flagship division, Sundown Vitamins, and today he runs it.

"That's something else that's great about being an entrepreneur," Carl interjects. "You can pick people from unorthodox places when you just feel that the fit is right."

That comment triggers a rapid-fire dialogue between Nick and Carl on the subject of entrepreneurship. My presence is acknowledged only by an occasional directive from Carl to "write that down" each time he believes Nick has uttered something quotable. I try but I miss some of it. They're talking too fast. Visible over Carl's left shoulder is a sign sitting on his credenza that reads: "Get to the point." They don't, but it is fun and interesting to watch.

"Carl is a pure entrepreneur," Nick announces.

"Everyone talks about entrepreneurs, but what does it really mean? It's not even an English word," Carl pronounces.

Maybe not, but looking back at the career of Carl DeSantis, one can get a pretty clear picture of what a true entrepreneur is and what it takes to be one.

Born in 1937 and raised in the Miami area, Carl grew up in modest surroundings. Events sad and joyful seemed to happen early in life. Carl's father died when he was just four. In the ninth grade he would meet a girl named Sylvia who later became his wife. He attended Florida State University—for exactly six months. Some three decades later he was awarded an honorary degree from the university.

"When the dean was introducing me to receive my degree, he explained to the audience that the reason I only attended the university for six months was because I was a very fast learner. He said the problem was that I had eighteen unpaid parking tickets left over from those six months and so the university had been holding on to my grades all those years!"

With his education "complete" and already a husband and father by the age of nineteen, Carl began what would be a seventeen-year retail drug store career with Super-X and Walgreen drug stores. Managing stores from Florida to North Carolina, Carl not only learned the nuts and bolts of running a business, but also saw up front and personally how consumers made purchasing decisions, what product pitches and presentations they either responded to or ignored, and how their tastes evolved over the years. He developed a keen eye and finely tuned ear for the slightest change in consumer concern and fashion.

Carl DeSantis's direct, everyday interaction with his customers and the almost "sixth sense" ability he had acquired to spot a trend or the opening of a product niche would prove to be invaluable assets in the mid-1970s when he began to search for a new direction in his career.

"I came to realize that my drug store career was really limited in scope," Carl said. "If I stuck around long enough, maybe I would get a gold watch at the end—not even that, more like a *gold-plated* watch! I wanted to find a way to break out on my own."

But now having three children to support (daughter Debbie and sons Dean and Damon) and little in the way of resources, Carl realized he could achieve that goal only by coming up with a good idea; finding low-cost, creative ways to turn that idea into business; and doing it alongside his job, which he couldn't afford to give up. That would mean a lot of hard work in the off-hours.

One thing Carl observed while managing a drug store in Miami Beach was the large number of "snowbirds" from the northern states who, after escaping the brutal winter for the sunshine of south Florida, came into the store in search of a low-cost product to protect and soothe their fair, sunburned skins. "The products already on the shelves were quite high in price, and I heard a lot of complaints." Carl and a pharmacist developed an inexpensive lotion called "Sundown" and sold it locally. It was Carl dipping his big toe into the waters of entrepreneurship, and he liked the feeling!

Shortly after that, Carl observed that a lot of calls and inquiries were coming into the store from customers looking for special blends and potencies of vitamins, particularly vitamins E, B-complex, and C. For millions of Americans, taking a daily multiple vitamin was nothing new. But Carl detected a growing interest in nutrition and health products, and he saw that consumers were becoming intrigued and captivated by the notion that particular vitamins and minerals were associated with particular health benefits. That savvy perception led Carl DeSantis headlong into the vitamin business in 1976.

"Some twenty-two years ago when we started the company, it was a family company. Just me, Sylvia, and the children," Carl recalls. "We practically ran it out of the house. As a matter of fact we did."

Beginning with several vitamin products under the SDV® brand, Carl turned a bedroom of the family home in North Miami

Beach into the company warehouse. The kitchen table was the packaging and order-processing department. Sylvia, with a background in accounting, kept the books. Dean and Damon pasted labels on bottles and prepared orders for shipping every afternoon after school. The front door was "shipping and receiving"—the UPS driver would back up to it each afternoon to pick the day's packages.

The marketing plan was simple—word-of-mouth customer satisfaction and $450 ads in the *National Enquirer*. "The ads in there were cheap in those days," Carl remembers.

"We did a lot of things here locally. We did most of it here from the bedroom. We stacked up the vitamins in there, we'd pack them, and UPS would come to the door and off they would go. We built ourselves a very successful mail-order business."

But Carl didn't stop there. "Then we decided to break out into the retail arena. I brought on board a number of good people, and soon we had opened up about 300 drug stores in southeast Florida and the Northeast. From there all good things happened."

By the early 1980s, Sundown Vitamins had become one of the most popular brands. Carl graduated from employee to boss. The consumer's intense focus on health, diet, and fitness—a trend Carl detected before most—was picking up steam.

In 1985, Carl attended an industry meeting in New York. Little did he know as he made his way to the city that, almost by accident, he would stumble on an opportunity that would mark a major turning point for his business and the entire preventative health care field.

"There has been a divine hand in my life and I truly mean that," says Carl. "I just happened to be in New York at an industry meeting. I met a number of people from the major drug companies. I also found out while I was there that the Rexall drug company, which was started in 1903 in Boston, was available.

"I got together with some people I know on Wall Street and they advised me if I wanted to make a move it would be a potentially very good one for our company."

Carl got on a plane the next day, flew to St. Louis, and struck a multi-million dollar deal to acquire the name, products, and assets of Rexall. "We were able to earn back what it cost us in seven months," he reports.

Rexall is one of the most respected brand names in America, recognized by 78 percent of the public thirty-eight years old or older. It is a name that people associate with trust, integrity, and health. And for many of us, it conjures up the image of a simpler, happier era in which the corner drug store was the focal point of small-town society. There you could find friends to socialize with at the soda fountain, helpful advice on how to treat your ailments from the pharmacist, and a myriad of products for everyday life sold by cheerful proprietors.

When Louis Liggett established the Rexall system of independent drug stores in 1903, he also determined that a respected, recognized name and a quality line of products would back these business owners. The idea proved so powerful that by 1952, there were some 25,000 Rexall drug stores nationwide. Even today, despite the emergence of big drug store chains and the decline of the town and city center as a focal point of American life, approximately 3,500 stores carrying the name Rexall still operate.

"We had bought a legend with Rexall," Carl DeSantis reflects. "Louis Liggett, who started the company, had a dream, and he fulfilled his dream. We then had to decide what was the best way to take this name and make the dream happen again." As we will see in the next chapter, Carl and his team would decide that network marketing was one way to make Louis Liggett's dream happen again.

Acquiring the Rexall trademark further strengthened Sundown's position in a nutritional health products industry that by the late 1980s and early 1990s was growing rapidly. In June 1993, the company changed its name to Rexall Sundown and, as noted, became a publicly traded company.

Today, as Chairman of Rexall Sundown, Carl has stepped back from the day-to-day management of the company, turning over many decisions to Chief Executive Officer, Chris Nast, and son Damon, who was recently promoted to President. But when it comes to strategy and future directions, these two understand who their greatest resource is. "Even when you're blessed with great people, it's not easy to take a step back," Carl confesses. "Especially when you've always been a hands-on person."

Right now Carl DeSantis's hands are on a bottle of Sundown Vitamins sitting atop his desk. He pauses, examines the label, and then talks about some of the design and packaging changes he has recently ordered. "Why not print your logo and label on both sides of the bottle?" he points out. "If it's on there just once and they don't stock it the right way on the store shelf, customers might not see your name. We started doing it and increased sales!"

Carl DeSantis may be sitting on top of a business empire in a well-appointed office on a well-manicured corporate campus in Boca Raton, but he hasn't lost his laser-like focus on the individual customer rushing down the aisle in a store anywhere in America ready to make a buying decision. He knows from years of front-line experience that you can't get too bigheaded about yourself or your product. Sometimes it's nothing more complicated than making sure the consumer can read your name on the bottle as he or she walks down that aisle.

Packaging issues resolved for the day, Carl grows philosophical as he tries to share his prescription for success with others.

"All of us have gone through tough times, but I've never known anything but the ability to win. I've never veered or believed that I couldn't do it.

"I think the same ingredient is necessary whether you have a fruit stand or are running General Motors. Success in business requires a lot of passion and a lot of integrity. And for crying out loud, don't do it for the almighty dollar. The dollar that we all have to be concerned about will come, but that's the last reason you should do things. Do it for the love of it. I really believe the sky is the limit as long as you set your sights on the correct thing in life."

Son Damon, who rose in the company from the kitchen table to the position of President, reflects on his father's approach to business and life and what it has taught him.

"I can remember back at the kitchen table helping with the mail-order ads. When I suggested changing one of the headline banners, he took my advice," Damon says. "I recall that fondly because I was just twelve then and he was already taking my advice."

"Even though I had to come straight home from school every day to pack the orders before the UPS truck arrived, I got to watch a business grow week after week and month after month. That made a big impression on me," he continues.

"A big reason my father was successful was his sales and marketing background and his experience in the retail drug business. That gave him the savvy to recognize what the consumer wanted. But even more important was his desire to succeed. His desire to achieve and his ability to stay totally committed to something. That truly is the definition of success."

In most great companies, a leader from the past or the present embodies the company's spirit, character, culture, values, and vision. At Rexall Sundown and Rexall Showcase International, Carl DeSantis is that leader and always will be. Today Rexall is no longer simply a family business. "But we have family in the business," says Carl. By that he means more than the fact that Damon plays a leading role or that daughter Debbie, with her pharmaceutical background, is Vice President of Product Development. Rexall Showcase International distributor Todd Smith recalls the first time he visited the company headquarters in 1991:

"When I made that first trip I was trying to make a very big decision. Here was a company that had just started its network marketing division, which was off to a bad start and really wanted me, Randy Schroeder, and Stewart Hughes to come in and get it going.

The Rexall name attracted me and the opportunity to work with Randy and Stewart excited me.

"But it was something that happened at the end of my daylong tour of the company that made the biggest impact. Carl DeSantis took me aside and said, 'I want you to know that God has been very good to me. We are really committed to this and we will stand by you and your family no matter what it takes, no matter what we have to do.'

"I can't tell you how impressive it was to see that kind of commitment extended not just to me but to my family whom at that time he had never met. That's Carl DeSantis."

CHAPTER THREE

A Showcase Decision

I was the one who had to go figure this thing out," says Damon DeSantis. The thirty-four-year-old President of Rexall Sundown and son of founder Carl DeSantis, was referring to his tough assignment in 1991 to take charge of the company's foray into network marketing, a project which had begun a year earlier and was not living up to expectations.

But then Damon had already taken on just about every tough assignment there was to perform at the company, so why not this one too?

Born in 1964 in Greensboro, North Carolina, where his father was managing a drug store, Damon grew up in North Miami Beach and at the age of twelve began preparing and packaging Carl's vitamin products for delivery to customers. "That business was built by a circle of family and friends around our kitchen table. It was a great experience," he recalls.

By the time Damon was of college age, he already had a thorough education in marketing and entrepreneurship, having studied since childhood under the tutelage of his father, Carl. He enrolled at the University of Florida and stayed exactly a year and a half. "Three times longer than my father," he notes with a laugh. One happy outcome of college life was meeting his wife, Cindy, there. Like father, like son, Damon married young. He wed at age eighteen, and the first of the couple's four children was born a year later.

Since that time, Damon has worked in a broad range of positions as Rexall Sundown has grown from a kitchen-table family business to a more than $500 million corporation publicly traded on Wall Street and selling more than 1,000 products in more than fifty nations. "I've had the good fortune to work on all sides of the business. It's given me a certain respect for all the people that work in different facets of the company."

In 1990, Damon, along with Carl and the other leaders of Rexall Sundown, concluded that network marketing offered a potentially powerful vehicle for the presentation of a unique line of natural nutritional products to a public that was clamoring for healthier lifestyles and alternatives to traditional prescription drugs. "Nutritional supplements are very much a word-of-mouth product," Damon explains. "There's not a tremendous amount a company can do through traditional marketing. People need to hear from others they know and trust that a given product is effective.

"More evidence is coming forward showing the positive impact of vitamins and supplements. As people became more and more interested in natural preventative care, it became a natural extension to offer them through the vehicle of network marketing," he continues. "And while we wanted to help people with their health, we also wanted to help them achieve the American dream. The beauty of network marketing is you can start at very low dollar input."

Carl underscores that the company's decision to start a network marketing division tapped two markets—the preventative health care market and a growing demand for entrepreneurial opportunities. "I did see that network marketing was on its way and that it was the wave of the future. I felt there were a lot of independent people out there who were capable of much more than they had the opportunity to create. So we collectively made the decision to start Rexall Showcase International."

Leading distributor Todd Smith agrees: "What Carl and Damon did by creating Rexall Showcase International was to reach out to entrepreneurs like me." But unlike the old franchise model where independent businesspeople would have to pay a franchise fee, and sometimes a very large one, to get the backing of a powerful brand like Rexall, "now all the financial risk has been taken away."

Stored in a cabinet in Damon DeSantis's office is a historical document from the old Rexall drug company. It includes a map of the United States, covered with dots, each one representing the location of a Rexall drugstore. Also depicted on the map is the route followed by the Rexall train decades ago—a train that carried a makeshift drugstore and new product displays. At each stop, current and prospective store owners met the train to learn about business developments and share in the excitement of the nationally recognized name many had purchased a piece of.

"We're building on a lot of history here and we never forget that," says Damon. What we're creating with Rexall Showcase International is a virtual Rexall, a Rexall without the bricks and mortar but with thousands and thousands of dots on a map, each representing an independent businessperson. Except it will be a map of the world, not just the United States. And the vehicle won't be a train, the vehicle will be network marketing."

When Carl DeSantis acquired the Rexall name in 1985, he pledged to himself then to "find a way to make the dream happen again." With the creation of Rexall Showcase International in 1990, Carl and Damon were certain they had found the way.

If At First You Don't Succeed

Yet almost from the start, things went wrong. "We just burst out of the gate in the wrong way," Damon explains. "It was very much a learn-as-you-go process. We had our ups and downs and then the thing just caved." The company was learning the hard way that finding just the right network marketing business model was a complicated mixture of art and science. You need a workable and comprehensive compensation plan, an easily duplicated system, professional support and effective training, and a core group of dedicated distributor leaders who were committed for the long haul and not just there to make a fast buck and move on.

At the outset Rexall Showcase International fell short in all of these, and with the division generating more headaches than sales, "it was very hard to see the light at the end of the tunnel," Damon remembers.

But Damon and his father remained absolutely convinced that network marketing was going to define the future of their company and would fundamentally change the way people buy, sell, and do business in the United States and around the world. "We knew what we had to do and why," Damon says. "We just had to get it right."

In 1991 help arrived in the form a group of experienced and successful Nu Skin distributors led by Randy Schroeder, Stewart Hughes, and Todd Smith. Concerned about the long-term prospects in that company, they took the DeSantises up on their invitation to visit the Rexall Sundown headquarters, then located in Fort Lauderdale. While very impressed by the overall company, they were surprised by what they saw happening in the Rexall Showcase International division—very little. A different cast of characters might have walked out the door. Not these three—they saw a challenge and great opportunity.

Randy recalls, "The first time I went there I saw one woman taking phone orders from distributors—and she wasn't busy.

"I thought, well maybe that moment was an unusual occurrence. But when I went back again, she still wasn't busy!

"I made a decision that day to participate because I saw that we would have a partnership. The company would create products and commission checks that would clear the bank, and we'd do everything else. We'd be the entrepreneurs."

It took Stewart Hughes a little longer to decide to sign on. What convinced him was "a deep level of commitment and integrity I saw in the person of Damon DeSantis. That had a huge impact on me."

Stewart recalls that the group was excited, not discouraged, by the fact they'd be entering a business at the ground level. "We saw the commitment the company had to really do it right." The day Stewart signed up, he took out a piece of paper and wrote out all the personal and financial goals he hoped to achieve in the Rexall Showcase International business. He saved that paper and looks at it from time to time to remind himself that he has accomplished every single one.

Enlisting a high-caliber group of distributor leaders who helped the company reconfigure its network marketing business opportunity almost from the start put Rexall Showcase International on a path of substantial growth. The result is an unusually strong partnership between the company's management and the distributors—a dynamic you don't find in all network marketing companies. "It has been a huge learning experience, but we learned it together. We built it as a team," says Damon.

Taking Charge of the Future

With Rexall Showcase International profits, sales, and distributorships all now rapidly increasing, the Rexall Sundown executive team knew it had a tiger by the tail. By 1997 it was time to bring on a strong leader who would develop a strategic plan for sustained growth and shape a vision for the future. That leader arrived in 1997 in the person of Dave Schofield.

Dave was born in Milwaukee in 1959 to a Japanese mother and an American father; his dad died when he was just six. Moving to

California with his mother, he attended high school there and later attended San Diego State University, where he majored in accounting. Dave would later go on to earn an MBA focusing on management from Pepperdine University.

From 1984 to 1994, he worked for the Los Angeles–based PIP Printing, one of the largest quick-print franchisers in the United States. Starting as a franchise auditor, "where I made $14,000 a year." Dave quickly moved up the ranks, reaching the level of executive vice president of domestic and international operations.

The years he spent working with franchisees provided valuable training for his later entry into the world of network marketing, Dave says. "I learned all about relationships with the franchisees," he explains. I learned how to consult with them, keep them motivated, communicate with them, and help them succeed. And I found myself really wanting them to succeed and taking personal interest in their growth. It became a passion for me that they succeed."

In 1994, Dave was recruited by Office Depot, where he managed more than 3,000 employees in a new Images Division, which provided printing, copying, graphic design, and other services to small and medium-sized businesses through each Office Depot store. He left in 1996, "hoping to take a year or two off," but was soon recruited by Carl and Damon DeSantis and the Rexall Sundown board to serve as Chief Operating Officer of Rexall Showcase International. He immediately put into place plans that further expanded the division's sales and distributor base. In February 1998 he was elevated to the position of Rexall Showcase International President.

"Dave has been instrumental in growing our business," says Damon DeSantis. "He has an acute awareness of the needs and expectations of the distributors. He has a plan and he has a vision. Most importantly, he has the passion to put them in place."

It's hard to miss that passion whenever you are in ear- or eye-shot of Dave Schofield. Given the chance before a large group or in a one-on-one conversation, Dave will fire off an array of statistics, pronouncements, and anecdotes about Rexall Showcase International's growth, its impact on people, and the direction the company is taking in the future. He's committed to what he does, and he exhibits the confidence and energy of one who believes he does it well—qualities he mixes well with easygoing humor and a measure of irreverence.

During a recent company conference, Dave was sitting in the audience as one distributor spoke of how unhappy those in corporate management jobs have become and how most wanted to escape—a familiar network marketing pitch. "I don't want to escape," Dave said under his breath. He later told me, "I like organizations, and I like to manage. My strength and experience as a corporate executive compliments the entrepreneurial side of our distributor force. This combination is very powerful and results in a well managed company along with a highly motivated distributor base."

Following a five-year strategic growth plan and a vision that he proudly posts on the company's web site, Dave Schofield and the new management team he has brought on board believe they can build the vehicle that turns Rexall Showcase International, and hence Rexall Sundown, into "a multi-billion dollar global powerhouse."

"In the last year, we've had more product orders, more calls, shipped out more product, and brought in more new distributors than in any other year," Dave relates. "We are truly changing the dynamics of what network marketing is all about. One thing we do to reward our distributors is offer stock options, and we pay among the highest levels of commissions in the industry. We're now expanding our computer systems and opening international markets. Next will be Japan, which is truly the crown jewel in the direct selling industry.

"In terms of the perception, the overall image of Rexall Showcase International is that it enjoys an elite status. In the past couple of years, we've had a lot of exposure that is showcasing our future potential. Outside the industry we're getting a lot of visibility and respect on Wall Street, where analysts there have called Rexall Showcase International the future growth vehicle for Rexall Sundown.

31

"This is a company that's on the move. The future won't happen by accident; it will happen by design. We've developed a five-year plan that we believe will grow the company to a multibillion-dollar company in the years ahead."

Direct Selling—A Global Phenomenon

To understand why entrepreneurs like Carl DeSantis, executives like Damon DeSantis and Dave Schofield, and distributor leaders like Randy Schroeder, Stewart Hughes, and Todd Smith are so committed to network marketing and have stuck with it through good times and bad, let's take a snapshot of this interesting form of business that has taken root around the globe.

Consider these statistics from the Direct Selling Association (DSA), the national trade association of direct selling, of which network marketing is a part, as well as its international counterpart, the World Federation of Direct Selling Associations (WFDSA).

Note that the DSA defines direct selling as "the sale of a consumer product or service in a face to face manner away from a fixed retail location."

- There are 9.3 million salespeople in the United States with 1997 sales of $22.2 billion. In 1993 there were 5.7 million U.S. salespeople who sold $15 billion of products and services.
- Approximately 79 percent of direct selling firms compensate distributors according to a multilevel compensation structure. These firms account for 80 percent of the distributors and 72 percent of the sales dollars. The remaining firms operate under a single-level compensation structure.
- About 55 percent of direct sellers are women, 26 percent are men, and 18 percent operate as two-person teams.

- Eighty-one percent devote 30 hours or less per week to their businesses, 8 percent spend between 30 and 39 hours, and 11 percent spend 40 hours per week or more.
- The major products sold by the industry include home/family care products (cleaning products, cookware, cutlery, and the like), accounting for 31.9 percent of all U.S. sales dollars; personal care products (cosmetics, jewelry, skin care), 27 percent; services and other miscellaneous products, 18.7 percent; wellness products (weight loss, vitamins, natural medicines), 17.7 percent; and leisure/educational products (books, encyclopedias, toys, games), 4.7 percent.
- Globally, the WFDSA reports that 30.9 million people engage in direct selling, up from 8.48 million in 1988. Some estimates peg the number of salespeople at closer to 36 million, since the WFDSA statistics do not include China.
- Worldwide sales in 1997 totaled $80.5 billion, compared to just $33.3 billion in 1988.
- The United States still ranks first in terms of the number of direct sellers. The top fifteen sales forces by country are:

United States	9,300,000
Indonesia	2,800,000
Japan	2,500,000
Taiwan	2,360,000
Brazil	1,838,044
Malaysia	1,800,000
Canada	1,300,000
Mexico	1,200,000
Philippines	1,008,513
Korea	909,000
Thailand	800,000
Australia	650,000
United Kingdom	400,000
Germany	395,000
Poland	350,000

- In terms of retail sales, Japan bests the United States. The top fifteen direct selling countries ranked by sales are:

Japan	$30.2 billion
United States	$22.2 billion
Brazil	$4.045 billion
Germany	$3.6 billion
Korea	$2.1 billion
Italy	$2.1 billion
Taiwan	$1.74 billion
Canada	$1.6 billion
Mexico	$1.4 billion
United Kingdom	$1.396 billion
Australia	$1.2 billion
France	$1.16 billion
Argentina	$1.074 billion
Malaysia	$658 million
Spain	$652 million

As you can see, direct selling is a rapidly growing global industry. Why are millions turning to this form of business activity? The short answer is that people from many walks of life bring to these businesses different levels of commitment and expectation. It is critical that companies devising network marketing arms, not to mention analysts in the media and elsewhere who examine the efficacy of this industry, understand that fact.

On many occasions, including discussions with me and in books such Richard C. Bartlett's recent book called *The Direct Option,* Direct Selling Association President, Neil Offen, has delineated several categories of network marketers:

- The first type is the person who signs up as a salesperson simply because they want to buy and use certain products themselves. They sign up to gain access to the products and any price discounts that may be offered.

- The second type is a salesperson with a specific, short-term goal in mind—for example to earn some extra money for a new car, an appliance, a vacation, or holiday gifts. These salespeople may stay in the business for years, but vary their level of activity throughout the year.
- The third category includes those who need the income on a year-round basis to supplement total household income, but cannot devote full-time to the direct selling business.
- The fourth type of salesperson is the career entrepreneur, for who direct selling becomes their primary source of income. These people work at the business full-time and beyond.
- The fifth type is more attracted to direct selling businesses for the non-monetary rewards—the meetings, friendships, contacts outside the home, and the recognition of achievement.
- The sixth type of salesperson joins because of his or her strong belief in the company's products. As you will see, many Rexall Showcase distributors started out with this as their primary motivation. They then learned to appreciate the other rewards a successful distributorship had to offer.

Motivation, whatever kind in whatever amount, can be easily snuffed out if a multitude of barriers to entry and success are thrown in the would-be entrepreneur's path. An article in *INC.* magazine delineates the following advantages network marketers and the companies who back them find in this mode of business over all others:

- It eliminates the need for slick advertising.
- In a world full of marketing noise, friends and family are the only salespeople many customers listen to and trust.
- It reduces the cost of acquiring customers.
- It reduces cash-flow risks, because merchandise has to sell before distributors get paid.
- It enables a company to build a large sales force very cheaply.

- It capitalizes on the growing supply of the self-employed, estimated at anywhere from 9 to 15 percent of the American workforce.

Many individuals with limited or no capital or experience find network marketing companies far superior to franchises and other more traditional business start-ups. *Entrepreneur* magazine is one of many sources to point out that in network marketing, the practitioner can avoid the purchase of expensive equipment. There are no licenses to apply for, inventories to maintain, employees to manage, or expensive legal and marketing bills to pay. Dealings with government agencies and banks are kept to a minimum. In sum, much of the overhead cost and time-consuming tasks associated with other small business ventures can be stripped away.

Richard Bartlett, whose direct selling career spans several decades, believes one of the most appeal qualities of the direct selling career is that it's a level playing field. Unlike many other fields where a premium is placed on youth, many successful direct sellers started their businesses relatively late in life. It's a better business model for the physically challenged as well, since most of the activity can be conducted from home.

Women and minorities find open doors here too, since the compensation formula and levels of achievement in a direct selling company are the same for everybody. And while formal education and prior work experience can be helpful, they are not required for entry. No one is going to keep you out of the field on the basis of a skimpy resume, Bartlett reminds us.

Doing It Differently

Look at the story behind many successful network marketing companies and it goes something like this:

A strong-minded individual gathers together a handful of partners, family members, and true believers. They find a product or service that is suited for word-of-mouth selling. They enlist their families and friends, who work day and night, out of basements, kitchens, and dens to scratch out some sales. Because they have spared themselves the huge costs of more traditional businesses (advertising, marketing, in-house sales staff), moving even a relatively modest volume of product generates an impressive flow of revenue. Those who come in at the ground level make a great deal of money, and their stories are transformed into legends, told and retold in speeches, audiotapes, and videos. In this way, they provide inspiration for aspiring recruits downline.

At some point, the company grows to the extent that more traditional business strategies are needed. It's what Nick Palin is talking about when he says the transition of a small company to a large one is like a spaceship jettisoning its spent fuel tank. Many of the initial entrepreneurs who helped put a company into orbit are jettisoned in a comparable fashion. (For some pioneers who hit it big, that suits them just fine. They have no interest in being part of a large corporate management structure. They're ready to move on and now have the money to do so!)

Some companies move into the big leagues by going public. Others expand through mergers and acquisitions. International operations are established, often under operating rules significantly different from those of the company's domestic business. Strategic partnerships are formed with leading consumer-product companies and service providers—firms that hope to take advantage of the network marketing company's loyal customer base and enthusiastic sales force. In today's competitive climate, a company that has managed to scratch out even a single percentage point of the market is worth the attention of larger, more established concerns.

From a business standpoint, these developments are fun to watch and hard not to admire. That's why I wrote *The Excel Phenomenon,* which told the story of Texas entrepreneur Kenny Troutt—a man who failed in other businesses at least three times before hitting pay dirt in telecommunications. Although he knew little about the industry, he decided to take advantage of deregulation and start a long-distance phone company. But he couldn't afford to build or buy a phone system. So he purchased excess long-distance capacity from the big companies and recruited friends and family to resell it to consumers in a network marketing system.

It was only after attracting hundreds of thousands of independent representatives and capturing up to 3 percent of the long-distance market that he actually started developing his own phone-switching systems. He took Excel public and became a billionaire. Having moved Excel into the residential market through reselling, he then sought to segue into the commercial market by acquiring a firm specializing there—and an in-house sales force came with it. Kenny Troutt's $1 billion company suddenly became a $2 billion company.

Then, in early 1998, Excel sold majority ownership to Canada's Teleglobe. Excel will remain a distinct entity with its own identity. It was Excel's way of bursting into the international arena, Troutt explained to his network marketing representatives.

The key challenge for any network marketing company as it makes the transition from the earliest stages of entrepreneurial development to the adoption of more traditional corporate growth strategies is how to continue to maintain the spirit, drive, and loyalty of the independent businesspeople it originally attracted to the business. Because these companies' successes are built on the people it convinces to sell its products, anything that shakes the faith and confidence of the sales force in the company, its leaders or products, can be a dagger at the heart of the business. Indeed, network marketing is replete with examples in which distributors fled or switched en masse to competitors.

It doesn't take much and it's not always the company's fault: An unfounded attack on products, bad publicity in the media, government scrutiny, a marketing plan that doesn't keep up with the competition, or the sense that the owners are in it for themselves can all be factors.

As we have seen, Carl DeSantis, his family, and his partners have followed a different path. While beginning in the true traditions of plucky entrepreneurship, they went on to build a strong corporate foundation and identity that included acquisition of one of the most respected brand names in American history—all *before* embracing the possibilities of network marketing. The strategy has been to build a strong foundation first—then on top of that foundation construct a business that offers unique products and an entrepreneurial opportunity designed to appeal to millions of aging baby boomers and others concerned about good health and sound finances.

That foundation, which is Rexall Sundown, includes a family of seven distinct divisions that together sell over 1,000 different products in more than fifty countries:

- **Sundown Vitamins** is the company's flagship brand and the number one branded vitamin line in the United States today. More than 250 products, including vitamins, herbal and nutritional supplements, minerals, and antioxidants are sold through mass merchandisers, drug stores, and supermarkets.
- **Rexall** markets more than 125 vitamins and nutritional supplements under its well-known brand name through dollar stores and food and drug wholesalers.
- **Richardson Labs®** is a leader in diet and weight management supplements. This subsidiary is known primarily for its supplement called Chroma Slim®.
- **Thompson Nutritional Products®** manufactures and markets more than 135 vitamins and nutritional supplements primarily to health food stores.
- **SDV Vitamins** is one of the largest mail-order nutritional companies in America, offering a complete line of vitamins, herbals, and other products directly to consumers by mail.

- **Rexall Managed Care®** provides vitamins and nutritional supplements to the managed care marketplace.
- **Rexall Showcase International (RSI)** is, of course, the network marketing division, offering more than 150 exclusive health and wellness products not available in stores or through the company's other divisions. It operates in all fifty states as well as in Hong Kong, Korea, Mexico, and Taiwan and—as of Spring 1999—Japan.

One of the most important questions prospective direct sellers ask about a company they want to join is, Is it real? Is it stable and secure with sound finances and a good business infrastructure? In an age of Internet companies that exist as little more than sites on the Web, it is more important than ever to ask these and other basic questions.

Does the company make its own products and have its own facilities and staff? What does its track record tell us? Is it growing or shrinking? Are the owners in it for the long haul or looking to build something fast and flimsy before they sell out for a big windfall?

Here are a few features about Rexall Sundown to consider:

- It is one of south Florida's largest businesses, with more than 1,200 employees. Its headquarters, manufacturing, packaging, distribution, and research and development facilities occupy more than 700,000 square feet in locations around the country.
- It is a publicly traded company listed on the Nasdaq National Market under the trading symbol "RXSD." As a publicly traded company, annual reports, quarterly reports, other legally required disclosures, and independent analyses are available for scrutiny.
- Rexall Sundown has experienced dramatic growth in recent years, earning recognition in September 1998 as one of *Fortune* magazine's 100 Fastest Growing Companies in America.

- In the 1998 fiscal year, the company recorded sales of $530.7 million, up from $290.6 million in 1997—an 83 percent increase in just one year. The Rexall Showcase International division accounted for $160 million of these sales in 1998, a 51 percent increase over the previous year.

Prospective distributors are encouraged to visit the company headquarters and facilities in Boca Raton, Florida. There they are treated to an exhaustive (and exhausting!) three-hour briefing and site inspection of the product-development, manufacturing, packaging, and distribution centers, located on a tree-shaded 20-acre corporate campus as well as at a nearby site in Deerfield Beach.

Visitors are typically impressed by the professionalism exhibited in the corporate offices and among the team of operators that busily process orders and help distributors. During the end-of-the-month rushes, when distributors are trying to push up volume to qualify for bonus pools and higher recognition levels, the team can be called upon to process $2 million in product orders in a single day. This will pale in comparison to the level of sales Rexall Showcase International will handle in the years ahead.

The manufacturing facilities, housed in an 82,000-square-foot plant are state of the art. While raw materials may be imported, all of the company's products are manufactured in the United States under exacting standards and rigorous inspection procedures. Twenty-four hours a day, five days a week, operators in sterilized clothing and masks pour different powders into huge blenders according to the product formulas developed by Rexall scientists and dietitians. The blended products are then put into packets or molded into tablets, coated, and bottled. The highly sophisticated machines can make 100,000 tablets in a single hour and more than 2 billion tablets a year.

Meanwhile, inspectors stand by to pull bottles at random and inspect them for quality and purity. Samples from each lot are logged and stored for up to three years, so that they may be reinspected in case any consumer complaints arise after a particular lot is sold in the marketplace. These precautions help explain why the facility has been awarded the highest rating ever given to a supplier of nutritional supplements by an independent auditor for the integrity and standards embodied in the manufacturing process.

A few miles south in Deerfield Beach, products are packaged and orders filled. Except for extreme rushes, if a Rexall Showcase International distributor or customer calls or e-mails in an order, it will be boxed and shipped the same day.

Among the many Rexall Showcase International distributors I spoke to, almost all recounted the importance of their visit to Boca Raton as a key factor in their decision to join the business. "You just have to see it, feel it, taste it yourself to get over whatever hesitation you have about joining network marketing," one said. "Hearing about it from someone else, even someone you trust, just doesn't do it."

Rexall Sundown's decision to add a network marketing arm completes the corporate support package that will provide a solid foundation for the individual who wishes to start his or her own Rexall Showcase International distributorship. Rexall is not one company but really a family of companies, each with its own distinct products, marketing strategies, and channels of distribution.

A New Business Model

Some may wonder why the network marketer should care about other divisions of the company. Others may ask whether the firm's strategy of promoting multiple brands through multiple distribution channels signals less than total commitment to the individual distributor force. Using more than one approach to putting products in the consumer marketplace—direct selling as well as mail order and retail arrangements with big chains like K-Mart—may strike some devoted network marketing advocates as something akin to practicing more than one "religion" at the same time!

In fact, this blending of approaches is the wave of the future. Much as they have disparaged direct selling in the past, consumer product and services companies are realizing they can no longer afford to ignore the potency of face-to-face (or phone-to-phone and computer-to-computer) selling. They crave the customer loyalty that is increasingly hard to come by with traditional advertising and marketing approaches. Changing demographics are causing an overall shortage of workers. Regulations are driving up the cost of maintaining those workers they do find. Again, these companies look with envy to the successful network marketing companies where a dedicated sales force works with no guarantee of income and no traditional employee overhead.

With mass media both multiplying and devolving simultaneously, with consumers becoming increasingly segmented, how do companies reach them? How do they cut through all the noise? How do they appeal to a public that is spending less and less time watching the major television networks and reading the daily newspapers, while spending more time on the Internet, watching videos, and channel-surfing around 100 to 500 different channels? During those times when the nation does come together, such as on Super Bowl Sunday, how many firms can afford the price of admission to a rarely unified market—$1 million for a single 30-second commercial!

The smart companies have come to understand that network marketing is an important part of the answer. *INC.* magazine has observed, "From the top of *INC.*'s 500 companies to the bottom are product and service companies that have adopted multilevel marketing to control overhead, create means of distribution, and build a national sales force on a budget. All of these companies have tapped into a growing contingent of displaced workers, professionals worried about their future, at-home moms and couples—all looking to get into business for themselves."

As for network marketing companies, what do they need from the more traditional companies? Answering that question requires some understanding of the environment in which these companies operate today.

- It is a highly competitive environment. With full employment and relative prosperity in the United States, the pool of eager participants in these businesses is limited, and the distributor forces that do sign up turn over continually.
- The regulatory environment is becoming more complex, particularly in the international arena that the United States' direct selling companies are counting on for a significant share of their future growth. Despite vast improvements in business ethics, spurred by pioneers like Amway and the Direct Selling Association, these companies are viewed with suspicion in many countries. As described earlier for example—in 1998, China overreacted to abuses by fraudulent domestic operators by shutting down the entire direct selling industry! Other countries require network marketing concerns to invest heavily in local manufacturing and other facilities before allowing them to sell products and recruit distributors.
- The development of unique products and services to be sold through network marketing is becoming increasingly expensive. To be competitive, you need capital. To keep on top of the competition, you need experienced executive management that understands changing markets. Yes, you even need lawyers to handle all the inevitable liability issues and to keep the class-action-lawsuit vultures at bay.

Few upstart network marketing companies have the resources and the skills to operate in this environment successfully over the long haul. That's why so many come and go—attracting little money, notice, or participation other than from a handful of roving multilevel marketing groupies. The transient nature of these companies and the inevitable disappointment and finger-pointing that comes with it further stymie the image-building efforts of an industry whose overall actual integrity far outstrips the public's perception of it.

The growth of the Internet and online usage has only fueled the fire. Users find they are deluged with unsolicited electronic junk mail describing the untold millions that can be made by selling some gadget through a network marketing scheme.

So what do network marketing entrepreneurs gain from joining forces with companies established along more traditional lines? The answer appears to be—the best of both worlds!

- The credibility and consumer recognition that comes with a well-known and highly respected brand name.
- A successful and profitable parent company, Rexall Sundown, which is publicly traded and therefore open to full public disclosure and scrutiny.
- A separate and distinct Rexall Showcase International corporate infrastructure of researchers who develop product breakthroughs that are exclusive to Rexall Showcase International, experienced managers and marketers who unearth and prepare new international markets, and lawyers who file and protect trademarks and patents and protect the business from legal poachers.
- Systems, training, and technologies—all very expensive and continually in need of updating—that allow the distributor to operate a lucrative business out of his or her home with just a fax and a couple of phone lines. Customers can order directly from the company, with the distributor getting the full credit.
- A chance to make unlimited income while retaining control over one's own schedule and level of involvement, benefits denied even the highest executives in the corporate structure.

Operating like an entrepreneur with a strong and established company backing you up. It's a good place to be—for the distributor and the company!

Rexall Showcase International is so intent on successfully blending a sophisticated corporate structure with a freewheeling entrepreneurial division that it offers as one of its key incentives for qualifying distributors stock options and a stock purchase plan in the parent company.

This is the total package that Carl and Damon DeSantis, Dave Schofield, and the top distributor leaders such as Randy, Todd, and Stewart have embraced. It's a formula as uniquely blended and finely balanced as the company's most noteworthy health care products. Having traced the roots of Rexall Showcase International and the key decisions that have made it what it is today, we're ready now to look at the products and the business opportunity that promise to have a major impact on two explosive industries: preventative health care and network marketing.

CHAPTER FOUR

A Gift of Health, a Gift of Finance

All network marketing companies say the products or services they offer are at the core of their business. For legal reasons, they have to say that. Standards that have been established to distinguish legitimate multilevel marketing companies from illegal pyramid schemes include a requirement that reasonably sufficient volumes of product be moved to consumers and ultimately consumed. Companies that place a heavy emphasis on recruiting, accompanied by heavy pressure on distributors to purchase expensive training materials and attend conferences, with products sold almost as an afterthought, can run afoul of the watchful eyes of state attorneys general and other authorities and regulators.

Most of the network marketing companies I have reviewed seem genuinely committed to the products and services that define their business. But in no company have I observed such a passion for the products as in Rexall Showcase International. Many of the most successful distributors, especially doctors using the products themselves or recommending them to patients, had no intention of starting a distributorship, but did so after positive results with the products. On the flip side, many distributors who have quit the business or never really got it going (a frequent occurrence in network marketing) continued to use the products even after leaving. The loyalty seems to be that strong.

In Chapter 7, we will discuss the powerful societal factors and medical developments that are today triggering an explosion of interest in preventative care and natural remedies—developments that make Rexall Showcase International's products attractive to consumers. In this chapter, we survey the products that lie at the core of Rexall Showcase International and the philosophy and technologies behind them.

Rexall Showcase International's product offerings fall into five categories:

1. **Total health systems** to promote cardiovascular health and weight loss, centered on the dietary fiber supplement Bios Life 2 and other food-based natural products
2. **Natural Health Remedies** (homeopathy)
3. **Showcase Nutritionals** (vitamins and herbal products)
4. **Aestivál** (skin and hair care products)
5. **Water-filtration systems**

Rexall Showcase International's Total Health Systems—Seizing the Power of Dietary Fiber

While the pace of change is slow, medical science is heading toward consensus on a back-to-basics approach that emphasizes prevention as preferable to disease treatment alone. Ongoing research worldwide continues to support many of the significant benefits of proper diet and exercise.

According to the Dietary Supplement Health and Education Act of 1994:

- The importance of nutrition and the benefits of dietary supplements to health promotion and disease prevention have been increasingly documented in scientific studies.
- There is a definite link between the ingestion of certain nutrients or dietary supplements and the prevention of chronic diseases such as cancer, heart disease, and osteoporosis.
- Clinical research has shown that several chronic diseases can be prevented with a healthful diet that is low in fat, especially saturated fat; cholesterol; and sodium. This healthful diet should also include a high proportion of plant-based foods.
- Healthful diets may mitigate the need for expensive medical procedures such as coronary bypass surgery or angioplasty.
- Preventative health measures, including good nutrition and appropriate use of safe nutritional supplements, will limit the incidence of chronic disease and reduce long-term health care expenditures.
- And the promotion of good health and healthy lifestyles improves and extends lives while reducing health care expenditures.

Unfortunately, many Americans grossly neglect the daily requirements for dietary fiber, despite conclusive evidence that deficiencies are linked to a number of health-related problems. Most get 8–12 grams of dietary fiber a day, far below the 25–40 doctors recommend as a minimum.

Other problems occur when the body does not get enough antioxidants. This problem has been documented in many medical journals and has become a major focal point in the nutrition industry. Antioxidants have been cited as having positive effects on the body's immune system, the aging process, and a number of other important health-related situations.

Rx for Life

To address both fiber and antioxidant deficiencies, Rexall Showcase International has introduced the Rx for Life system, which it believes to be one of the most comprehensive and advanced nutritional programs of its kind. It contains three selected products formulated to address the dietary deficiencies of a growing number of Americans:

> **Bios Life 2®,** the featured product in the system, is a nutrient drink mix designed to reduce serum cholesterol; it is supported by two patents for its method and composition. The patented matrix of fibers contained in this product has been associated with lowering LDL (low-density lipoproteins, the "bad" cholesterol), lowering triglycerides, and decreasing the risk of heart disease and cancer.
>
> Bios Life 2 also contains a wide array of vitamins, antioxidants, and chromium in a patented form. It is not a chemical appetite suppressant or a meal replacement, but when mixed with water and taken prior to meals, Bios Life 2 creates a comfortable, full feeling. Each serving of Bios Life 2 contains a scientific complex of dietary fibers. These fibers, both soluble and insoluble, are widely recognized for their health benefits and also contribute to a well-balanced, complete weight management program.
>
> How does it work? Fiber encompasses an array of substances indigestible by the human intestine—whereas proteins, fats, and carbohydrates are almost entirely absorbed in the small intestine. Dietary fiber consists of both soluble and insoluble components. Generally, soluble fiber is found in grains and legumes and gives the mushy texture to certain cereals, and insoluble fiber is found in fruits and vegetables.
>
> Soluble fibers help reduce bowel transit time and have a lubricating effect on the intestine. They are also known to help

control and maintain normal cholesterol in two ways. First, they prevent the reabsorption of bile acids from the small intestine. To replace the lost bile acids, cholesterol is drawn from the body, thereby reducing its cholesterol supply. Second, the fermentation process in the intestine produces short-chain fatty acids which block the synthesis of cholesterol. These properties give Bios Life 2 it's special action and it's great value in maintaining overall cardiovascular health and fitness.

As you read about the many doctors and individuals with health problems who have become converts to Rexall Showcase International products, you will hear a great deal about "Bios"—it is the single most discussed and praised product in the Rexall Showcase International line.

A significant number of people who have been on the Rx for Life program report that their serum cholesterol levels drop thanks to the use of Bios Life 2 as part of these systems. In many cases, they see cholesterol levels dropping significantly within the first thirty days, and decreases continue after that. These programs work best when used in conjunction with a responsible lifestyle of rest, exercise, and a healthful diet. They are natural food-based products that are nontoxic and non-addictive and carry no side affects or adverse reactions as so many prescription drugs do.

Nature Force® the second product in the Rx for Life system, is a whole-food antioxidant. Nutritionists, physicians, and many other health industry experts believe that the best place to get antioxidants is directly from food, which is what this product is made of—foods that contain high amounts of antioxidants. Nature Force is not a vitamin pill or a dietary supplement—it is a real food in tablet form. Through a unique distillation process, Nature Force combines the powerful antioxidants in real food pigments and cruciferous vegetables (such as broccoli and odor-modified garlic) with high-quality antioxidant vitamins and minerals.

51

Why are antioxidants getting so much attention? Essentially, antioxidants are substances that help fight against the damage that time and the environment can do to the body. The principle villain is an element vital to every living thing on Earth, oxygen. As oxygen is drawn into the body, it releases unstable, incomplete oxygen molecules that need to bond with something in order to become stable. These unstable molecules are called free radicals, which often steal the substances they need from healthy body cells, causing them damage. Free radicals can also come from external sources such as environmental pollutants, smoking, and medical conditions such as viral infections. Antioxidants act as free radical scavengers that bond with free radicals and thus help them limit the damage they do to cells.

Optimal Performance® is an enhanced energy formula composed of ingredients that have been shown to increase endurance and stamina, increase alertness, and aid in the body's recovery time after a workout. In this product, several potent botanical and mineral nutrients synergistically combine to help boost your energy levels. It does not provide a quick energy high, but rather a longer term overall elevated level of achievement.

Taken together, Bios Life 2, Nature Force, and Optimal Performance—the products that comprise Rx for Life—represent a powerful back-to-basics preventative health system.

One thing you seldom hear a Rexall Showcase International distributor do is make a sale on the basis of price. Quality and results are the selling points here. For example, a sixty-packet supply of Bios Life 2 (a month's supply for most) costs about $54—$1.80 per day. Not cheap but about the same price as a hamburger and fries at a fast-food restaurant. The question is, Which is better for you?

Cellular Essentials®

Even if you're in good health, if you were to look at photos of the inside of your arteries at birth and then in adulthood, you would be shocked at the buildup of arterial "plaque." Heart attacks can be caused by the development of cholesterol and these fatty deposits on the walls of the arteries and the heart. Cholesterol particles and other fatty particles deposit in the blood vessel wall because some are coated with a specific kind of "sticky" fat molecules which form a biological "adhesive tape" around the particles of fat. This leads to deposits and eventually to the clogging of the arteries.

Rexall Showcase International's Cellular Essentials have been developed to promote cardiovascular health and includes a special formulation of vitamins, nutrients, minerals, and amino acids which act synergistically to provide optimal nutrition at the cellular level. Its use of the natural amino acids L-Lysine and L-Proline are believed to act as "Teflon" agents which can prevent and neutralize the stickiness of the particles. Thus, the spread and buildup of new deposits are prevented and existing deposits are loosened. The Cellular Essentials program includes:

Cardio-Basics®, a multi-nutrient compound in tablet form specifically designed to promote the structural stability and health of the cardiovascular system. It contains a balance of vitamins, nutrients, minerals, and amino acids, along with other cell-fuel nutrients to help maximize function and antioxidants for cell protection.

Bio-C™, contains four forms of Vitamin C, plus bioflavanoids which promote absorption of Vitamin C in the body.

Vascular Complete®, a daily supplement of nutrients that work to optimize the healthy function of blood vessels. This formulation of vitamins, nutrients, minerals, and amino acids has been found by many to stop and reverse the "clogging of the arteries" that typically advances with age.

Breakthrough Products in Weight Loss and Maintenance

Americans spend nearly $50 billion a year on weight loss programs and products, probably having something to do with the fact that more than 100 million of us are overweight! Rexall Showcase International is today poised to revolutionize the weight loss industry.

Those looking to manage and maintain their optimal weight as part of an overall healthy lifestyle have found Rexall Showcase International's **Rx for Life™ Weight Management Program** particularly effective. The program includes the Rx for Life pack detailed earlier along with a companion pack. The routine calls for an additional serving a day of Bios Life 2. You take Bios about ten minutes before each meal, and the product forms a soft solution in your stomach, which creates a feeling of fullness.

Also part of the program is one of RSI's homeopathic products called **Metaba-TROL®,** which is formulated with specific medicines proven to control the appetite. The final product in the program is **Enzygen®,** which can aid the majority of Americans who are deficient in digestive enzymes. The lack of these enzymes can lead to increased fat deposits and weight gains.

Yet an announcement anticipated during Rexall Showcase International's 1999 Annual Convention in Albuquerque, New Mexico, is sure to throw the weight loss industry into a frenzy—the introduction of **BodySynergy™,** a breakthrough weight loss system that safely and naturally reduces the craving for food by rechanneling the brain's impulses that produce the feeling of hunger. **BodySyngery,** a complete weight loss program with proprietary products and technologies, is more fully described in Chapter 12, New Frontiers. This new product will surely push the frontier on the stubborn and serious problem of weight control in an exciting direction.

Natural Health Remedies

Rexall Showcase International also offers a line of products that is based on the science of natural homeopathic medicine and designed to activate the body's own healing processes.

The term *homeopathy* comes from the Greek word *homoios* ("like" or "similar") and *pathos* ("suffering"), and homeopathic medicine is based on the premise that "like cures like." While many of the concepts of homeopathy were first postulated by Hippocrates, the modern science was developed two centuries ago by a German physician named Samuel Hahnemann. As described by the *Los Angeles Times* in a recent major series of articles on the growing interest in alternative medicine, "homeopathy is based on the theory that extremely diluted and potentized extracts of various natural substances could neutralize symptoms. When large amounts of a natural substance are given to an otherwise healthy person, mild symptoms of the disease develop. Hence the name, homeopathy, which means 'like treats like.'"

While controversial in many medical circles, homeopathic treatments are widely used and accepted in many countries. For example, 32 percent of the French have used homeopathic medicine, while 42 percent of British physicians refer patients to homeopathic practitioners. In the United States, growing numbers of people are becoming genuinely concerned with the dangerous side effects associated with many prescription drugs and are therefore turning to more natural forms of health care, such as homeopathy.

To help ensure that its line of natural remedies is effective and safe, Rexall Showcase International has called upon one of the world's leading experts in homeopathy, Dr. Tariq Kuraishy, to help develop its products.

"There still isn't a school where you can get a degree in homeopathy. It is only taught at the postgraduate level," Dr. Kuraishy explains. "So I was coming into this science with a solid background in mainstream pharmacology and medical research and all of the disciplines that go with it."

Blending this traditional experience with the fresh approaches embodied in homeopathy, Dr. Kuraishy and Rexall Showcase International have developed treatments that serve as an adjunct to—rather than a replacement for—standard medicine. "We'd all worked within the traditional medical system and brought all the structure and standardization to homeopathy," he explains. "We were able to look at what were considered 'alternative' systems, such as homeopathy, and see them as 'adjunctive' instead."

Applying this training and blend of skills as he developed products for Rexall Showcase International, Dr. Kuraishy focused his attention on three aspects of homeopathic science: extraction, ingredient combination, and delivery systems. "Applying modern scientific standards and techniques to the extraction process has resulted in more control and standardization," he says. "Having worked with homeopathic practitioners all over the world for twenty-five years, I've learned a variety of methods and techniques—and I've applied that accumulated knowledge to the task of combining ingredients in appropriate strengths for truly synergistic formulas."

As for delivery systems, the doctor believes Rexall Showcase International's formulations are unique in the field and insists that no "gimmicks" be involved.

"Over the last two centuries, the most widely used form of homeopathic medicines has been a tiny pill which you allow to melt under your tongue," he says. "There's nothing wrong with that, and for most single remedies that works just fine." Noting that for most people, placing a tiny pill under the tongue is an unfamiliar experience, he has worked to develop delivery systems such as capsules, lozenges, and topical creams that enhance the activity of the medicine and fit easily into people's lifestyles.

"Rexall Showcase International has done more to open doors for homeopathy in the past five years than has been done in the previous sixty years. Part of this is due to the growing number of physicians, dentists, and chiropractors in our business, but I feel a significant part is due to an overall increase in the awareness level of distributors," he concludes.

The most popular Rexall Showcase International natural homeopathic remedies include:

In-Vigor-Ol®, a formula specifically indicated for the temporary relief of everyday fatigue, including general tiredness, lethargic feelings, and exhaustion.

Calmplex-2000®, designed to treat everyday stress, nervous tension, and insomnia with all-natural, nontoxic, and non-habit-forming ingredients. It is made of a blend of extracts from common oat, valerian root, chamomile flowers, and other ingredients.

Defend-Ol®, a product formulated to aid in the initial and on-going symptomatic treatment of and protection from the effects of many environmental pollutants. Many people report significant relief from allergy symptoms when using this product daily.

Reliev-Ol®, which provides temporary symptomatic relief of nasal congestion, coughing, laryngitis, post-nasal drip, and other symptoms common to colds and allergies.

Orarex®, which provides systemic treatment of sensitive and bleeding gums and tooth decay. It is a tooth cream and homeopathic remedy all in one and can be used in place of regular toothpaste.

Intern-Ol®, a product that provides immediate and long-term relief of stomach acidity, heartburn, and indigestion.

TraumEx®, both capsules and a topical cream formula that provide relief of minor aches and pains due to arthritis, backaches and muscle aches, strains, and sprains.

PMS Balance®, a natural homeopathic medicine formulated to provide relief of menstrual discomfort and menstrual stress and irritability.

Nutritionals

Ideally, we would get all the nutrients we need from the foods we eat—fresh fruits and vegetables and healthy meals low in fat and high in vitamins and minerals. But that's not realistic. Furthermore, our dietary needs change as our ages and lifestyles change.

Rexall Showcase International's third category of products is an array of nutritional supplements containing vitamins, herbs and other botanicals, amino acids, and other natural ingredients that have been formulated to address some of the most compelling health needs and concerns facing us individually and as a society. For example:

Men's Formula Plus™ has been created as an integral part of a nutritional program to support prostate and urinary tract health. Scientifically formulated with cernitin and Calcium D-Glucarate (a patented ingredient available exclusively to Rexall Showcase International distributors) in combination with a unique proprietary blend of beneficial herbs and nutrients, Men's Formula Plus supports the body's natural immune functions and cellular health.

This product addresses one of the most serious health concerns facing men—maintaining a healthy prostate gland and urinary tract. When men reach the age of forty, they should begin taking specific steps to address this concern. A proactive approach includes regular exams and good diet and exercise—and Men's Formula Plus.

Women's Formula Plus™ is a nutritional program to promote breast health and address the tragedy of breast cancer with natural preventative measures. Breast health is a major concern for women, and many constantly search for ways to address this concern. Factors that can negatively affect breast health include increased age, a family history of breast health problems, and late menopause. Exposure to pesticides and other chemicals, alcohol consumption, weight gain, and physical inactivity may also be contributing factors.

Preventative measures are extremely important and should include regular self exams, mammography, a diet rich in fiber and antioxidants, and maintaining your ideal body weight. Women's Formula Plus is an integral component of an overall breast health program. It contains a specialized combination of herbs and nutrients to support and maintain breast health, including Calcium D-Gucarate to boost the body's immune system and natural cleansing processes.

Vision Complete™ (formerly known as Vision Essentials) is a product for maintaining optimum eye health, including strengthening the eyes' sensitivity to light and enhancing night vision, increasing blood circulation, and maintaining healthy eye pressure.

Clear Thoughts® is a select combination of herbs and nutrients formulated to enhance short-term memory, increase energy and concentration levels, and stimulate mental function.

In addition, Rexall Showcase International's nutritional products include a wide range of specially formulated all-natural vitamins and other food-based supplements such as: Senior Essentials™, a vitamin and nutrient formula enhanced with extra iron; Essential C 6+6, a specially developed complex of natural vitamin C sources with bioflavonoids; and Meno-Basics® Companion Pack, a dietary supplement and a natural homeopathic remedy for women experiencing perimenopause and menopause.

Aestivál Skin and Hair Products

Most people use some kind of skin and hair care product almost every day, which is why this is a $23 billion industry in the United States alone.

Rexall Showcase International has developed a skin and hair care line called Aestivál. The products—including moisturizing creams, sprays, shampoos, and sunscreens—are designed to nourish, revitalize, and protect the skin and hair from the damaging effects of the sun, pollution, chemicals, and harsh environmental conditions.

The products feature a GlycoActive® system—an exclusive system that is designed to both prevent and correct skin problems. Because they are therapeutic products, not cosmetic, both men and women use them. The most popular products in the Aestivál line included:

The Aestivál Facial Care System

This unique, five-step facial skin regimen, designed for all skin types and conditions, is formulated to help restore the natural health and glow to all skin, while invigorating and beautifying damaged and aging skin. Each step in the system—including a facial cleansing gelee, gentle skin polish, skin renewal treatment, firming eye gel, and protective moisture cream—is designed to benefit the skin in a specific way. In addition, the steps act synergistically to maximize each other's effectiveness, resulting in a system that corrects, protects, and moisturizes.

The Aestivál Body Care System

This three-step system provides progressive, therapeutic skin care. The products include a Hydrating Body Cleanser, an Advanced Exfoliating Body Polish, and a Total Protection Body Moisturizer. Using a unique combination of botanicals, natural cleansers, and moisturizers, the products are used in place of harsh, drying soaps and help cleanse, exfoliate, and moisturize your skin daily.

Aestivál Outdoor Body Protection Formulas

These three exclusive and uniquely formulated sunscreen products have natural ingredients including free radical fighting antioxidant vitamins, a natural blend of essential oils, and Parsol (a patented Swiss sunscreen). The formulas are PABA-free, non-sensitizing, non-irritating and contain no synthetic fragrances. They are ideal for all types of skin including sensitive skin and provide effective protection for the face and body.

The Aestivál Hair Care Collection

This collection of hair care products—which includes Sea-Mineral Shampoo, Sea-Nutrient Shampoo, and Sea-Complex Hair Conditioner—is carefully blended with naturally rejuvenating ingredients from the sea. Each product is rich in vitamins, antioxidants, botanicals, and minerals to revitalize, nourish, and protect your hair and scalp from the damaging effects of pollution, chemicals, and styling appliances.

Water-Filtration Systems

Residents of developed and developing countries alike are growing increasingly concerned about the quality of their drinking water. In the United States, water-filtration systems for residential use represent a $10 billion industry and the future growth projections are staggering.

Recognizing this market and the growing concerns about water quality, Rexall Showcase International has introduced a line of ClearSource® water filters, using a new technology called halogen reduction media, which can be found exclusively in the beverage, brewery, and pharmaceutical industries. These filters help remove chlorine, sedimentation, and bad taste and odor. Two more advanced systems are also available. These systems remove more than 97.7 percent of the lead in water, 95 percent of the chlorine, and more than 99 percent of dangerous waterborne parasites.

A central question any current or prospective network marketer must ask is, Can I get excited about the products? Do I believe in them? Are they products I would use? Are they important products that make a substantial, positive difference in people's lives? In the chapters that follow, we will hear from many people whose personal experiences with the products have led them to answer those questions strongly in the affirmative. This initial introduction to the products of Rexall Showcase International will help you begin to answer them for yourself.

The Rexall Showcase International Business Opportunity

As a network marketing business, Rexall Showcase International does not sell its preventative health care products in stores or directly to consumers through the mail. Rather, it relies upon a sales force of independent distributors to move these products to the market. These distributors are not employees of the company, but men and women who build, own, and run their own businesses. In essence, they derive income from selling the products, capturing the difference between the wholesale price and the retail price, and recruiting others to do the same.

It's a powerful concept that is today being embraced by many companies in many industries as a more effective means of marketing and selling products. And it is attracting millions of participants who are looking for a low-cost, few-hassles opportunity to start their own business. Yet there is fierce competition within the network marketing industry for distributor prospects—and the task of keeping independent distributors motivated and satisfied is always a tough challenge, when they can walk away anytime with seemingly few consequences.

For this reason, a successful network marketing company must have two strong and outstanding sets of products in order to thrive—the *physical* products (or services) it sells to consumers and the *opportunity* products it sells to its current and prospective distributors. A company's centerpiece opportunity product is its compensation plan.

Although this book is not the place to set out in detail the technical features of Rexall Showcase International's plan, I will discuss in general terms the approach and philosophy developed by Rexall Showcase International to attract what it hopes will be a growing force of professional, highly motivated independent distributors.

Rexall Showcase International's distributor leaders, who played a key role in helping the corporation devise its compensation plan, remind us that there are three prominent methods by which most Americans earn their income.

The first is linear income, where the worker is employed by someone else and exchanges his or her time for money.

The second way is residual income, where one earns commissions from repeat sales in industries such as insurance.

The third and most lucrative method is leveraged income, where one earns money based in large part on the efforts of others. As the billionaire J. Paul Getty once said, "I would rather earn one percent of the efforts of 100 people than 100 percent of my own efforts."

Rexall Showcase International has built into its compensation program, called ProfitPlus™, a number of strategies to help the distributor earn strong residual income as well as leverage his or her time by benefiting financially from the efforts of others.

As a distributor you can make money in four different ways. Let's call them profit centers.

The first profit center is the income derived from retailing Rexall Showcase International products. Distributors are paid a 25–40 percent margin on all products they personally sell. Thousands of

Rexall Showcase International participants continue in their regular occupations but enhance their income by several hundred dollars a month through this simple process.

The second profit center allows you to earn money through group commissions. As you begin to sponsor people into the business, and those you sponsor do the same, you will earn commissions on the entire group's sales volume.

As the sales volume of all the distributors in your group increases, you will earn promotions to higher levels in the business. With each promotion comes a higher commission level for both your personal sales and those of your group, up to 20 percent. In this fashion, you can progressively earn more money for doing the same thing!

The position of Director brings with it the highest commission levels. Rexall Showcase International distributors strive to achieve this position as quickly as possible. Although the only *required* cost to enter this business is $49.50 for a distributor kit that contains instructions, rules and procedures, product information, and tips on how to get started, many busy professionals and eager entrepreneurs choose to start their businesses in this more dramatic fashion—and by doing so they position themselves to immediately access other features of the compensation plan.

That brings me to the third of Rexall Showcase International's profit centers. As a Director, when you help others reach Director status, you earn overrides based on their sales volume even as they break away from your original group.

The fourth profit center consists of a series of bonuses that are paid each month based on your sales and sponsoring achievements. Newer distributors particularly benefit from a Growth Bonus Pool that is a kind of profit-sharing program to reward those with the highest levels of new sales volume.

One of the most innovative features of Rexall Showcase International's compensation plan is a stock option program. Rexall Showcase International is one of the only companies within the

Group Commissions

◆ Step Up to Success & Earn 5%–20% Commissions!

In addition to your retail profile, you may also promote to higher levels of leadership and qualify for monthly commissions based on your total number of group points within one *commission* month. And, of course, the higher your sales volume, the more you can earn!

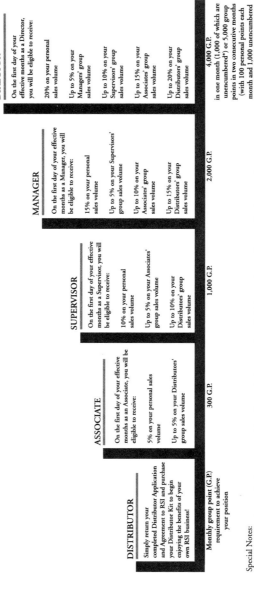

DISTRIBUTOR

Simply return your completed Distributor Application and Agreement to RSI and purchase your Distributor Kit to begin enjoying the benefits of your own RSI business!

ASSOCIATE

On the first day of your effective months as an Associate, you will be eligible to receive:

5% on your personal sales volume

Up to 5% on your Distributors' group sales volume

SUPERVISOR

On the first day of your effective months as a Supervisor, you will be eligible to receive:

10% on your personal sales volume

Up to 5% on your Associates' group sales volume

Up to 10% on your Distributors' group sales volume

MANAGER

On the first day of your effective months as a Manager, you will be eligible to receive:

15% on your personal sales volume

Up to 5% on your Supervisors' group sales volume

Up to 10% on your Associates' group sales volume

Up to 15% on your Distributors group sales volume

DIRECTOR

On the first day of your effective months as a Director, you will be eligible to receive:

20% on your personal sales volume

Up to 5% on your Managers' group sales volume

Up to 10% on your Supervisors' group sales volume

Up to 15% on your Associates' group sales volume

Up to 20% on your Distributors' group sales volume

Monthly group point (G.P.) requirement to achieve your position

300 G.P.	1,000 G.P.	2,000 G.P.	4,000 G.P. in one month (1,000 of which are unencumbered*) or 5,000 group points in two consecutive months (with 100 personal points each month and 1,000 unencumbered points during month two)

Special Notes:
• To be promoted to any level, you must achieve the required group points of which a minimum of 100 need to be personal points.
• In addition to the requirements above, to earn monthly commissions, you must have at least 100 personal points per month.
• The month in which you achieve any position in the RSI ProfitPlus Program is your "qualifying month," and you may start to earn commissions or overrides based on this position in the following month, which is your "effective month" (except for those commissions earned under the RSI Instant Qualifier Program).

*Unencumbered points are any points not used by another Distributor in your group who is qualifying for Director status in the same commission month. All personal points are unencumbered.

Director Override Programs
◆ Receive Generous Overrides on Downline Directors!

Overrides— When you become an active Director with one or more active Director legs, you will begin receiving a 5 percent monthly override on the group sales volume of Directors in your downline.

Bonus Overrides— When you achieve four or more active Director legs, you may qualify to receive Director bonus overrides. Combined with you regular monthly overrides, you may receive total overrides on your fourth, fifth and sixth generations from 7 percent to 10 percent!

Director Levels (Number of Active Legs Shown in Parentheses)

Eligible Generations	Silver (1)	Gold (2)	Pearl (3)	Ruby (4)	Saphire (5)	Emerald (6)
1	5%	5%	5%	5%	5%	5%
2		5%	5%	5%	5%	5%
3			5%	5%	5%	5%
4 Diamond Level*— Receive a 2% bonus override when you have two legs with 5,000 organizational points each and two legs with 2,000 organizational points each. Combined with your 5% override, your total override is now 7% on your fourth generation.				7% OR 5%	7% OR 5%	7% OR 5%
5 Double Diamond Level*— Receive a 3% bonus override when you have two legs with 10,000 organizational points each and three legs with 3,000 organizational points each. Combined with your 5% override, our total override is now 8% on your fifth generation.					8% OR 5%	8% OR 5%
6 Triple Diamond Level*— Receive a 5% bonus override when you have three legs with 25,000 organizational points each and three legs with 5,000 organizational points each. Combined with your 5% override, your total override is now 10% on your sixth generation.						10% OR 5%

*Due to the active leg requirement, Ruby Directors may only qualify for bonus overrides at the Diamond level. However, Sapphire Directors may qualify for bonus overrides at either Diamond or Double Diamond levels, and Emerald Directors may qualify for bonus overrides at any one of the three bonus levels. Please refer to additional requirements under "Standard Distributer Definitions and Requirements" listed at the end of this brochure.

network marketing industry to allow distributors to earn stock options in the parent corporation, Rexall Sundown. It's one more reason to reach the Director level as quickly as possible, for Directors in 1998 had the chance to earn up to 2,700 options. Higher-performing distributors are also given the opportunity to participate in a stock purchase plan that features a 5 percent discount off the prevailing rate and no commissions.

The stock option and stock purchase plans represent a creative and clever strategy on Rexall Showcase International's part to:

- Build on its strength as a publicly traded company
- Enhance its appeal to upscale professionals
- Minimize potential tensions that sometimes arise in network marketing companies between the distributor force and corporate management by making distributors stakeholders in the company's overall performance.

No matter how varied and lucrative a company's compensation plan may sound, the bottom-line proof is in the number of actual dollars that are returned to distributors. Rexall Showcase International President Dave Schofield emphasizes that "our distributor compensation plan pays out a maximum of 63 percent of every sales dollar that goes back to the distributor in the form of commissions and bonuses. Combine that with our stock option programs and other special incentives and we feel that we have the best distributor compensation program in the entire industry."

Recognition Money Can't Buy

With stubbornly high rates of turnover among its practitioners, motivation is essential in network marketing. So is recognition—recognition that extends beyond monetary rewards

One of the most common myths about independent businesspeople is that they have gone out on their own to be alone. Like most of us, those building their own businesses still seek and are motivated by recognition from their families, their peers, and the leaders of their industry. Rexall Showcase International has developed an ascending series of business levels that distributors "promote themselves to" as they increase sales volume and sponsor other distributors. Each achievement carries with it additional income opportunities—but also the respect and admiration of those one respects and admires. While there are many rungs available to climb on Rexall Showcase International's achievement ladder, most distributors agree that two important recognition milestones are the Century Club Elect and the Century Club.

To reach **Century Club Elect,** during a qualification period, a Director will earn 50,000 or more organizational sales volume points (roughly $50,000) for two months, as well as have three or more active "legs," two of which must have 10,000 organizational points. "This is the first truly meaningful achievement level for the most serious people in our business," says distributor leader Stewart Hughes. Members are recognized at national conferences and in the company's magazine and are included in a number of special events and programs.

To reach **Century Club,** a Director's organization will attain $100,000 or more of volume for two months during a qualification period, as well as have at least four active "legs," two of which must have 20,000 organizational points. "When you've made it to the Century Club," Stewart explains, "what that means is you have built a business that has such deep roots, it won't go away." Century Club members also receive national recognition at conventions and in publications, are sponsored on a yearly trip, and are consulted about the company's future direction. In essence, when you've made it to the Century Club, you have become a substantial leader at Rexall Showcase International and in the industry of network marketing.

There are also Amway-style achievement and recognition levels based on business performance, such as diamond, double diamond, and triple diamond—the level at which leaders like Stewart Hughes, Randy Schroeder, and Todd Smith reside. A new and higher "diamond presidential" level has recently been established. No one has reached it yet, but it won't be long. And a representative ten-member panel of top distributors called the Presidential Board of Advisors plays a vital consultative and leadership role at the company.

As treasured as these positions are, top distributors emphasize over and over that the Rexall Showcase International business opportunity has been designed with this reality in mind: Most people who take advantage of it will not work at it full-time and will not initially give up their primary career to pursue it. They will attempt to build it on the side, some with the goal of diversifying their sources of income and never leaving their job, others with the dream of some day replacing their principal income and quitting their job. What has already attracted tens of thousands of active distributors to Rexall Showcase International is that backing up an array of natural preventative health products is a low-cost entrepreneurial opportunity that is simple to comprehend and can be built at one's own pace.

"A gift of health and a gift of finance" is how we've seen Rexall Showcase International business leader Jim Moyles describe the Rexall Showcase International products and business opportunity. As we turn now to the tumultuous changes that are rocking our economy, re- shaping our society, and placing unbearable burdens on traditional health care and retirement programs, we'll see why more people in the United States and around the world will find themselves in great need of those gifts.

CHAPTER FIVE

Navigating an Ocean of Change

Today we are witnessing the steady destruction of the traditional employment economy, where workers sell their time to a company in exchange for money and sell their experience in exchange for security. This traditional economy is being replaced by a single, massive interconnected economy in which money, people, companies, ideas, and technologies are totally fungible. In this new economy, spectacular growth and severe dislocations are occurring side by side. It is an economy that is choking off the more traditional methods of generating secure income but is at the same time spawning new opportunities.

The new economy, defined in equal measure by both turmoil and opportunity, is the first of three profound sea changes that are dramatically altering the way people live and work in the United States and around the world. An organization like Rexall Showcase International will be propelled forward because its products and business opportunity give the average person a holistic program for navigating this ocean of change.

This Is Not Your Father's Economy

The changes reshaping the traditional economy and the search for a better opportunity have taken John Hargett and his family over a long and winding road.

"I've seen both sides of traditional business as a business owner and a corporate executive," he explains. "In the early 1980s my family owned a wholesale grocery business. I spent eight years fighting high interest rates, employee problems, taxes, and larger competitors. All this for fifteen-hour days and hypertension!"

Acting on a tip from his father, who had retired from the pharmaceutical industry, John then entered the corporate world, working for an expanding company in the generic prescription business. "The first five years were incredible," he reports. "I was promoted early on to the position of vice president for the Western United States. This title and responsibility gave me a much larger income and a job security that led my wife Brenda and me to build a new custom home for our family."

But then disaster struck the Hargetts. The company went through a hostile takeover, and John's position was eliminated. He spent nine months looking for a comparable position, but a downturn in the industry made such positions nonexistent. He ended up settling for a lesser job at 35 percent less pay, working for a small drug company.

"The combination of being out of work for nine months and the reduction in pay cost my family all our savings, our 401K, and the down payment on the home we were building. My oldest daughter was forced to leave college. We put our current home up for sale, but the housing market was depressed and no one was buying." Finally, with no other options left, in 1993 the family filed for bankruptcy. "Our home was eventually foreclosed on," John explains, "and Brenda went back to work. Then I found out that my company was up for sale. I knew I was about to go through the same process of elimination all over again."

71

One day during these difficult times, Brenda Hargett—who happened to work with Pam Crosetto, the wife of leading Rexall Showcase International distributor Bob Crosetto—came home and told John that she had learned that the couple were involved in a company that sold preventative health care products through network marketing. "Bob's going to be calling you to invite you to a briefing to check it out," she told John. John told her he was planning to say no when the call came because of his preconceived image about network marketing.

But when Brenda told him that the company was Rexall Showcase International, he was willing to investigate the opportunity. John used to call on the company as an account in the drug industry.

"I knew preventative health care was going to be the future and I became convinced that the products Rexall Showcase International had developed would be in high demand from our aging population," he explains. "What was challenging was the concept of network marketing."

But at work John saw the handwriting on the wall. He knew his job could soon be eliminated. So despite misgivings, he joined the business and worked it during every spare moment he could find. "My immediate goal was to double what I was making in my corporate job so we could buy a home and put our daughter back in college. Within two years, this was accomplished," John reports.

Shortly after that, John left his corporate job to develop his Rexall Showcase International business full-time. Three months later he learned that the company he had worked for was sold, and the entire sales force of which he had been a part was eliminated. "My regret is that not one individual believed they were at risk. Some spent up to a year looking for work rather than invest in owning a business like Rexall Showcase International."

Today, after just four years, John and Brenda Hargett have a Rexall Showcase International organization that extends throughout the United States and parts of Asia. They are among the top twenty earners in the company. "Rexall Showcase International has provided our family not only with a more beautiful home than before but also with a lifestyle that never could have been accomplished in so short a time in traditional business," John says.

He reflects on the lessons he has learned and what others should draw from his experience:

"My father worked for thirty-eight years for the same pharmaceutical company and retired with a terrific pension. My mom stayed at home to raise four sons. It was a good life.

"I wanted to be like my dad. He had always told me to go to college, get a good education, plug into one of the best corporations in America, work hard, and keep your mouth shut and you'll be blessed.

"Up until the early 1990s, my dad's philosophy actually worked. But all that has changed. You have to look really hard to find a single person in corporate America below the CEO level who believes that the next five to ten years is going to be as good as the last five to ten."

Is the Grass Really Greener?

Joan Florence knew all along that there was a better path than working for a big company. Instead, she shared the dream of the overwhelming majority of working people everywhere to "be your own boss." But many who reach that dream—particularly in today's economy—find that it's not all that it's made out to be.

Born and raised in Cullman, Alabama, Joan was one of ten children—five of whom, including Joan, became nurses. She was good at her profession and was recognized for it when she landed a job in blood services nursing with the American Red Cross in Birmingham.

Yet after more than a decade in nursing, Joan saw an opportunity to jump into the weight loss business which, in the mid-1980s, was a lucrative and popular place to be. A franchise opened up in Tuscaloosa, so she moved there, invested her savings, and joined the growing legions of women who own and operate their own small businesses.

As in nursing, Joan was successful. She made that business profitable virtually from the day she bought it to the day she sold it.

"But I learned that being your own boss isn't all that it's cracked up to be," Joan says. "There is a lot of volatility in the weight loss business. I had employee problems. I had overhead expenses. There are regulations and taxes and liability. You're affected by the ups and downs in the economy, changing consumer trends, and even the weather."

For a time, Joan was not only running her own business, but also helping her brother run his—a two-hour drive away "I was just getting burned out," she recalls.

Early in 1996, she received a tape in the mail from a friend who was in a different kind of business called Rexall Showcase International. "But I was so busy, the tape just sat there for three or four months before I even bothered to listen." When she did listen, she was impressed. More importantly, something she heard struck a very personal chord.

"I learned that Rexall Showcase International had a product called Cellular Essentials that could help maintain cardiovascular health. My mother died of heart disease, and so this had a very special meaning for me," Joan says. While she had tried network marketing in the past and never made any money from it, she was sufficiently impressed and intrigued to travel to Rexall Showcase International's headquarters in Boca Raton, where she toured the facilities and met the company management. The next day she attended a regional distributor meeting and joined the business. "It was the caliber of the people that did it for me," she reports.

Starting at ground level in the fall of 1996, Joan began sending tapes to everyone she knew and following up to determine interest. "Within months, the business started taking off. It grew very fast, reaching all across the country." Such quick growth entitled Joan to not only handsome commissions but also company bonuses. "By the end of my first year, my check for October had already reached $16,000 in bonuses and I sold my weight loss business."

After just over two years in Rexall Showcase International, Joan Florence has already attained the triple diamond level and is a member of the Century Club. She accomplished those feats faster than 98 percent of the distributor force. But to Joan, the most striking things about this business is how it differs from her franchise business. "I work out of my home, according to my own schedule, and there are no employees. In most small businesses you may think you're the boss, but the employees are really running you. In this business you have great teammates and a professional company backing you up, without any of the headaches!"

Joan Florence and John Hargett each had to confront the realities of an economy where, even when you make substantial money, you always have to worry whether it's going to disappear overnight—an economy in which you work harder and harder in order to maintain a steadily diminishing quality of life.

If you simply look at the numbers economists love to cite, it's hard to argue with the performance of the American economy. Inflation barely exists. Unemployment is at a ten-year low. Consumer demand and confidence are high. Gasoline prices for our beloved cars and sport utility vehicles are so low that in some places it's cheaper to buy a gallon of gas than it is to buy a gallon of drinking water!

But there's big trouble churning just beneath the surface.

Global Meltdown—How Far Will It Go?

Recently, six leading economists gathered at the headquarters of the U.S. Chamber of Commerce in Washington to help businesspeople assess the impact of Asia's growing financial crisis on the U.S. economy. Prime Minister Goh of Singapore visited later in the day, and when he learned of the presence of these six economists, he smiled and said, "If you have six economists here, then that means you'll get twelve opinions about what's going to happen!"

While the economists at this session did differ in their outlooks, what struck me was that while the topic was supposed to be Asia, they spent as much time talking about Brazil, Latin America, and Russia as they did about Japan, Indonesia, or Thailand.

This underscores the truly global nature of the current economic crisis. Problems that began in Asia have spread to at least three continents. Forty percent of the world is now in a recession.

How long could it be before this turmoil reaches the shores of the United States? The impact has already been felt:

- U.S. exports to Asia dropped sharply in 1998. This is significant because trade with Asia accounts for four million U.S. jobs. The World Trade Organization has estimated that total global trade has been cut in half because of the crisis.

- Corporate profit growth has registered its first year-to-year drop since the recession of 1991.

- Severe economic contractions in some Asian countries as well as Russia have generated varying degrees of political upheaval, social unrest, and even violence. In Russia, concern is growing about a Communist resurgence and a renewed nuclear threat. America may soon have to increase defense expenditures.

- Japan, with the world's second largest economy, is saddled in its banking system with more than $1 trillion in bad debts. Additional closures of major Japanese financial institutions would trigger worldwide upheaval.

- All these factors have helped generate volatility in stock prices—and that has undercut investor confidence.

What are the prospects that Asia and the world economy can pull out of this tailspin?

The international financial structure must be strengthened—with clear and responsible practices for lending, investing, and banking that are adhered to by all. The economies of Asia must proceed vigorously on the path of economic reform—lower taxes, fiscal discipline, legal and financial transparency, and open markets. China should continue the stabilizing role it has played in resisting the temptation to devalue its currency.

Many economists believe Japan holds the key to recovery. The nation needs a complete financial overhaul and the responsible disposal of bad debts. Deregulation of the economy, making it more open—not only to foreign competitors, but also to homegrown small and medium-sized enterprises—is critical as well.

You must have a great deal of faith in the collective leadership of our country and others to envision the speedy implementation of such a program!

Will You Become a "Just-in-Time" Employee?

Despite the happy-face economic statistics that still accurately describe the U.S. economy in many respects, more than a few Americans are worried about their income security. They're beginning to realize they have bought homes and cars they can't afford, delayed implementing a serious savings plan, and overextended themselves in both work and debt.

Their concerns are not surprising when you consider what is happening in corporate America.

A recent report in the *Los Angeles Times* concludes, "For many corporations, downsizing has become a strategy that is used in good times and bad. Senior managers, under considerable pressure from stockholders to increase profits, often take the easiest way by cutting employment costs."

All told, the Department of Labor reports that despite sustained economic growth, 3.6 million workers were laid off during the last two-year period for which statistics are available. These workers had held their jobs for three years or longer. An estimated six million more who had been with the companies less than three years also lost their jobs.

The situation has grown worse since that report. In October 1998 alone, firms announced planned cutbacks of 91,500 jobs, the most in three years. In the first ten months of 1998 alone, 523,000 jobs were cut, a pace exceeding the previous year by 200,000.

Whether the job cuts are attributed to big mergers, loss of Asian export sales, or the need to economize to satisfy investors, the list of major corporations cutting staff is growing longer and longer.

In 1998 alone, the downsizing hit list includes:

AT&T	18,000
Motorola	15,000
Raytheon	14,000
Seagate	10,000
Xerox	9,000
BankAmerica	8,000
Travelers Group	8,000
First Union	7,480
Sunbeam	6,400
United HealthCare	5,400

And as 1998 drew to a close, two other major employment developments came to light: 9,000 workers are slated to lose their jobs should the merger between oil giants Exxon and Mobil be approved; and Boeing announced a two-year downsizing program that would trim its workforce by 53,000.

In the 1980s, the concept of "just-in-time" delivery was popularized in American industry; in this business practice, companies achieve shipping, warehousing, and production efficiencies by ordering raw materials and components only as they are needed and turn them into finished products only as they are ordered. A more efficient transportation system and sophisticated information technology made this commonsense idea possible.

Stanford University Management Professor Jeffrey Pfeffer sees a parallel in the increasing industry practice of layoffs as a strategy of first resort, calling the result for workers "just-in-time employment."

"There are some companies that wouldn't hold workers one minute more than they're needed," he told the *Times*. "They will hold inventories of goods for a long time, but they don't want to hold inventories of people."

Financial manager and commentator John Dorfman notes the cruel irony that announcements of mass firings often trigger increases in a company's stock price. "It's a knee-jerk reaction," he writes. "Practically every time a company announces job cuts, investors bid up the stock. It peeves me to no end."

Furthermore, Dorfman points out that if companies are trying to impress investors, the impression usually doesn't stick around for very long. "Not only are job cuts callous and evidence of bad corporate planning, they aren't even good for the stock's performance over the following year or two." His own survey of companies who had previously downsized discovered that seven out of ten had stocks performing more poorly than the market as a whole.

Echoing Dorfman's conclusion in its own survey, the *Times* reports that "Experts say they're surprised that so many companies are using layoffs as a first resort, especially since studies have shown that downsizing alone doesn't achieve the desired financial results." The paper cites Cornell University professor Theresa Welbourne, who emphasizes that a company should consider the workplace climate it creates when laying off employees. "Downsizings often lead firms into downward spirals. Your high performers seek out other jobs, and that eventually has an impact on the company's earnings."

Being laid off is perhaps the most extreme manifestation of the overall upheaval in the corporate employment environment. The *Times* cites survey findings which discovered that "more than half of all working Americans have been downsized, have worked for a company that has merged or been bought out, or have moved to a different city because of their job."

Moreover, the phenomenon is no longer confined to blue-collar workers on the factory floor. In recent years, workers with at least some college education made up the majority of people whose jobs were eliminated. Better-paid workers—those making at least $50,000 per year—now account for twice the share of lost jobs that they did in the 1980s.

It is no wonder that employees feel less attachment, loyalty, and commitment to their companies—and more competitive with their colleagues, as a "them or me" mentality consumes the workplace. In one survey, 75 percent of employees say companies are less loyal to employees than they were ten years ago. Seventy percent agree that most working people compete more with co-workers now, rather than cooperate with them.

There are also indications that the climate of economic fear has spread from the workplace to the community and the home. When *USA Today* recently asked baby boomers between the ages of thirty-two and fifty to write to the newspaper about how they felt about the security of their white-collar professional jobs, the responses included bitter and poignant tales of lost respect, broken marriages, and even thoughts of suicide. One respondent sadly chronicled the decline of his once-friendly and prosperous suburban neighborhood: "A bunker mentality has replaced neighborhood fellowship. A nomadic existence has usurped the concept of roots—of living in one place for a lifetime. The security that comes from stability is what boomers want most. And it is the very thing that today seems so hard to possess."

Another reader, who worked for a big oil company for twenty-five years before losing his job, put it bluntly: "They can call it reengineering, restructuring, downsizing, but it still means you're fired."

That significant layoffs are occurring in the midst of a growing economy and a booming stock market seems like a contradiction. So does this: At a time when some employees are being let go, others are being brought into the country under special work visas to fill jobs companies say they can't fill with domestic workers.

Other employees claim they are being required to work increasing amounts of overtime. One phone company worker was actually fired after twenty-four years on the job for refusing overtime work because as a single father he had to care for his children. Thus many employees who survive the spate of downsizings find their work environment more competitive, time-consuming, and tense. Succeeding in the corporate "rat race" forces many to put family and quality of life in second place.

To be fair to employers, several points must be kept in mind.

First, the competitive environment requires that companies hold a tough line on costs, or else *everyone's* job at the firm could be at risk.

Second, research shows that most laid-off workers find new jobs within a short period of time. While some earn less, many others actually earn more than they did in their previous position.

Third, many companies are attempting to adapt to individual employee needs, offering overtime work to those who have the time to earn more, while allowing others to cut back their hours, work four-day weeks, or work from home in order to balance employment and family responsibilities.

Fourth, rigid government hiring and firing rules, burdensome regulations, spiraling payroll taxes, and an explosion of employee-related litigation mean that the company's cost of maintaining a worker now extends far beyond that worker's actual salary. Unions and trial lawyers fight to preserve this status quo. In short, there is plenty of blame to go around.

And finally, the economic system with which many find fault has, after all, produced a strong, productive economy with very low unemployment and virtually no inflation—an economy that is admired all around the world. U.S. Chamber of Commerce president and CEO Thomas J. Donohue puts it bluntly: "Don't ask business to apologize for being the one institution in this country that has really worked!"

Indeed it has. American free enterprise has brought untold prosperity and opportunity to our society and to countries around the world that have emulated our system. But that system is undergoing profound change, and many Americans have come to realize they must change with it. They can understand that a bank going bust in Thailand can set off a chain reaction of economic events that could cause them to lose their jobs here in America. But understanding it and accepting and living with it are entirely different matters. Millions of Americans are leaving that uncertain environment or building alternatives around it so that they can achieve more secure, prosperous lives for themselves and their families. They want to take charge of their own lives once again.

Looking for the Right Opportunity

For millions of Americans, the answer has been the same as it was for Joan Florence—be your own boss by starting a small business, buying into a franchise, or becoming a network marketer. The path of entrepreneurship attracts so many because it affords an opportunity to build something on your own. Ideas and creativity count. Hard work pays off. You have the right to succeed and the right to fail. You feel in charge of your destiny.

The men and women who own and run the small businesses and who are self-employed represent a significant economic and social force that brings much of the creativity, energy, inventions, and new jobs to our country. Consider these developments:

- There are more than 22 million small businesses in the United States today, businesses that collectively employ half of all the workers and create two out of every three new jobs.
- Women own more than 33 percent of these businesses and are starting them at a rate faster than men. Compare that to the corporate world where, according to *Business Week*,

women account for just 11.2 percent of the officers of the top 500 firms. In just 32 of those companies do women constitute 25 percent or more of top management. At 125 firms there are no women in those ranks.

- One in eleven American workers are self-employed. The 12.1 million who are self-employed exceed the number of Americans who belong to private-sector unions. We hear a great deal about those unions in the news—but not nearly so much about this strong and growing independent workforce.

- And as discussed in Chapter 3, an estimated 9.3 million Americans own or participate in direct selling businesses, including network marketing businesses like Rexall Show-case International.

Thanks to the availability of relatively low cost information technology and communications, small business owners, the self-employed, and even many in the corporate and professional worlds are doing more work out of their homes. This has become a promising path for many who are trying to meet family responsibilities and avoid long commutes.

Link Resources has been conducting an ongoing survey of people who work at home and found they have been steadily increasing in numbers throughout the 1990s. At least one-third of all adult workers perform some work at home in at least one of the following categories, as detailed by *INC.* magazine:

- Primarily self-employed home workers (12.1 million as of 1995) for whom self-employment is the primary source of income.

- Part-time self-employed home workers (11.7 million) who hold multiple jobs and spend part of their time working from home.

- Telecommuters (6.6 million), employees who work from home part- or full-time during normal business hours.

- Corporate after-hours home workers (8.6 million), who use computers, phones, and faxes to do company work at home after normal business hours.

In recent years, telecommuting in particular has become a popular and highly valued mode of work for professionals. *Business Week*, using more recent data than the Link survey cited earlier, reports that "9.9 million people work outside their main corporate offices at least three days a month, up from 9.1 million in 1997 and 5.4 million in 1993."

Telecommuting's acceptance by mainstream business is highly relevant to Rexall Showcase International as it tries to attract legions of distributors with much the same pitch: By working out of the home, you can better balance family and professional responsibilities; avoid long commutes and live where you want; and, in many cases exercise more control over your own time and schedule. The embrace of telecommuting by top companies and professions helps break down a stigma that suggests if you work out of your home it's because you can't find a prestigious job, you're "just a housewife," or "you must not be very important or successful."

The appeal to employees is obvious. But why are big companies like AT&T, IBM, and Arthur Anderson and others stepping into this still largely uncharted terrain? "Telecommuting has gotten an added boost from a strong economy in which employers must make accommodations to attract the best and brightest workers," *Business Week* concludes. "There are also environmental and political pressures as companies respond to Clean Air Act provisions that aim to cut traffic. And businesses want to pare real estate costs by creating 'hoteling' arrangements in which, say, 10 people share a single cubicle on an as-needed basis."

Starting a small business and being your own boss or seeking a more flexible home-based work schedule from your company or organization—these represent two responses to the growing uncertainty and the deteriorating quality of life found in mainstream employment. They prove to be satisfying accommodations for millions of people. Yet many others find that these supposed solutions create new sets of problems.

In 1996 just over 170,000 new businesses were formally created in the United States. That same year, 72,000 businesses failed. Indeed, most small businesses shut their doors within the first five years of their establishment.

Starting a small business can drain your family's life savings and force you to go deeply into debt—even mortgaging your house—to get the necessary financing. You'll likely need that financing if, for example, you want to buy a good franchise in a substantial business; they can cost you from $100,000 to $500,000!

If you have little or no track record, it can be very difficult to get those needed bank loans. A recent survey by the Census Bureau found that even with the current low interest rates, nearly 49 percent of small businesspeople said it had become more difficult to get financing than in the past. And, even with what is reputed to be a strong economy, the number of small businesses reporting a growth in sales fell to its lowest level since 1968. This is an ominous development because smaller enterprises account for just over half of the output of the entire American economy.

To add to the small businessperson's headaches, governments at all levels continue to pile on burdensome and often contradictory layers of regulations. Safety inspectors from the federal Occupational Safety and Health Administration (OSHA) have recently put out the word that they are going to start applying rules designed for big companies—companies that have at their disposal large human resources and safety staffs, not to mention teams of corporate lawyers—to small ventures as well. We've already seen in congressional hearings how the IRS had been targeting smaller business and family farms, which don't have the resources to fight back.

Look for payroll tax hikes, new health care mandates, and additional mandatory increases in the minimum wage to add substantially to the cost of maintaining employees. And should one of those employees become disgruntled or seek to exploit you, he or she can always find an eager trial lawyer to help take you to the cleaners.

Thankfully, the United States is home to millions of entrepreneurs who are courageous, stubborn, or both and who continue to fuel the vital small-business engine of our economy. Yet, as Joan Florence and many others have discovered, "being your own boss" did not lead to the kind of income security, time freedom, and lifestyle they dreamed of. It may have been an important step on the journey to financial independence, but it was not in itself a satisfactory destination.

Getting on the Right Side of Change

As he surveys the economic changes that are buffeting big companies and their employees as well as small businesses and their owners, Rexall Showcase International distributor leader Todd Smith believes that "the majority of the population could be self-employed in the near future whether they are ready or not. You can no longer depend on your employer or your job to provide for your security or even to be around tomorrow. How long could you last?

"If you are an employee who works for someone else, you should find a new model to take control of your finances."

The same is true for business owners or those with their own medical, legal, and other professional practices. "If you own a business you're not exempt," Todd says. "Most are being crushed with overhead, taxes, and employee headaches. Owning a traditional small business can be a financial death trap—you pay a fortune to get in and all you pull out is an average income."

Just as with the situation facing employees working for someone else, the old model of owning your own business and being your own boss is gone too.

Many people confront this new economic landscape and ignore the changes. They continue to rely on that which can no longer be relied upon for their financial security and quality of life. Others play the blame game, lashing out bitterly at corporations, the government, or the state of the world in general. But Todd Smith and many others at Rexall Showcase International believe you can put yourself on the right side of these changes.

"You can protect yourself and free yourself from dependence on the old models," Todd underscores. "You have options."

Along with every period of tumultuous change come exciting new possibilities for those willing to see them and seize them. Rexall Showcase International believes it has developed a new business model that responds to the changes and makes them work for you. How is this new business model defined, and how does it differ from traditional job and small business models?

- It is a home-based business opportunity. There is no store, no lease—just a phone, a fax, and a personal computer. Your commute lasts for as long as it takes you to walk down the hall.
- There are no employees, payroll, schedules, payroll taxes, workers compensation claims—no employee headaches.
- It operates synergistically with a parent company as what Todd Smith calls that company's "entrepreneurial arm." The old way for companies to move products to consumers was to hire a huge sales force, launch expensive ad campaigns, and sell expensive franchises. Under the new model, the company sticks to developing the products and delegates the marketing to its "entrepreneurial arm."
- There is a potential for a rapid increase in income and for high income, because when you are freed of all the headaches inherent in the old model, you are able to focus all your attention on customers, sales, and income.
- And you develop a secure diversified income, a residual income that pays you over and over for the same activity, one where you get paid for the efforts of others you bring into the business.

Putting yourself on the right side of global economic change does not necessarily mean throwing your current career and lifestyle overboard. It does mean managing your career in a highly reflexible, entrepreneurial fashion. The days of working one job for one paycheck are dying. An entrepreneurial career means diversifying your activities and developing several streams of income. For some, that may mean a job or practice with a Rexall Showcase International business on the side. Others may pursue their Rexall Showcase International business full-time and invest some of the profits in other businesses, stocks, or properties. But for all it can mean retaking control of your financial and personal life—successfully navigating an ocean of change!

We should not overemphasize the fears of those who remain wedded to the old employment or small-business-ownership models. I suspect many more are excited by the possibilities of pursuing more than one job, career, business, and stream of income. An entrepreneurial career can be fun and stimulating, once many of the risks and headaches are removed. At a time of great economic upheaval, Rexall Showcase International is stepping in with an opportunity for people to make a transition, as quickly or as gradually as they like, from a traditional career to an entrepreneurial career. As the pace of this economic change accelerates and as more people realize they need and indeed have better options, I believe Rexall Showcase International's distributor force will grow at a tremendous rate in the United States and around the world. Let's look at the stories of two families who, each in their own fashion, have made this transition.

A Better Way to Live

Rick Jordan of Laguna Niguel, California, has been in the commercial insurance business for more than nineteen years; it is a business he loves, but he realized some time ago that it was changing and becoming less lucrative. He was first exposed to network marketing in the late 1980s and actually sat on the board of a network marketing company. Intrigued by this business model and concerned about changes in his own industry, Rick decided to become a distributor.

"I hired a CPA to analyze various companies' financial statements and compensation plans," Rick recalls. "He also put together many financial models to see which compensation plan was best. Rexall Showcase International was by far the best and the only one I would associate with."

With the support of his wife, Lori, Rick began building his Rexall Showcase International business in 1993. But doing so didn't mean shutting off his involvement in other business ventures. "I have other business interests," he explains. "I own two insurance agencies, a full-service hand car wash and custom detail center, and partnerships in several fast-food restaurant franchises.

"I have worked the Rexall Showcase International business completely part-time," Rick emphasizes, but even so he has been able to build an organization that sells more than $1 million of products every month. He is one of the company's top twenty income earners and is a triple diamond director.

"I feel I exemplify the ability to build a successful network marketing business without giving up your current career or other business interests," Rick believes. "Time is a very important consideration in building this kind of business and I have built mine part-time."

Indeed Rick Jordon illustrates one attractive approach to building an entrepreneurial career that is exciting, challenging, and bolstered with several distinct streams of income. A few miles away in Orange, California, Gary and Debbie Mooers took advantage of the Rexall Showcase International business opportunity to follow a different path.

"I had been working for a multi-billion dollar savings and loan for nine years when one of my customers gave me a tape outlining the Rexall Showcase International products and business," Gary explains. "I was hesitant to even consider multilevel marketing because I thought it meant door-to-door sales."

It's not that Gary didn't want a business of his own. "I often thought about going into the mortgage business," he says. "But that would have taken substantial capital as well as the confidence enough to believe that I wouldn't end up working eighteen hours a day to open a mortgage business only to end in failure.

"So when I saw this opportunity to be an entrepreneur without taking that huge risk associated with traditional businesses, I couldn't resist."

Keeping his job and working his Rexall Showcase International business on the side, Gary was driven to succeed by the fact that Debbie, a vice president for a Fortune 100 company, "was working a treacherous sixty hour week in the rat race of corporate America. She was never out from under the pressure." Moreover, with a young child under the care of a nanny, the Mooers wanted a life where they, not the nanny, could be the real parents.

Things happened fast. "Within twelve months, we saw the light at the end of the tunnel," Gary says. "Within sixteen months, we had completely replaced Debbie's income. Within two years, we had replaced both our incomes.

"Debbie 'fired her boss' in the twenty-fourth month and stayed home. I waited two more months and did the same."

Concludes Gary, "We are now true entrepreneurs, working out of our home with no boss. This is not just the cleanest way I know to do business, nor is it only the cleanest and most efficient way to move product. This is a better way to live!"

CHAPTER SIX

When Boomers Become Elders

Are You Ready for the Impact?

If Bob Crosetto had any doubts that he had made the right decision to give up his lucrative insurance business for a full-time career with Rexall Showcase International, they were eliminated when he opened up his morning newspaper in Bellevue, Washington, one day in 1995. There he read that his former office manager, whom he had fired before selling the business, had been arrested on charges of paying to have her ex-husband murdered so that she could collect on the life insurance policy Bob had sold her.

"I couldn't believe it," Bob said. "I sold this woman and her husband their life insurance policies. That was before I realized what a disruption she was in the office and had to fire her. Later on, after I sold my business I heard the couple divorced and she moved to Phoenix. Apparently she went to a bar one night, struck up a conversation with a guy who she then hired to kill her ex-husband. Then he drove up to Washington, knocked on the ex-husband's door, and when he answered it, slit his throat."

The authorities were soon on the woman's trail; and while a policeman was interviewing her in Phoenix, she realized the hit man she had hired could be a star witness against her. Incredibly, she proceeded to offer the cop another chunk of the life insurance proceeds to hit the hit man!

Bob's ex-employee is now serving life in prison. The whole macabre experience "reminded me why I got out of that business and maybe explained why before I did, I always seemed to get a stomach ache when I pulled into the parking lot for the day's work."

Bob never expected to be in the insurance business anyway. What he had always wanted to do was to go into education. "Both my parents were teachers," Bob relates. I had hoped to follow their lead, but in a slightly different fashion. I wanted to be the superintendent, so I could be the boss."

There may be one or two school superintendents in America who feel as if they're the boss—even with the competing demands of school boards, parents, taxpayers, teachers, students, and unions! It didn't take long for Bob to recognize reality. Despite a strong educational background that included a master's degree in counseling as well as classroom teaching experience, by the mid-1960s Bob had "graduated" into the world of business. He became a successful life insurance salesman and later established his own firm, which produced a substantial $500,000 annual income for the Crosetto family.

But as Bob marched through his fifties, his outlook on life began to change. "It was getting harder and harder to manage a small business," Bob remembers. The hours were grueling, the regulations and taxes were crushing, and the employee problems generated a steady supply of headaches—and stomach aches! The Crosettos also made some investments that didn't pan out. "I realized I was headed for retirement with nothing much put aside," Bob says.

During this period, Bob jumped at the chance to go diving in the Bahamas with a good friend. The brief escape provided him with an opportunity to reassess his life. "I didn't want to come back to my business," he remembers. "I realized then that I had to look for something new and different to do." The central question for Bob was, "What would that be?"

Guiding him to an answer was some advice from his friend that Bob to this day shares with anyone he can. The key to success is to "make your strengths productive and your weaknesses irrelevant."

"If you think about it, that's very perceptive advice. Most people spend a lot of time and effort trying to address their weaknesses and correct their flaws. You know what that means? It means they eventually work themselves up to 'average,'" Bob reasons.

Feeling invigorated with a fresh outlook, Bob returned home to Washington and told his wife, Pam, he wanted to change course. "She assumed I was going through a mid-life crisis at age fifty-eight," Bob says with a laugh.

Undeterred, Bob first hired a friend to manage his insurance business. Then he set out to find a new venture where he could make his strengths productive and develop the kind of income security and quality of life insurance failed to provide.

Coincidentally, the friend Bob brought on to run his business told him about a new product that many people were finding would lower their cholesterol, something Bob needed and wanted to do. It was Rexall Showcase International's Bios Life, and after using the product for a short period of time, Bob saw his cholesterol drop fifty points.

When Bob found out there was a business behind the product, he was excited, especially because it appeared to be a business where he could put his strengths—the ability to network and the desire to teach—to productive use. But first he checked the company out thoroughly. "I had to be damn sure it would still be around a few years down the road."

The strength of the Rexall name counted a lot for Bob. "It brought back memories of my childhood in Langley, Washington. I loved going down to the corner Rexall drugstore and having a 'Green River'—which was a very sweet, refreshing lime drink," he recalls fondly.

After completing his inquiry and taking Pam on a few long walks around the lake to explain his thinking, in February 1994 Bob sold his insurance business and within a few months was devoting all his professional energies to building a Rexall Showcase International distributorship.

Finally finding a venue where he could pull together all of his skills and interests in teaching, counseling, and networking, Bob Crosetto has enjoyed tremendous success, moving more than $10 million in product with the help of the thousands of distributors and 1,200 directors who constitute his organization.

Now at the age of sixty-two, Bob has focused a great deal on what this kind of business can mean for people his age. "One of the main reasons I sold my insurance business was the realization that it really wasn't preparing me at all for retirement. I could envision myself still driving up to that office every day for years and years and years."

And there was more at stake than finances. It was about personal renewal. "People get old if they don't have goals," Bob says. "This is a great business for people at or near retirement age. We haven't done as much as we should to focus on this group. I'm going to help spread the word.

"I really believe the best part of my life is ahead and I want to make that possible for others my age too."

The Second Sea Change

The 76 million baby boomers, those of us born between 1946 and 1965, are getting old. Boomers are turning 50 at the rate of 10,000 a day. Beginning in the year 2011, when the first boomers reach the age of 65, the ranks of America's elderly will explode. At the same time, overall population growth will continue to decline, and the ratio of working-age Americans to retired Americans will decline, perhaps as low as two workers for every retiree. The elderly are living longer, and at the same time young adults are having fewer children.

The aging of America, a pattern that is being replicated all over the world, is the second great sea change that presents both profound challenges for society and exciting possibilities for a company like Rexall Showcase International. Rexall Showcase International products will be highly attractive to baby boomers as they proceed through middle age and toward retirement and grow increasingly concerned about the onset of major health challenges such as heart disease and cancer. They expect and hope to be living longer than their parents and grandparents and want to do so in good health for as long as possible.

At the same time the Rexall Showcase International business opportunity responds to their desire to be financially secure when they retire and to maintain an interesting activity that challenges them and gives them a purpose. Boomers represent the most affluent generation in human history. They've grown accustomed to a life of hard work that brings rich rewards, and they don't want to have to give it all up. Yet they are coming to understand that because they are so large in number, there is no way the government's social safety net of retirement and medical insurance programs can possibly survive the onslaught of boomer retirees intact.

Like Bob Crosetto, millions of us now realize how poorly prepared we are for retirement. By one estimate, 96 percent of all pension plans will pay at most 20 percent of our current salary when we retire. Can you live on that?

According to *Success* magazine, a person 35 years old today making $60,000 will need $150,000 a year at age 65 just to maintain his or her current lifestyle. That means this person would have to save $44,000 a year—100 percent of after-tax income—to live at that level in retirement.

Many Americans are taking some steps to prepare. Twenty-five million participate in 401k plans that collectively have amassed a trillion dollars in assets. Thirty-seven percent of U.S. households invest in mutual funds. Yet still, only an estimated 2 percent who reach the age of 65 are financially independent.

The Demographic Time Bomb

If you are one of the majority of people who have not put into place an effective strategy to retire in good health and sound finances, you've picked the worst possible time to be in that condition. That's because all around the world a demographic time bomb is ticking away. When it explodes, rich and poor countries alike will be flooded with retirees looking to governments and a proportionally shrinking population of younger workers to provide for their income, medical, and lifestyle needs.

Statistics from the Bureau of the Census are usually dry and antiseptic but in this case they tell a dramatic story:

- America's population continues to age. In 1860, half the population was under the age of 20. In 1994, half was 34 or older. By the year 2030, half will be 39 or older.
- From 1900 to 1994, the elderly population—those aged 65 and older—increased eleven times over, compared to just a threefold increase for those under the age of 65. Until the year 2010, the rate of growth of the elderly will be relatively modest; but it then explodes from 2010 to 2030 as the baby-boom generation retires.
- Since 1960, the number of Americans aged 65 or older has increased 100 percent, compared to 45 percent for the population as a whole. The number of people aged 85 and over has increased 274 percent.
- By 2000, America will be home to 35.3 million people aged 65 or older, 12.8 percent of the population. By 2030, 70.1 million Americans will be 65 or older, 20.1 percent of the population.

- By the year 2000, 12.4 million will be between the ages of 75 and 84; 4.3 million will be 85 or older. By 2030, those numbers will explode to 23.3 million and 8.8 million respectively!
- Globally, 357 million people were aged 65 or older in 1994, about 6 percent of the world's population. The world's elderly are growing at a rate of 2.8 percent a year, compared with 1.6 percent growth for the population as a whole. Over half of the world's elderly live in poorer developing nations today. By 2030, two-thirds of the elderly will live in those countries.

Much of America's aging process has been brought about by the welcome news of longer life expectancies. When the nation was founded, life expectancy at birth was just 35 years. In the mid-1800s it was 42. By 1900 it was about 48. And as we enter the new millennium, it will reach 78! Social and financial impacts aside, this has been a remarkable human achievement, owed in large part to medical advances as a well as a free economic system that has improved living standards.

But longer life spans are not the only demographic shift we're seeing in our country and many others. Lower birth rates mean that fewer workers are available to take the place of retirees—and that presents a tremendous challenge for the "mature" developed economies of the West. In Japan, a country with the one of the longest life expectancies in the world, the percent of the population aged 65 and over has already exceeded 16 percent—and by 2030 the total population in that country is projected to be less than it is today. How do you sustain economic growth and collect sufficient taxes to support growing numbers of retirees who have ever-increasing medical needs, when there are relatively fewer and fewer workers coming into the system?

In 1950 there were 16 workers for every retirement-age Social Security beneficiary in the United States. By 1960 the ratio had narrowed to 5 to 1. Today it is just over 3 to 1. And by the year 2030, it will be 2 to 1. That means in effect that every working couple that year will have an extra person to support in addition to their own family!

The United States is not alone in grappling with a declining ratio of workers to retirees. According to the *Los Angeles Times,* here is the current situation in some of the world's major economies:

Country	Number of workers	Number of retirees	Ratio
Britain	27 million	9 million	3:1
Canada	14 million	4 million	3.5:1
France	25 million	11 million	2.3:1
Germany	32 million	11 million	2.9:1
Italy	20 million	21 million	0.95:1
Japan	70 million	17 million	4.1:1
U.S.	147 million	44 million	3.3:1

Life expectancy in each of these countries actually exceeds that of the United States. As citizens live longer and birth rates hold steady or decline, expect these ratios to decline throughout the world's most advanced countries, severely testing both their prosperity and their social cohesion.

The Census Bureau concludes: "Demographers have called out an early warning that the Baby-Boom generation is approaching the elderly ranks. American society has tried to adjust to the size and needs of the Baby-Boom generation throughout the stages of the life cycle. Just as this generation had an impact on the educational system (with "split shift" schools and youth in college) and the labor force (with job market pressures), the Baby-Boom cohorts will place tremendous strain on the myriad specialized services and programs required of an elderly population.

"A window of opportunity now exists for planners and policymakers to prepare for the aging of the Baby-Boom generation."

Social Insecurity

But will those planners and policymakers heed the early warning and act judiciously to shore up the programs designed to support retirees in their old age? Can you count on politicians in Washington to make necessary changes now to forestall the need for more drastic changes later? And even if they find the political backbone to do so, will government programs under any scenario provide the income security you need to retain a semblance of your current lifestyle?

Started in 1935, Social Security worked reasonably well for the first half-century of its existence. In fact, it helped substantially to reduce poverty among the elderly. It worked because there were many more workers paying in than there were retirees pulling money out—not to mention the fact that the initial retirement age of 65 actually exceeded a man's life expectancy at the time!

And with so many boomers in the workforce, as well as a long string of payroll tax increases, the Social Security trust fund will continue to take in more than it sends out until 2013. Then the draining of the fund starts, as fewer workers pay into the system and retiring boomers begin to retire. Interest on the current surplus will close the gap for a while, but by 2030, without changes in the system, Social Security will become insolvent.

The burdens on the system are growing, and yet many Americans are highly dependent on the program's benefits:

- For 63 percent of beneficiaries, Social Security provides at least 50 percent of their total income.
- For 26 percent, it provides 90 percent of total income.
- For 14 percent, it is the only source of income.

Seniors and soon-to-be seniors are worried—and they should be. A recent poll conducted by the American Association of Retired Persons (AARP) found that 55 percent of Americans agreed with this statement: "In theory, Social Security is still a good idea, but I doubt if this country can afford it anymore." Baby boomers are the most skeptical—just 16 percent expressed confidence in the viability of the system.

Those who expect to join the approximately 37 million seniors who depend on the Medicare program to take care of their health needs should understand that this program is under the same threat of collapse as Social Security—except that Medicare's day of fiscal reckoning comes even sooner.

In 1996, Medicare gobbled up nearly $200 billion, about 12 percent of the total U.S. budget. Expenses have exceeded receipts since 1995, a trend that will only accelerate as medical procedures get more expensive, the ranks of the elderly grow, and life expectancies further increase.

The most immediate problem is that the trust fund that finances inpatient hospital care under Medicare Part A will spend its last nickel shortly after the turn of the century.

Medicare is caught in the same demographic squeeze as Social Security. In 1995 there were 3.9 workers paying taxes to cover each Medicare beneficiary. The Medicare trustees estimate that by 2030, there will be just 2.2 workers for every beneficiary. Meanwhile, abuse of the system is rampant. A recent Inspector General's report found that the Medicare program wastes $1.03 billion a year by overpaying for certain prescription drugs.

The problem for workers and retirees is that each time politicians try to fix these problems, they only come up with two responses: increase taxes and reduce benefits.

For the typical American, Social Security is already an expensive program with low benefits and a poor rate of return on investment:

- The average monthly benefit for today's retiree is $663 for those retiring at 62 and $925 for those retiring at 65. The maximum monthly benefit is just over $1,300 per month.
- Employers and their employees each pay a tax of 7.65 percent (for Social Security retirement and disability as well as

Medicare) on the first $72,600 of income, for a combined payroll price tag of 15.3 percent.

- Self-employed entrepreneurs, the engine of our economy, are hit particularly hard. They pay the whole tax themselves. Moreover, the amount of income subject to the Social Security payroll tax was hiked on January 1, 1999; and further scheduled increases have already been signed into law.
- Low inflation is on the whole a positive development, but it means that benefit increases tied to the inflation rate have in recent years been minuscule.
- Benefits are now taxed as well. Currently, retired seniors on Social Security can earn up to $14,500 without any taxes on benefits. But after that they lose one dollar in benefits for every three dollars in additional income.
- The retirement age is going up. It will gradually increase to 67.
- And a particularly sore point for investment-savvy boomers is the fact that the average rate of return for their dollars "invested" in Social Security is less than 2 percent—worse than even a passbook savings account. Most believe they could do much better in the stock market, which explains the growing interest in a partial privatization of the system.

What a bargain! Higher taxes, a poor rate of return, delayed retirements, and benefits that for most won't come close to sustaining their current lifestyle. On top of that, the system is threatened with insolvency due to the aging of the population. The question facing boomers is, Can you get ahead of all this through savings and investments alone? For most the answer is no.

The same dilemma confronts prospective retirees all over the world. The *Los Angeles Times* recently reviewed the status of government retirement programs and the taxes required to pay for them:

Japan. Retirement age to increase from 60 to 65; shared payroll tax to rise to 29.8 percent by 2026.

Britain. Maximum benefit from government pension reduced from 25 percent of wages to 20 percent. Retirement age for women to be increased from 60 to 65.

Canada. Shared payroll tax to rise from 5.85 percent to 9.9 percent in 2003. Benefits to be gradually reduced, particularly for upper-income retirees.

France. Retirement age to increase from 60 to 65. Benefits to be calculated on best 25 years of earnings rather than 15. Workers must pay into the system for 40 years, up from 37.5.

Germany. A 1 percent increase in the federal value-added tax will be imposed to help pay for pensions. Benefits will be reduced from 70 percent of previous earnings down to 64 percent.

Italy. Retirement age, now 57 for women and 62 for men, will increase to 65 for both. Civil servants will work until age 67.

"Social Security does face a crisis in 2013 and beyond," concludes James K. Glassman of the American Enterprise Institute. It is a system that must be reformed."

Will it be? Astute political observer David Broder of the *Washington Post* recently echoed the doubts shared by many, despite pronouncements by the president and members of Congress that they were ready to tackle the issue: "Privately, many in the administration are far more pessimistic," he writes. "While Democrats did not make Social Security as much a partisan issue in the 1998 campaign as in some past years, the lines are now being drawn.

"Conservative think tanks such as the CATO Institute and the Heritage Foundation want Republicans to insist on converting a portion of future Social Security taxes into individual savings accounts. Labor and its allies, who are owed a lot by the Democrats will . . . block any such change.

"An administration official said, 'There's a substantial chance that by March [1999] the Republicans will be attacking the Democrats as socialists and Democrats will be accusing Republicans of wanting your grandmother to survive on cat food.'"

Recovering a Sense of Purpose

The impact of age on our society extends far beyond the pressures it puts on our nation's fiscal health and our personal finances. As Bob Crosetto emphasized, maintaining a sense of purpose and embracing a set of interesting and challenging goals is important for everyone, but particularly for those in or near retirement.

It's a troubling but well-documented fact that suicides among the elderly, especially men, are on the rise. In fact, the Census Bureau reports that elderly men are more likely to commit suicide than to die in motor vehicle accidents. Sometimes they take their elderly spouses with them.

George and Elnor White were married for fifty-eight years. In November 1998, the *Washington Post* reported, their bodies were found in the garage of their suburban Baltimore home. Elnor was killed by her husband with his World War II army pistol. He then turned it on himself. "In homicide-suicides involving older couples, depression is often as much the killer as any bullet," the newspaper concluded. "With cruel speed it transformed . . . one of Maryland's most respected trial lawyers into a despairing, paranoid man, a man certain that the future held only penury and pain for himself and his wife. No balance sheet, no doctor, no loved one could convince him otherwise."

The *Post* goes on to report that in Florida, "where retirees make up about 20 percent of the population, an elderly homicide-suicide is reported on average at least once a month." This troubling trend underscores the need for countries with growing legions of elderly to open up and make room for their experience and continuing contributions—for their sake and for the benefit of society as a whole.

Indeed, in a report called "The New Millennium American," analysts at PaineWebber note that the desire to remain productive,

useful, and challenged is a central part of the profile of the baby
boom generation: "Unlike their parents who grew up amid the
hardships of the Depression and World War II, baby boomers today do not view a leisurely retirement as their reward for years of
hard work and sacrifice. Boomers have always been work centered
and will remain so. . . . For many boomers, work is a career and a
way of life, not a job; it provides a social network of professional
contacts and is the source of inner satisfaction as well as a way to
pay the mortgage."

The authors go on to cite a recent survey in *Business Week* that
revealed:

- A large majority—75 percent—of baby boomers expect to
  keep working after they retire from their current careers.
- But only 15 percent want to do so in their former occupation at reduced pay.
- Another 28 percent want to work part-time in a different
  occupation.
- And 10 percent want to start a new business.

"Boomers will not retire," the analysts conclude. "They will re-
tread. As they will grow older, they will restructure their lives so as
to relieve stress and work on their own terms."

Driving aging boomers' search for new projects and directions is the sense among many that as life progresses, their current goals are going unfulfilled. The PaineWebber report found
that "in recent years, many baby boomers have increasingly felt
the pang of unmet expectations. Now that most of them are in
their forties—and despite continued material prosperity—many
boomers feel that they haven't 'made a difference' or 'made the
world a better place.'"

The analysts continued: "Many boomers have still not found inner happiness—to the contrary they are probably the most stressed

generation in history." Reviewing survey research, they identify this stress as coming from:

- The normal responsibilities of middle age—career, finances, caring for children and elderly parents—with additional pressures coming from a sense of no job security and the failure to save for retirement.
- The disappointment of their expectations. "Boomers are for the most part, middle-class, middle-aged and middle of the road, a state that many of them revolted against when they were growing up."
- Too many decisions to make. "The downside of the Information Age is that people are overloaded with information and choices." In a recent survey of all Americans, a full 40 percent said that the lack of time was a bigger problem for them than the lack of money.

Echoing a point discussed in the last chapter, the PaineWebber authors conclude that we have indeed entered a period of cradle-to-grave entrepreneurialism. "More and more Americans are being forced to behave like entrepreneurs in managing their careers, supervising their children's education, and planning their retirement," they write. "Many people of 'retirement age' are likely to choose the stimulation of work over the monotony of having nothing to do."

Rexall Showcase International is thus ideally positioned not only to fill a "health gap" for consumers of its products and an "income gap" for its business builders—but also a "meaning gap" for those at or near retirement as well as for middle-aged boomers dissatisfied with their current contribution to society. It's easy to dismiss Rexall Showcase International's vision of "making a positive difference in people's lives" as corporate sloganeering. But it's a vision that drives many in and out of the Rexall Showcase International business who understand that greater personal happiness can flow from being part of something larger than themselves.

Remembering the Young

The aging of society impacts more than just the elderly; in fact, it portends huge consequences for succeeding generations of younger Americans. Many elderly or near-elderly are concerned not only about their income and health security in later years, but also about being a burden on children and grandchildren. Those family members in turn wonder how they can properly maintain their elders in comfortable surroundings.

Longer life expectancies are creating several phenomena seldom seen before:

- The old are taking care of the very old. According to the Census Bureau, more and more people in their fifties and sixties are likely to have surviving parents, aunts, and uncles. They "will face the concern and expense of caring for their very old, frail relatives since so many people now live long enough to experience multiple chronic illnesses," the Bureau reports.

- Furthermore, a sizable proportion of the baby boomers have remained childless (26 percent as of 1990). That will translate into big increases in the number of seniors who are unable to count on children for care and must therefore be institutionalized.

- A so-called sandwich generation has emerged, consisting of those boomers who find themselves paying for their children's college education and the care of their elderly parents or grandparents all at once. How many of us are financially equipped to do that and at the same time save and invest for our own retirements?

These accumulating financial pressures, coupled with the insecurities now inherent in the workplace, have in recent years pushed the concerns of children to the background. The traditional family is under serious strain:

- Since 1970 there has been a 548 percent increase in the number of unmarried couples with children under 16 years of age.
- In 1993, 31 percent of all babies were born to unwed mothers—up dramatically from 10.7 percent in the 1970s. In 1950, it was just 3.9 percent.
- There are nearly 8 million single-parent households with children at home.

A majority of working-age women are now employed outside the home. This has been a positive development for most women, but the impact on children of both single-parent households and working-couple households is unmistakable. Denied the close supervision and nurturing of times past, many youth are drawn into or are victims of destructive behavior.

Youth crime is on the rise, even as crime rates overall level off. More than 1.5 million young people in America are arrested for crimes each year. Young men under the age of 18 commit 17 percent of all violent crimes.

Drug use among young people is on the way back up after a hopeful but short-lived dip in the mid-1980s. A recent comprehensive survey of junior and senior high school students uncovered these troubling findings:

- Since 1991 the proportion of eighth-graders who had taken any illicit drug in the previous twelve months has almost doubled, from 11 percent to 21 percent.
- At the same time the proportion of tenth-graders taking those drugs rose by two-thirds, from 20 percent to 33 percent.

- The proportion of twelfth-graders taking an illicit drug in the past twelve months has increased from 27 percent to 39 percent.

Researchers are finding further consequences for children when parents find they must both work harder and longer outside the home. "Parents are right to be concerned about the squeeze on family time," the *Washington Post* concluded in an in-depth report. "Specialists say that children benefit intellectually and socially when the whole family is together—by listening to adult conversation, learning to relate to siblings, and getting a clearer sense of the family's moral values."

A recent study by Search Institute, an organization specializing in research on children, examined 270,000 sixth- to twelfth-graders in 600 communities nationwide. According to the *Post,* the Institute discovered that "children who spent at least four evenings a week at home with their families and had frequent, in-depth conversations with their parents were less likely to have sex and use alcohol or drugs." Another study that involved the taping of dinner conversations between parents and children in the Boston area for eight years uncovered this interesting result: "Preschoolers who were exposed to mealtime discussions among parents and siblings did better on vocabulary and reading tests in elementary school than those who weren't."

Many busy parents, intuitively aware of research findings like these, have made well-intentioned efforts to reserve so-called quality time with their children. But further research shows that the notion of scheduling their children as if they were just another entry on their appointment calendars doesn't work and misses the point. In a recent report *Newsweek* states: "Experts say that many of the most important elements in children's lives—regular routines and domestic rituals, consistency, the sense that their parents know and care about them—are exactly what's jettisoned when quality time substitutes for quantity time. . . . Parents who race in the door at 7:30 P.M. and head straight for the fax machine are making it perfectly clear where their loyalties lie, and the kids are showing the scars."

Working women appear particularly conflicted by the dilemma of reconciling the demands of work and home. "I *think* she's doing okay," one working woman told *Newsweek* about her young daughter. "If it were up to me, I'd spend more time with her. I wish I were able to stay home, but that's just not possible."

Eager to aid the family finances, pursue career aspirations, and raise a family all at once, many women attempt to carry a near-impossible burden. While *Newsweek* found that men are picking up a greater share of child-rearing and household responsibilities, the burden still falls most heavily on women, whether or not they are also working outside the home.

Specifically, women employed outside the home were found to devote an average of 6.6 hours per week to the most essential child-care responsibilities, such as bathing, feeding, reading, and playing. The average employed man devotes just 2.5 hours to these activities.

None of these figures includes the many more hours spent on housekeeping, shopping, laundry, cooking, and other errands. When married couples working outside the home were asked how such duties were divided between the spouses, "We share it 50-50" was the response of 43 percent of the men but only 19 percent of the women.

Someone's not telling the whole truth. Who do you think it is?

As we saw in the case of Rexall Showcase International couples like Gary and Debbie Mooers (in the last chapter) and will see repeatedly as we meet other Rexall Showcase International distributors, the right opportunity in network marketing offers working parents a chance to put their family first, while still enjoying the financial benefits and personal satisfaction that comes from building their own business. Why should anyone make the awful choice between a rewarding career and good parenting when there is a way to do both?

Target of Opportunity

"I'm 58 years old. In my life I've had only one employer and am still married to my high school sweetheart from 1957. You see, I don't make hasty decisions about important matters in life," says John Kercher of Tampa, Florida.

Several years ago while in his early fifties, he decided to set a goal of retiring from his career as a management consultant and partner at Price Waterhouse by the age of 55. The reason was simple: "I had seen too many of my partners retire at 60 and die at 61 or 62. My own father never made it to retirement." Having had coronary bypass surgery himself at the age of 48, John had ample reason to be concerned that he would repeat that pattern.

Still, it wasn't an easy decision. Ever since John was 15 years old, he had wanted to be in the business world—building businesses, running them, advising them. As a teenager, he and a friend started a house-painting business in Kettering, Ohio, that became the largest operation of its kind in that Dayton suburb. "Even then," John told later told *Florida Business* magazine, "both of us knew we wanted to be management consultants. We had a very strong service orientation. We wanted to help people in some kind of business management pursuit."

The house-painting business paid for John's bachelor's degree in economics at Ohio Wesleyan University. He later received a scholarship to attend the University of North Carolina, where he earned an MBA.

Shortly thereafter, John landed a job at Price Waterhouse. Before he knew it, he was on his way to Australia with his wife Diane and their 18-month-old daughter. He played a leading role in building the firm's practice there. By the time the Kerchers returned to the United States in 1971, the family had grown by one more child, and John and Diane had acquired a love of travel and the South Pacific that has yet to diminish.

Back in the United States, John took on increasingly important management consulting assignments for Price Waterhouse, first in Pittsburgh and later in Tampa. His last responsibility for the firm was directing a $20 million regional business unit in the southeast part of the United States. But after thirty-one years, it was time for something new.

"I found myself getting grouchy on Sunday afternoon at five o'clock in advance of a partners' meeting I had the next day," John recalls. "I thought there's got to be a business where I could have some fun, where I could set my own pace, and where I would enjoy some time freedom."

John set his criteria and started looking. But why look at all? Why not just retire for real? "I don't like to waste time," John replies. "I wanted to do something that's productive and lucrative and I didn't want to be forced into some leisure activity that I never liked before.

"Besides I've got some very expensive habits sitting in the drive-way!" says John, referring to his beloved Porsches.

When a friend told him about Rexall Showcase International and advised him that this would be the business that met all his criteria, John "spent five weeks trying to tear it apart." But he couldn't do it.

"After three years full of full-time activity," John reports, "I now have a business in the United States, Mexico, Korea, Hong Kong, and Taiwan with 1998 revenues of almost $7 million. My personal income in the first year in this business was $20,000. My income this year will be about $400,000—a retirement dream come true."

But John appreciates even more the health benefits he says the Rexall Showcase International products have provided him. "On the Bios Life product, I lowered my cholesterol from 270 to 215 during the five weeks I was evaluating the business. You can imagine that helped convince me! Today my cholesterol is 163 with the LDL at 102. I'm not at cardiac risk at all."

To John Kercher, the target of opportunity for Rexall Showcase International in the future is obvious. "I'm targeting my age group," he says. "There are many people in their fifties who have built no equity, who haven't prepared for retirement, and who are now afraid of being downsized. Many of them also have some kind of weight or cholesterol problem.

"And like me, they're old enough to identify with the Rexall name. That counted a lot for me. If the name of the company was Smith, I probably wouldn't be doing this business."

As America ages, as pension programs are cut back—and as parents work harder and longer away from home to provide for old relatives, young children, and their own retirement—Rexall Showcase International's approaches to both health and business will significantly grow in their appeal. Like the economic changes ripping through our professional lives, the social changes brought about by our aging population pose a danger to many but new opportunities for those ready to seize them.

CHAPTER SEVEN

The Preventative Health Revolution and the Coming Collapse of Conventional Care

There are six satin roses sitting on the fireplace mantel in Dr. Daria Davidson's Seattle-area home. Her goal is to have a few dozen roses there. Daria explains why: "Six years ago at age forty-one, I was diagnosed with breast cancer. It was super-malignant. I went through it all—surgery, radiation, chemotherapy. That experience forced me to take a good hard look at my life. How could I, whose profession as a trauma care physician is devoted to restoring the health and saving the lives of others, have been so negligent about my own health and let my own life get so out of control?"

Daria's serious illness touched off a period of soul-searching that led this highly successful health care professional, whose career had been dedicated to rescuing people in the midst of life-threatening illness and injuries, to Rexall Showcase International. Today she is one of the most passionate champions of the twin engines of the company's growth—the preventative health care revolution and the

113

explosion of home-based entrepreneurship. Daria now believes that "maybe I got cancer so that I would have an opportunity to change my life and help people change and improve theirs." And so to mark this new phase in her life and to reflect on the fact that according to the odds she shouldn't be around today, on each birthday since the onset of cancer, she places an additional rose in that vase.

Breast cancer, unfortunately, is nothing new to Daria's family. Her mother and grandmother had it too. Daria has since discovered an inordinately high incidence of the disease in the area where she grew up—the Long Island, New York, town of Littleneck—causing her to question the environmental and lifestyle factors that could be behind it. Intent on pursuing a medical career, Daria's first step was to become a nurse. She climbed up the ranks quickly, being hired to run a pediatric intensive care unit with forty-four employees in Tulsa, Oklahoma. By the late 1970s, it was time for medical school. Daria Davidson became Dr. Daria Davidson, after graduating from the University of Oklahoma Medical School with a specialty in emergency medicine. She then went to work in a Level One trauma care "ER," where the pressures and surroundings are much like what we see on the popular prime time television show. Later, she was put in charge of running a large trauma care center. Also serving on the board of the American Heart Association, Daria was highly focused on becoming a successful leader in U.S. health care.

But then came the disastrous diagnosis at the young age of forty-one. After her initial recovery, she began to question the truisms of her profession, challenge her prior definition of success, and reassess her goals. "I made a list of all the things that were important to me professionally," she recalls. "I wanted a career where I could make the same income, which was never less than $300,000 a year. I wanted to live where I wanted to—and for me that was an area with mountains and trees. I wanted to work primarily out of my home. I wanted to apply my medical knowledge to helping people. I wanted to serve humanity in some capacity and, finally, travel and teach."

Today as Daria reviews that list, the name Rexall Showcase International of course jumps right out at her. But initially and—some might say—inexplicably, her response was to go to law school! "Well, I had no intention of practicing law, but I thought that with that degree and the many contacts I had, I could build up a great consulting business with doctors, hospitals, and insurance companies as clients."

But in June 1995, Rexall Showcase International dropped into her lap. "A doctor I knew urged me to evaluate the products, which he said were producing great results in terms of lowering cholesterol in many people," she recalls. "I was very impressed—until I learned that they were sold through network marketing. Basically I thought it was a scam. If the products were so good, why weren't they being offered in stores like everything else?" she wondered.

The only reason Daria took a second look was "because of the strength of the Rexall name." When she found out that the company was able to get the products directly to the end user, pay out 63 cents of every wholesale dollar to distributors, and still make more money for itself, the picture became clear. From a business, health, and consumer-awareness point of view, network marketing made perfect sense for the dissemination of these products.

But an even greater hurdle presented itself—a giant mental barrier, a barrier of ignorance, stubbornness, and even arrogance in the minds of many doctors when it comes to preventative health care and the role it plays in ensuring good health. Daria knew where these doctors were coming from. "I spent my whole career in medical intervention, not prevention. Most doctors of my generation or older got no training in nutrition in medical school. So what they're being asked to do now is shift their whole way of thinking—that's a hard thing for most medical professionals to do."

For Daria, her own brush with death and the grueling treatment that followed—along with the growing weight of evidence validating the claims of food-based nutritional supplements and other natural remedies—changed her perspective completely. "I'm good at trauma and those in my profession will continue to do heroic things to save lives. But if you're about to drive over a cliff, where would you rather have me—down on the rocks below struggling to keep you alive? Or up on the road trying to get you to slow down and stop before you reach the edge?"

Noting the growing mountain of evidence—even in journals attached to the medical establishment—Daria states, with her trademark directness, "Not even the staunchest detractor can stand by his antiquated position that solid nutritional support is not necessary for optimal health. Anyone who continues to do so stands in defiance of overwhelming evidence."

As Daria Davidson's own resistance to both network marketing and preventative health care crumbled, law school quickly became a thing of the past. "On reflection, being a consultant and having to suck up to all those hospitals and lawyers didn't look so appealing after all," she snaps. She struggled with her own conclusions about Rexall Showcase International. "If it's legitimate, and I concluded it was, I'd feel very stupid if I didn't do it. Rexall Showcase International offered a much quicker path to the goals I outlined before I started law school." Relocating to the Seattle area, Daria began as a part-time distributor while continuing a full-time medical practice. Just over two years later, in March 1998, she left her practice to devote all her energies to building her Rexall Showcase International business. She travels the country, speaking to prospective consumers and distributors, particularly in the health care field. And hers is a frequent voice on Rexall Showcase International's training videos and audiotapes. "I still work four shifts a month at the hospital—but I don't take any money for it," she adds.

"I have a life now that is unbelievable. The income and time freedom is great, and I'm being of service to people in the field I love. I believe passionately in these products. You have to understand, they're not just 'okay' in terms of their health benefits—they're shocking!"

From intervention to prevention—there's been a gap between those two approaches to health care that's as wide as the Grand

Canyon. Doctors like Daria Davidson know. Patients like Ron Weitz know it too.

"It was Thursday evening, March 7. We had just closed our restaurant. I was sitting at the desk balancing the day's receipts when it hit me." Ron has told the story many times and can feel the pain each time he tells it again.

"I'll never forget that night. I called out my wife Barbara's name. She came in and took one look at me and said, 'We're going to the hospital.' She later told me my face was completely gray in color. We started to the car and it hit again. I grabbed the counter to keep from falling.

"On the way to the hospital a wave of nausea came over me like nothing I've ever experienced in my life. At the hospital, lying there stretched out on the gurney, I looked up and saw six or eight people standing over me. One of them said, 'just try to relax—you're having a heart attack.'"

Ron Weitz was just forty-seven years old and until that terrifying night was convinced he was in perfect health. What he didn't know then was that the terror had just begun.

"The rest of that night I kept slipping in and out of consciousness. Each time I wondered if I would survive. Who would take care of my family?" The next few days were full of worry and uncertainty, tests, tests, and more tests. "On Friday, March 17, I went through the dehumanizing experience of open heart surgery," Ron says.

"And when it was over, I realized that there were two important lessons staring right at me. First, it doesn't always happen to somebody else. It can happen to you.

"Second, they don't fix you with open heart surgery. They just treat the symptoms. Before I even left the hospital I was told I'd be back in seven to ten years to do it all over again!"

Today Ron is fifty-seven, and he has yet to make that second trip under the knife and all indications are that he has continued to improve these last years. But it has been a long journey from then to now.

"The day after I was released from the hospital I was back at work," Ron says. "When you own a small business, there's no six weeks of rest and recovery." Ron went through twelve weeks of cardiac rehabilitation where he learned about proper diet, stress management and exercise. He followed the instructions he was given to the letter.

"But you know what the result of all that correct behavior was?" he says. "Two years out of surgery during my annual physical they told me my arteries were clogging up again. Two weeks after that I found myself in the hospital with a blood sugar level of 496, which signaled full-blown adult onset diabetes." In the year that followed there were tests, drugs, and more tests and drugs. "I just felt lousy," Ron remembers.

Then a friend told him about some new and natural products made by a new division of the Rexall company—products that were producing promising results in many people. "If it wasn't for the Rexall name I wouldn't have listened and if I hadn't listened, I truly believe I wouldn't be alive today," Ron states bluntly.

He began taking Rexall Showcase International's Prescription for Life products, which feature Bios Life 2. "Within six months I was completely off of diabetes medication, my cholesterol level has dropped 100 points, I lost 40 pounds—and I feel great," he reports.

Ron emphasizes that there is no need to wait until you have a life-threatening illness to recognize the value of the Rexall Showcase International products in the maintenance of good health. Indeed, he has become an articulate advocate of not just a line of products, but also a different, more natural approach to health. He struggles to contain his concern with a medical establishment that places total focus on treating symptoms of people who are already sick rather than helping people to keep from getting sick. "We're smart enough to recognize the value of maintenance when it comes to our cars (i.e. change the oil, rotate tires)—why not do the same with our bodies? Why not prevent illness, not just treat illness?" he wonders.

A bout with an aggressive form of skin cancer followed Ron's struggle with diabetes. He has made numerous trips to Mexico for alternative natural treatments not available in the United States; and while he is not out of the woods, the cancer is in 5½ year's remission. This experience has further convinced Ron that our approach to health care must broaden. "Here they cut you, they burn you, or they poison you—all which damage your immune system, which is your body's chance to fight back. My treatment in Mexico is designed to build my body and immune system for the fight of its life. And I'm still here."

Ron, who is now fifty-seven, has become a successful Rexall Showcase International distributor, but all of his passion seems to spring from products that he is convinced have prolonged his life. "After what they did for me and so many others, I have a moral obligation to be in this business and share the Rexall Showcase International products with others," he explains. "It seems like the only product Rexall Showcase International hasn't come up with yet is one that grows hair!" adds the balding Ron.

No conversation with Ron Weitz lasts for very long before his concern for you and your health shows. "I just don't want you to go through what I've been through," he says. As a forty-four-year-old man, I should be using the Bios Life 2 product to lower my cholesterol and Cellular Essentials to reverse existing buildup in my arteries. "And, Jim, if you do nothing else, at least take Men's Formula Plus for prostate health," he says.

A Movement Catches Fire

The painful, heroic, and, so far, triumphant stories of Daria Davidson and Ron Weitz embody, from both the patient and caregiver perspective, the third profound sea change that is reshaping modern life in both troublesome and positive ways: the coming collapse of the health care system as we know it and the rise of a powerful preventative health care movement.

It is a movement that encourages individuals to take greater responsibility for the maintenance of their own health through proper diet and exercise, aided by a wide range of food-based nutritional supplements, natural remedies, and other treatments broadly labeled "alternative medicine." It is a movement that seeks to put the humanity back into our health care system by restoring the relationship between the patient and the caregiver. Fundamentally, it is a movement based on the common sense idea that it is better for both the patient and the system to take all steps possible to prevent the onset of serious health conditions before they occur, rather than having to intervene with drastic and expensive procedures later.

You'd have to be stuck in orbit on the Russian space station MIR to have missed the explosion of media attention now focused on this growing movement:

- A comprehensive series of front-page articles in the *Los Angeles Times* called "Hope or Hype" (August 30, 1998): "The alternative medicine movement is going mainstream, experiencing astonishing growth."
- A front-page story in the *Washington Post*, "Widening the Medical Mainstream" (November 11, 1998): "The number of Americans who are using 'alternative' treatments such as herbal supplements, massage therapies, and megavitamins is increasing dramatically and visits to alternative practitioners have become more common than visits to the family doctor."
- A *Time* magazine cover story titled "The Herbal Medicine Boom" (November 23, 1998): "More and more Americans are supplanting and replacing prescription medicine with a profusion of pills and potions that contain various medicinal herbs, vitamins, and minerals."

- One week later, a cover story in *Newsweek* called "Cancer & Diet: Eating to Beat the Odds—What You Need to Know" (November 30, 1998).

- Another report in *Newsweek,* "What's Alternative?" (November 23, 1998): "Remember when alternative medicine was a fringe thing? To say those days are gone would be a terrible understatement. Last year some 83 million Americans— more than 40 percent of the adult population—sought out herbalists, chiropractors, and other unconventional practitioners. We paid more visits to these healers (629 million) than to primary care physicians (386 million), and the cost of the whole affair topped $27 billion."

- Still another report in the *Los Angeles Times* called "Herbal Renewal" (November 30, 1998): "Conventional medicine once dismissed botanicals out of hand. Now a new round of studies says some of the remedies show promise."

- And perhaps most noteworthy of all, in November 1998, the *Journal of the American Medical Association (JAMA)* released an issue devoted entirely to alternative medicine, triggering a spate of television and print reports around the world. Never before had the authoritative house organ of the medical establishment lavished such serious research attention on preventative care and alternative treatments.

What's going on here? Why is this happening now? Clearly both the conventional medical establishment and the mainstream media have finally caught on to a trend Carl DeSantis saw coming more than twenty years ago as he watched and listened to customers in his Miami Beach drug store. It is a trend seen not just in the United States, but around the world:

- The baby boomers, who grew up in the environmental and "back to nature" movements of the 1960s and 1970s, have carried into middle age their interest in health, wellness, and products formulated with natural ingredients as opposed to human-made chemicals.

- As the boomers age, their focus on staying fit and healthy has sharpened. They expect to spend more years in retirement than has any previous generation—perhaps as much as a third of their lives—and want to take steps now to forestall serious illness and old-age dependency for as long as possible.

- Growing evidence about the role of a proper diet in health maintenance, as well as the effectiveness of natural food supplements like dietary fiber in reducing risk factors known to cause heart attacks, strokes, and cancer, have further accelerated this interest. To a growing number of people, taking preventative measures now—particularly when they involve natural food-based products with no side effects, products approved by the Food and Drug Administration—is just simple common sense.

- Lastly, as I will outline shortly, heightened interest in low-cost preventative care approaches is also driven by patients' growing discomfort with the strategies of modern medical science and serious doubts about their ability to afford and obtain such expensive care in the future.

We should note that the tremendous level of media and medical attention now being paid to this new health care philosophy is hardly all positive. A period of intense scrutiny and debate is underway, and that's as it should be. (For example, the *Los Angeles Times* report questions the potency of some herbal products, including one of Rexall Sundown's. The company disputes the paper's results and testing method.)

One challenge facing observers and analysts as they report on such developments is how to sort through all the jargon, buzzwords, and clichés. What is described as "new," "alternative," or "unconventional" may be "old," "mainstream," or "traditional" in other countries and cultures. Chinese medicine, for example, with its emphasis on herbs, minerals, and other natural ingredients, has been around for thousands of years. Even in the United States, it strains accuracy to describe such practices as taking vitamins, visiting a chiropractor, getting a therapeutic back massage, or taking a product like Metamucil for fiber and irregularity as "alternative." To millions of Americans, it just seems "natural!"

Furthermore, some commentators, for reasons either intentional or unintentional, toss every conceivable offbeat health practice—from "bee-sting" therapy to the use of magnets to draw poisons from bodily organs—into one big grab bag they call alternative medicine. This unfairly diminishes the credibility of products and strategies—such as Rexall Showcase International's fiber products—that are backed by serious science, mounting medical evidence, and even government patents.

Newsweek highlights this definitional dilemma in its article "What's Alternative?" "What distinguishes the 'alternative' from 'mainstream' medicine?" the magazine asks. "Alternative practitioners have been known to put belief before evidence—but so have conventional physicians.

"As Dr. Jerry Dalen writes in the current *Archives of Internal Medicine,* fewer than half of the protocols now used to prevent blood clots in people with cardiovascular disease have been evaluated in controlled clinical trials. Yet no one calls the untested ones unconventional. 'In my opinion,' he writes, 'the principal distinguishing characteristics of unconventional and conventional therapies is their source of introduction. . . . American academic medicine has a bias against outsiders."

Recognizing the confusion that comes from applying such broadbrush terminology, Rexall Showcase International, as we have seen in Chapter 4, carefully delineates its product lines, for each carries with it its own science, history, proof of effectiveness, and quality and safety protocols. For example, the Bios Life 2 fiber product is backed by two U.S. government patents and a preponderance of evidence even from "mainstream" medical quarters confirming the role of dietary fiber in reducing serum cholesterol and therefore heart attack and stroke risk. Similarly, the company's vitamin products, such as its proprietary formulations of vitamins C, B, and E, hardly strike one as being controversial or on the "fringe." The homeopathic products, which Rexall Showcase International calls "natural remedies," represent the company's most controversial line, despite the fact that homeopathy has a modern history spanning two centuries and is widely accepted in other advanced nations such as France and Great Britain.

In their exhaustive and insightful study of the alternative medicine movement, *Los Angeles Times* reporters Terence Monmaney and Shari Roan adopt an expansive definition: "The label 'alternative medicine' covers a range of products and treatments, some derived from centuries-old spiritual and healing traditions of non-Western societies, others as new and high-tech as pressurized oxygen chambers." The reporters detail several benchmarks signifying the breadth and growth of alternative medicine:

- It is already an $18 billion industry. (Other analysts peg the number at $27 billion.)
- Nationwide, 16 percent of Americans used chiropractic services within the last year; 17 percent used herbal products; 13 percent took high-dose vitamins; and 5 percent took homeopathic remedies.
- In terms of attitude, 40 percent of Americans report that they have grown more positive in their outlook toward alternative care in the past year. Just 2 percent have become more negative. Of those feeling positive, 47 percent said it was because they learned more about it; 41 percent reported their own positive results with a treatment.
- The herbal supplement market has grown from a $2.09 billion business in 1994 to a $3.65 billion business in 1997 and an estimated $4.3 billion in 1998. "No alternative ap-

proach has grown more quickly than herbal supplements, from St. John's wort for mild depression to black cohosh for premenstrual syndrome," the newspaper reports.

• Estimated sales of vitamins and mineral supplements rose 20 percent between 1995 and 1997—from $4.3 billion to $5.1 billion.

Reviewing the reasons for such substantial expansion of these markets, Monmaney and Roan confirm much of the anecdotal evidence Rexall Showcase International distributors are uncovering "in the field."

"Alternative medicine is flourishing partly because of the successes of scientific medicine and public health," they conclude. "As more people have survived into old age, a spectrum of chronic, debilitating disorders has become more common. The reporters cite Dr. Michael Goldstein, a professor of public health at UCLA, who distinguishes between conventional medicine's success in "heroic life-saving measures" and its comparative failure in making progress against chronic diseases and pain.

The Coming Collapse of Conventional Health Care

One other critical factor is certainly driving Americans, as well as residents of other modern societies, to a stronger emphasis on nutrition, wellness, and preventative treatments: the visible, ongoing disintegration of our health care system. Consider these disturbing reports and developments:

• Nearly 15 percent of the entire output of the U.S. economy is spent on health care, a share that will rise to 20 percent by the year 2020 and a greater share than that of other major developed nations, where the average is 8 percent.

- Despite this enormous cost, 43.4 million Americans—16.1 percent of the population—have no health insurance. Approximately 1.7 million Americans lost their coverage in 1997 alone, the biggest one-year increase in five years.
- An estimated 10.7 million American children are unprotected by health care coverage.
- The majority of Americans—61.4 percent—depend on employers for health insurance. Yet many smaller companies, finding costs skyrocketing and the potential for more government regulation and increased liability increasing, are preparing to bail out of the system if necessary. According to a Public Opinion Strategies survey conducted in February 1998, 57 percent of small employers say they would be very likely or somewhat likely to stop providing health care coverage should major new regulatory measures, now under consideration in Washington, be enacted into law. Forty-six percent of those surveyed say they would be likely to stop providing coverage if health premiums rise another 20 percent. Since more than half of working-age Americans are employed by these smaller firms, the findings portend a substantial future threat to the mainstay of our health care financing system—employer-sponsored coverage.
- A recent article in *INC.* magazine concludes that "companies with fewer than 100 employees get little attention in the [health] insurance marketplace; they are the small fish that everyone throws back." Even a low number of claims won't stop massive premium increases for many small companies, the magazine reports.
- Sixty-one percent of insured Americans now get their coverage from managed care organizations and, fair or unfair, many of them don't like it. A recent *Newsweek* poll found that more than half of Americans believe HMOs are harming the quality of medical care. A recent *New York Times*

survey found that by a margin of 58 percent to 17 percent, people believe that managed care organizations are impeding doctors' ability to control treatment. As we will see in the next chapter, many doctors deeply resent what they view as the intrusion of accountants, insurance companies, lawyers, and health care bureaucrats in their relationships with patients. That is driving many to Rexall Showcase International, where they can reaffirm the tradition of care-giving that brought them to medicine in the first place.

- And under intense pressure to both hold down costs and at the same time increase service options, some insurance companies are bailing out of the system. Reacting to the announcement in December 1998 that Prudential Insurance Company would sell its ailing health care operations to Aetna, the *Los Angeles Times* called the move the latest in a "flood of defections from the ravaged managed care business. Prudential is the most dramatic example yet of an insurance company exiting the troubled health care arena. The proposed sale alarmed doctors and consumer groups, who fear the new company would have the power to force patients to accept fewer services and doctors to accept lower fees."

The growing dissatisfaction of both patients and health care professionals with the conventional system is helping to fuel the boom in preventative care as well as the growth of Rexall Showcase International. "Another impetus has been the rise of managed care, which many patients say has brought out the worst in mainstream medicine," report Monmaney and Roan in the *Los Angeles Times*. "In contrast to managed care's reputation for medicine by stop-watch, many types of alternative healers are known for listening to patients' stories, offering comforting treatments, and perhaps charging less as well."

Can You Count on Medicare?

Millions of working Americans are finding the cost of health insurance rising, its availability slipping, and the quality of care declining. If that were not enough, the government's Medicare program, designed to cover all seniors as well as the poor, is on the verge of collapse. The last thing it can afford is an onslaught of millions of retiring baby boomers after the turn of the century.

Senator John Breaux of Louisiana, who chairs the national Bipartisan Commission on the Future of Medicare, says it bluntly: "We have problems today with 39 million people on Medicare. What are we going to do when 77 million baby boomers start walking through that Medicare door in the year 2010 and saying, 'Here's my card, where's my treatment?' We are going to have a system that is insolvent and can no longer afford to pay for the treatment."

Stanford University Professor Victor Fuchs told *Business Week* recently, "Although people justifiably worry about Social Security, paying for the old folks' health care is the real 800-pound gorilla facing the economy." By the year 2020, the share of the U.S. gross domestic product spent on seniors' care alone will double to 10 percent. Meanwhile, Medicare's health insurance trust fund is projected to go broke in 2008. That's less than a decade from now.

As is the case with the impending insolvency of Social Security farther down the line, the familiar government response to Medicare's dilemma is to raise taxes and cut benefits. But add the crises facing both programs together and it's impossible to envision closing the gap with taxes. The payroll tax rate on young Americans that would be required to maintain these programs "as is," figures Hudson Institute Fellow William Styring, would "probably be 37 percent by 2020 and 51 percent by 2030."

Those rates, he continues, "are not only unthinkable but politically impossible and an economic wrecking ball that would kill an incentive for the young to work, save, and invest."

The more likely reality that will face boomers and their families will be "fend for yourselves!" Professor Fuchs, according to *Business Week,* "estimated that annual health care spending per senior will soar from $9,200 in 1995 to almost $25,000 (in 1995 dollars) in 2020—a hike that would strain the resources of both the government and seniors themselves, who on average shoulder over a third of their own health bills."

Even government's more innovative attempts to reform Medicare by opening it to competition from HMOs are showing strains. "The Medicare HMO business, which began with great fanfare in the early 1980s, has proved to be less profitable for health care companies than they once imagined," reports Kathy Kristof in the *Los Angeles Times.* During the last fifteen years, some 6 million of Medicare's retired beneficiaries joined HMOs with the promise of better coverage at a lower cost.

But with federal budget writers holding down Medicare reimbursement rates at relatively low levels, HMOs are finding the promise tough to keep. As a result, some are pulling out of the Medicare marketplace altogether.

Considering the myriad financial pressures and increased demands placed on our health care system, Hudson's William Styring believes there's only one logical prognosis to be issued, as stark as it is—the "financial collapse of the U.S. health care system."

Taking Control of Your Health

Have you ever stopped to consider what the "story of the century" will be as we cross into the year 2000 and look back on 100 tumultuous years of tragedy and triumph? At the end of each year, journalists are fond of trying to rank the previous year's top ten major events or developments. Doing it for an entire century is far more challenging, but lots of observers and commentators will try anyway!

What would you list—the development of the computer, the rise and fall of Communism, the advent of the nuclear era, the invention of the jet airplane, the evils perpetrated by Adolph Hitler?

Recently on a television tabloid show, an editor of *People* magazine actually declared that certainly the tragic death of Princess Diana was "the story of the century."

My own nominee for the "story of the century" is the expansion of the longevity of human life. In the United States, almost thirty years have been added to life expectancy in this century. For all of its problems, the modern, conventional health care system has without question played a central role in this remarkable achievement.

As we address conventional medicine's shortcomings and help it sustain the crushing new demands that an aging population will place upon it, we must not ignore its achievements and we cannot deny its essentiality.

Preventative health care will, in fact, help heal the institutions we may all count on one day to save our lives with emergency trauma care or a major operation. It will help heal it by reducing the number of times we would otherwise call upon it for its life-saving services.

The question Rexall Showcase International distributors like to ask is, Are we prepared to cede responsibility of our own health to a system that can't possibly take adequate care of us in the out years? Or will we take charge by taking the simple and satisfying steps offered by Rexall Showcase International's products and business opportunity?

Distributor leader Jim Moyles sums it up: "The time is right for preventative health care in the United States and around the world." Along with dramatic changes in the global economy and the graying of the world's population, the preventative health care revolution marks a fundamental transformation in society that Rexall Showcase International is ideally positioned to build upon.

The Doctor
Is In

There is no better evidence of the viability of Rexall Show-case International products or the workability of its business opportunity than the fact that thousands of doctors, surgeons, and other health professionals are recommending the products to patients and are becoming distributors. Most important for the long-term health of the medical profession in which our aging population is placing so much trust, Rexall Showcase International has helped countless medical practitioners become once again the care-givers most have dreamed of being since childhood. Many worked their hearts out and went deeply into debt to get their education, only to see the profession to which they aspired lose its soul. Rexall Showcase International has helped many of them be the kind of doctors and health care providers they always wanted to be.

From the moment I began my inquiry into this company, I began looking for one overriding piece of evidence that would satisfy me as to its long-term viability. Many entrepreneurial ideas are clever and ingenious. Remember the fellow who invented those cardboard screens to put behind our windshields when we park our cars in the sun? He took millions out of that idea. In network marketing, many companies put together a good plan, grab hold of a hot product, and for a time ride the wave of success.

If the companies are up-front and honest, there is nothing wrong with this kind of trendy, niche entrepreneurship. But here we are talking about people's health, and we are asking whether Rexall Showcase International really has a future of continued spectacular growth ahead of it. It can be established that the company is solid and professional, the marketing plan for independent distributors is lucrative, and the trends and audiences the products appeal to are growing. But with these facts established, one central question remains: Does Rexall Showcase International—its products, company financials, and business plan—win the support of a broad range of health care providers? Let's explore this question.

"Getting By" in Kansas

Thirty-six-year-old Neal Secrist can't remember a time when he *didn't* want to be a doctor. "I decided that at an early age," he says, noting that his family lived modestly and he was the first to attend college. Agreeing to serve in the United States Air Force after his medical training was, in fact, the way Neal, financed his education—but it wasn't so bad because he was able to pursue at least two of his life's passions, medicine and flying. He became an Air Force flight surgeon and was stationed in Kansas and practiced emergency medicine on the side.

Neal, it seemed, was living the life he had dreamed of. But about five years ago, he noticed that the practice of medicine was changing in a fundamental way. "Health care has gone through a complete devolution," Neal believes. "The physicians have lost control of the way they practice. Between managed care and liability issues, someone else is dictating to us now. There's a lot of frustration among doctors and I felt that frustration. It seemed like I would work one-third more hours, see one-third more patients, and earn one-third less money. This sage advice began to ring true to me: 'If the horse you are riding dies, we suggest you dismount.'"

Actually Neal had no intention of giving up on medicine—which was and is today his true life's calling. But he thought he'd better look for ways to diversify economically and change the way he cared for others.

"I tried two or three other home-based businesses, but they failed miserably. I thought about network marketing, but it had such a stigma. I thought if I ever did that, I'd have to run around the hospital with a bag over my head!"

Neal kept searching until one day someone he held in great esteem, a man named Richard Epley—who had in the 1980s enjoyed great success in real estate—told him about Rexall Showcase International. Neal's first reaction? "I said 'aw man, not you too Richard!' It was network marketing and I just didn't want to do it. But then I thought here was a guy who was a proven success at business, someone so good at what he did that at one point he almost convinced me to start selling real estate for him.

"I was worried too. What if it goes real big and I was the one who turned Richard down?" Neal instead decided to "lift the hood" and really investigate the inner workings of the Rexall Showcase International business and products. He examined the medical literature and later on traveled to the Boca Raton headquarters and examined the company leadership, laboratories, and production facilities. "When I did that," Neal reports, "my early snap judgment changed. This isn't what I first thought. This is a solid company with a good team and products behind it."

Neal was ready to jump in, but several serious roadblocks still stood in his path: lack of time, lack of money, and a pregnant wife, Kimberly, who opposed the idea.

"You have to understand that at the time I really wanted to start this business I had zero time. Full-time active duty with the

Air Force as a flight surgeon plus two emergency medical practices added up to a seventy-plus-hour workweek. But even so, I thought I had to carve out just ten to fifteen hours a week and give this business a serious try. Otherwise, five years later, I'd be in the exact same position, doing hard time with less and less to show for it. For all those who plead 'no time' as an excuse for joining this business, they really should look at my example—because I really *didn't* have any time!"

A further complication occurred when Neal told his wife, Kimberly—who was then eight months pregnant with their daughter Ashley. "She was livid. Where I saw the prospect of serious income, all Kimberly could envision was serious outgo," Neal remembers. In fact, he used their credit card to borrow the money to get started.

"To sum it up, I'm someone who came to the table with no business skills, no money, no time, and a hostile spouse," Neal reports.

But steady and impressive results with the business and the products turned things around. After the birth of their daughter, Kimberly struggled to restore her physical appearance and lose the weight she had gained during her pregnancy. She began using Rexall Showcase International's Rx for Life Weight Management System. Within six months she lost the excess weight. "At that point, Kimberly moved from hostile to neutral when it came to Rexall Showcase International," Neal says.

Four months after that, Kimberly had lost another ten pounds, and the couple began receiving monthly checks from the company ranging from $3,000–$4,000. "This business is kind of neat," Kimberly began saying.

After two years, the monthly checks had grown to $6,000–$8,000—and still Neal was working the business only part time, investing 15–20 hours a week. It was at this point that his wife started referring to the Secrists' Rexall Showcase International distributorship as "our business."

That's not all. Neal started to wonder, "What would happen if I really threw some serious energy into this?" He significantly scaled back his medical practice and poured much more energy into Rexall Showcase International. Today, four years after he started the business, Neal is a top leader. He is a member of the Presidential Board of Advisors, and the Secrists receive income that more than doubles his medical income. "We can get by on that in Kansas," he jokes.

Equally important to the Secrist family is the change in lifestyle. "I still practice one morning a week, from eight until noon," Neal emphasizes. "When I leave, I tell my colleagues I'm headed off for lunch and I come back next week after lunch!"

Neal runs the business out of the family's home. "My commute is just thirty steps down the hall. It used to be fifteen, but we just bought a bigger house! We've got no staff. All that's needed are a couple phone lines, a fax, and a few airline tickets."

Perhaps most important of all, Neal believes he has finally found the best way to answer his life's calling—being a caregiver and making people well. "When I was just a doctor," he explains, "I treated forty to sixty patients a day, one at a time, depending on how busy the ER was. And I earned a living.

"But because I said yes to this opportunity, I was able to find six people who then grew into thousands in my business organization. Today I indirectly help thousands of people on a daily basis with their care. There is also time now to do mission work and participate in benevolent projects. I now make a contribution to health care, and as a result I earn a better living. And the beauty is you don't have to be a doctor to do it!"

Neal Secrist is one of thousands of doctors and other health care professionals who both make the products available to patients and build their own Rexall Showcase International businesses. He and others acknowledge that the reactions they receive from colleagues cover a wide spectrum; there are those whose sense of professional curiosity and responsibility make them want to immediately review the medical evidence about the products, and those who are far less enthusiastic and suggest it would be a conflict of interest for a physician with a Rexall Showcase International business to recommend products he or she profits from. Neal Secrist acknowledges giving this question serious thought. He says the key is not to treat the patients as prospects for the business, but to simply make the products' information available if appropriate to the individual case. Furthermore, he believes as a doctor that it would be ethically wrong not to suggest care he truly believed would help just because he is part of the Rexall Showcase International business. "Once you research the product line as I have and review all the case studies and scientific evidence available, and come to the conclusion that the products provide serious life-prolonging benefits for many patients who have put their trust in you, to not make them available would not just be a conflict of interest—it might be considered negligent."

Good Doctor, Lousy Genes

When Dr. Lou Pack of Atlanta spoke before a group of physicians at a Memphis hospital, the highly respected founding fellow of the American Rheumatology Association and past clinical instructor on medicine at Emory University began his talk with a sardonic slap at what had become of his profession: "For the fifteen hours of my trip here," he said, "I don't have to worry about OSHA fining me $500,000 because I put the gauze in the wrong bucket. I don't have to worry about Medicare saying I filled out the wrong code and I have a $2,000 per line penalty. I don't have to worry about the insurance company coming back to me six years after the fact saying they overpaid me and want all their money back.

"I don't have to look at another managed-care contract sitting on my desk. And I don't have to worry about removing a hangnail from someone who is then going to say that as a result she's sexually dysfunctional, got divorced, and her grandmother can't have prunes anymore."

136

Headquartered in beautiful Boca Raton, Florida, Rexall Showcase International is one of the fastest-growing divisions of Rexall Sundown, Inc., a true leader in the burgeoning health products field. Rexall Showcase International occupies a 58,000 square foot headquarters (shown above) and 465,000 square feet of manufacturing, packaging and shipping facilities.

Rexall Sundown founder and Chairman Carl DeSantis saw a vast need for health and wellness products and began a mail-order vitamin company from his garage. Years later, he saw an opportunity to deliver unique, specialized health products to consumers while giving entrepreneurs the chance to fulfill their dreams, and RSI was born.

Under the leadership of Damon DeSantis, Rexall Showcase International grew from a $1.3 million company into a $76.5 million corporation in just six years. Today, Damon guides Rexall Sundown as its President and Rexall Showcase International as Chief Executive Officer.

As Rexall Showcase International's President, David J. Schofield oversees the company in all functional areas, including: marketing, sales, product development, operations, information technology, international expansion, distributor support, and distribution. Dave played a leading role in crafting the company's strategic plan, which is designed to develop RSI into the best multilevel marketing company and a multibillion-dollar corporation.

Quality is a true signature of Rexall Sundown and Rexall Showcase International products. Each batch of product is rigorously tested at in-house laboratories to ensure quality. The company's commitment to quality has consistently earned high scores from one of the most prestigious independent quality audit firms in the health product manufacturing industry, Shuster Laboratories, Inc.

Twice a year, thousands of distributors from across the country gather at the Rexall Showcase International National Conference to witness exciting product launches, be among the first to hear about new programs designed to enhance the RSI opportunity, celebrate each other's success, network with the industry's finest, and re-energize themselves.

Current and previous members of our Presidential Board of Advisors were recognized at the Long Beach, California, National Conference in August 1998 for their dedicated service. From left to right, top row: Janie Fischer, John Berta, Jeff Mack, Gordon Oswald, Dr. Neal Secrist, Todd Smith, Randy Schroeder, Jim Moyles, Stewart Hughes, Bob Crosetto, and David J. Schofield (RSI President & Chief Operating Officer). Bottom row: Damon DeSantis (company Chief Executive Officer), Rick Walsh, Renee Stewart-Chittick, John Haremza, Dr. Richard Kurtz, Cliff Overvold, Tom Bissmeyer, Eddie Stone, Doug Overvold, and Jerry Rapplean (company Vice President of Sales).

With RSI since its inception, Randy Schroeder is the company's top earner and is a member of the prestigious Presidential Board of Advisors. Randy has built a thriving business that spans the United States, and he has been instrumental in developing RSI's international markets as well.

Todd Smith is one of Rexall Showcase International's top leaders and highest earners. His successful business—which began when RSI opened its doors—reaches across the United States and abroad. Todd supports all RSI distributors by serving as Chairman of the Presidential Board of Advisors, and he has developed the highly successful Team Building System.

A dynamic leader, Stewart Hughes helped launch Rexall Showcase International and today leads an exceptionally successful organization that covers the United States and parts of the Pacific Rim. Stewart, a member of the Presidential Board of Advisors, devotes great time and energy to supporting not only his organization but also all of RSI by traveling throughout the world to support others.

An RSI distributor since August 1991, Jim Moyles (shown here with his daughter, Ashley), has supported the growth of Rexall Showcase International in numerous ways. He serves as a member of the Presidential Board of Advisors, frequently shares insights as a National Conference speaker and has helped many distributors within his own organization achieve Century Club status.

John Berta and Julie Berry found more than thriving careers through Rexall Showcase International—they found each other! While building separate, successful Distributorships, John and Julie met and married. Together, they have been instrumental in guiding the company's growth.

One of the top female earners with RSI and a member of the Presidential Board of Advisors, Renee Stewart Chittick has developed a vast organization that spans the United States. Renee frequently shares her insights while speaking at National Conferences as well as regional and local programs.

Jeff Mack (shown here with his wife, Lisa) has built a successful business that touches virtually every state in the country. In addition to having served on the Presidential Board of Advisors, Jeff has been instrumental in developing RSI's presence in the Pacific Rim.

RSI distributors since March 1994, Bob and Pam Crosetto have diligently and enthusiastically developed one of the most dynamic organizations in the country. In addition, Bob has served as a member of the prestigious Presidential Board of Advisors. Both Bob and Pam continue to support others by hosting regional training schools throughout the United States.

Janie Fischer (shown here with the legendary former Dallas Cowboys quarterback, Roger Staubach and his wife) has built—on a part-time basis—a thriving organization with literally thousands of distributors that spans the United States and reaches international markets. A former member of the Presidential Board of Advisors, Janie relishes the opportunity to be professionally productive and generate a substantial income while having time to be an ever-present mom.

Gordan Oswald (shown here with his wife, Megan) became an RSI distributor in March 1993. Since that time, he has established a nationwide organization and has built a successful international business, helping to strengthen RSI's Asian markets. Gordan has served on the Presidential Board of Advisors, and he frequently presents at National Conferences.

Dr. Neal Secrist (shown here with his daughter, Ashley Nicole) has supported Rexall Showcase International's growth and success by serving as a member of the Presidential Board of Advisors and by aggressively building a dynamic organization. Neal frequently leads regional training schools throughout the United States.

Jack Smith joined Rexall Showcase International in June 1992 and has developed a thriving organization by which he has achieved Century Club status. Highly supportive of others, Jack invests great time and energy traveling around the country to help others achieve their goals. Jack also leads frequent regional training schools.

Clearly frustrated by developments in traditional medicine, Dr. Pack nonetheless believes that the most important consideration for the medical profession is not what has become of the medical practice or even the soundness of the Rexall Showcase International business opportunity. "What's got to be the most important consideration for doctors is, Do the products work? Are we advancing something that's credible and effective?"

In an earlier chapter, we discussed the exploding interest in preventative care, natural remedies, and alternative approaches to medicine. A great deal of controversy surrounds this movement because it is new and different and because it challenges established thinking. And, yes, some of the controversy is generated because, undoubtedly, some of the products and therapies being pedaled have not been proven to be effective—or worse, are fraudulent.

How do we clear the smoke away from this debate and find the truth, particularly if we are not schooled in medicine and health? We "lift the hood," as Dr. Neal Secrist advises. We listen to the doctors. And how do they know? The humorist Will Rogers once remarked: "Who are you going to believe? Me or your own eyes?" Thousands of highly respected and qualified doctors from a broad range of medical disciplines have seen with their own eyes the positive impact of various Rexall Showcase International products on their patients, on their colleagues' patients, and in many cases on themselves.

Dr. Pack was one who needed to look no further for a case study than his own body. "I've got lousy genes," he says. "I have a very serious cholesterol problem. My father, my cousin, practically my whole family has ended up having bypass surgery. Everyone told me there was no way I could do anything about it other than prescription medication.

"I have a background in pharmacy, so when I was approached about Rexall's Bios Life product, I was as skeptical as you can be. I struggled to be open-minded and finally concluded after studying the ingredients of the product that at least there was nothing in there that could harm me. I decided to give it a try."

Within two months, Dr. Pack reduced his cholesterol level by fifty-eight points. His own internist, who had monitored and treated the doctor's problem for six years, was so taken aback that he immediately got involved with the Rexall Showcase International products and business.

The Rexall Showcase International approach suddenly took on a compelling clarity for Dr. Pack. "I spoke to the chief of cardiac rehabilitation at Emory and he told me that only about 7 percent of post-operative patients actually change their behavior after bypass surgery. The rest keep dying," he says.

Dr. Pack points out that, ironically, there is nothing particularly revolutionary about the Rexall Showcase International products. "We've known about fiber for years. These products are so good that even if a patient changed nothing else in terms of diet or exercise, there would be some beneficial effect.

"Rexall Showcase International did not really come up with a new cure. What it did was take everything we know that already works and put it into a unique formulation—a better combination that's more highly absorbable. That's why it works.

"I called physicians all over the country, and they have all seen the same results."

Perhaps the most significant contribution a product like Bios Life can make to health is to refocus attention on prevention. Using an interesting analogy, Dr. Pack says, "In medicine we have been paying more attention to fixing flat tires instead of doing front-wheel alignments. What we need is a run-flat heart just like we now have the run-flat tire that you can still drive even when it springs a leak."

But if the key to a healthy heart—summed up in the word "fiber"—is so clear, why can't the public and the medical profession figure out an effective way to seize upon it? Are we really that dumb and that stubborn?

It's not as easy at it sounds. "If you take 25–30 grams of fiber a day, you enter a health envelope that's a good place to be," Dr. Pack explains. "But how do you do that? If you rely on food alone, you'd have to eat something like a pound of broccoli, a dozen bananas, and seventeen apricots every day! That's not going to happen.

"What Rexall Showcase International has done is unique. They've come up with a product that you take two or three times a day. Combine that with a typical American diet and you are now approaching that health envelope."

The doctor cites other attributes and advantages. Prescription medicines often have side effects. Bios Life does not. It is so low in cholesterol, it can help you lose weight too. And because it is a food-based product, the fact you are taking it does not have to be reported to insurance companies, thus reducing the risk of cancellation. The product is produced under two U.S. patents, one on its method and composition for reducing cholesterol and the other on its absorbability.

"A recent article in the *Journal of the American Medical Association* reported on a study of 43,000 people over a six-year period and found that by increasing their fiber content, the cardiac risk factor was reduced by 41 percent," Dr. Pack reports. "I don't know a prescription drug on the market that can do that and have no side effects.

"But the medical community is slow to change. In the past, treatments for problems such as rabies and scurvy were found decades before they gained acceptance and common usage." Given the resistance he finds in many quarters, Dr. Pack's strategy is often to zero in on the one fact no one can question, that at the very least Rexall Showcase International's fiber product, as the Hippocratic oath says, will do no harm. "I say, Why not try this out on patients first? The bottom line is that it offers a better quality of care."

Whether they like to admit it or not, most doctors are also businesspeople at heart. And it didn't take long for Dr. Pack to consider that there must be a very interesting and lucrative business behind Rexall Showcase International's Bios Life and hundreds of other food-based products.

When he found out that the business behind the products was based on multilevel marketing, "then I got really skeptical." Nonetheless, just as he had done with the products, Dr. Pack decided to carefully examine this growing but controversial form of business. He took a course in multilevel marketing from a teacher whose doctorate work at Harvard focused on multilevel marketing.

"What I learned was that despite what they'd say about it, most major companies are engaging in this form of distribution in some fashion. Look at all the highly respectable brand-name companies such as Coca-Cola, Colgate-Palmolive, and Mercedes Benz that are selling their products through the Amway catalogue," Dr. Pack explains.

"I also learned that in the 1950s and 1960s, about 80 cents of every dollar a company spent was used to manufacture the product. If it wanted to increase profits, it had to squeeze cost out of the manufacturing process. But today, about 80 percent of the cost is in the marketing and distribution of the product. To be profitable, companies have to find ways to cut those costs, which is why so many of them are turning to multilevel marketing in some fashion."

Dr. Pack came to understand that the direct selling form of business amounts to nothing more than eliminating the intermediaries—a process that is being greatly aided by technology. In Rexall Showcase International's case, the distributor need not have any physical contact with the products, since his or her customers can use the Internet and an 800 number to place an order directly with the company, with the distributor still getting the sales credit and commission.

Also helping to overcome this doctor's skepticism about network marketing is the time-honored Rexall brand name. "This is a hundred-year-old name that to me has always represented integrity and trustworthiness."

To Dr. Pack, Rexall Showcase International's approach to preventative health care is poised for explosive growth. "How can it be otherwise?" he asks. "There are 78 million baby boomers, one-third of the population. Ten thousand of them are turning fifty every day. Standard medical practice can't possibly handle this onslaught of retiring and aging Americans. A fresh focus on health and fitness and preventative care is the only way."

Taking It Personally

Dr. Lou Pack is not the only prominent physician whose exposure to Rexall Showcase International began with a serious personal health concern. Dr. Franklin Murphy of Beverly Hills, California, is an internist and cardiologist who for ten years developed and ran a preventative health care program at UCLA. He knows what he's talking about when it comes to separating the proven products from the fads.

Dr. Murphy had his eye on the role of fiber in the diet for a long time, but in the 1980s there wasn't a commercially viable product available. He needed one desperately. "I had my own cholesterol levels checked and found my triglycerides at nearly 1,300, posing a significant risk of pancreatitis and death. My cholesterol level was 316. I knew I had to do something. So I started taking the Bios Life fiber product and in four months I dropped 35 pounds, my cholesterol normalized at 174, and the triglycerides fell to less than 200.

"There is no doubt that because of the Rexall Showcase International products, I have added years and maybe decades to my life," he concludes.

When Dr. Murphy found out there was a business associated with the product he credits with prolonging his life, he was excited about the prospect, chiefly because of what he saw happening in medicine. As part of a family with four generations of doctors, a family that is renowned for its contributions to medicine, there is a sad undercurrent to Dr. Murphy's dissatisfaction with developments in the profession.

"I'm down in the trenches. I do some HMO medicine, some capitated care. If I'm getting nine dollars a month to take care of you, I can't give you a lot of care. My family has been in medicine since my great-grandfather graduated from the University of Cincinnati more than a hundred years ago. There is a tradition of caregiving in my family that I simply can't live up to under the current system," he explains. "I want to do fee-for-service medicine, and I believe the concept behind preventative medicine is so powerful."

"What the Rexall Showcase International business does for me is give me a vehicle to provide the kind of care I'm supposed to," Dr. Murphy continues. "Likewise, anyone who gets into this becomes a doctor in the sense that he or she is providing care to a lot of people."

Like Dr. Murphy, Dr. Maurice Harris, a cardiologist in one of the largest cardiology practices in the southeastern United States, began by taking the Bios Life product. His personal health situation was not as serious. He had a cholesterol level of 198, which quickly moved down to 160 when he started taking the product once a day. "My staff noticed that I wasn't getting as upset, I had more energy and less fatigue," he also reports.

Dr. Harris decided to try the products on some of his more intractable patients. "I had one eighty-year-old patient who had had bypass surgery, and the best I could do for her with prescription drugs and a strict diet was get her cholesterol level down to 285. I put her on Bios Life for a month, and her cholesterol level dropped to 216. It really blew me away."

Even so, Dr. Harris still sees a lot of resistance to the products among the medical establishment. One who used to be skeptical was Dr. Waynard Miller of South Carolina. "I think we have good drugs to lower cholesterol," he says. "But many patients remain above the guidelines even when they're taking the maximum dose. Others can't or won't take them for a prolonged period of time."

It was the U.S. patent on the method and composition of the Bios Life product that led Dr. Miller to undertake a simple experiment. He put thirty patients on Bios Life—one spoon two or three times a day for six weeks—with no other change in diet or exercise. What he found was a 23–41 percent reduction in the cholesterol levels of these patients. "I was convinced," the doctor says. "These products now play a major role in my treatments."

Dr. Bill Pierce, a member of the board of directors of a multi-specialty practice of 100 doctors, was convinced too—convinced that the products wouldn't work. "I had high cholesterol and I just knew from my training that natural products would not lower it. And I certainly didn't want to damage my reputation in the medical community by embracing them," he says.

"But I took the Bios Life product anyway. Why? Because my wife had a Rexall Showcase International business, and I had to show her the products didn't work."

Pretty soon it was time for Dr. Pierce to eat some crow along with the little packs of Bios Life. "My cholesterol level dropped from 251 to 195, basically moving me from high risk to low risk in just four weeks!

"It was very difficult to tell my wife I was wrong. But I had to fess up. My passion in medicine is to save the limbs and the lives of seriously diabetic patients. What I have been able to do through products like Rx for Life and Cellular Essentials is transform the lives of so many of my diabetic patients. In fact, I share these products with anyone I come in contact with.

"I mean, that's my job as a doctor, to take care of patients. Now I am better able to help them take care of themselves. This is a company of high integrity with superior products—and the hard truth is that my wife's business through Rexall Showcase International has done more good for the health of more people than the last thirteen years of my practice, or the next twenty."

Dr. Tim Beasley, an obstetrician-gynecologist practicing outside of Nashville who has been in the Rexall Showcase International business since 1995, admits he took an equally stubborn approach to the Rexall Showcase International products at first. Again it was personal experience that turned him around. He tried the products on his patients. "You have to understand that we doctors are obnoxious, obsessive-compulsive, perfectionist, and extremely individualistic—so we don't believe anything until we prove it to ourselves. That's how I approached these products and this business," Dr. Beasley says. He and the doctors in his practice gave the products to thirty patients, and the results "made believers out of my peer group. In Tennessee, Rexall Showcase International is rapidly expanding not because of me or even the Rexall brand name but because it works. Patients are switching from prescription medicines and in some cases are now being reimbursed by their insurance or finding their HMOs amenable to the treatment."

Dr. Beasley notes particular success for obese patients and those with high cholesterol. "I've seen borderline anorexics benefit too," he says. "There was one twenty-three-year-old woman who was very thin. For five years, she refused to eat in public. It was putting a strain on her marriage. She started taking just half a pack of the Bios Life a day and then moved to full treatment. She says she has never felt better and you can see it. Her color is back, she has more energy, and her face looks fuller."

Closer to home, the doctor's eighteen-year-old daughter alleviated some serious problems by using the products. "When she was a senior in high school she would experience excruciating pain before a big test or at other times of high tension," Dr. Beasley explains. "Since going on Bios Life, she's much less moody, her social life has improved, her eating habits have stabilized, and her weight has stopped fluctuating."

This doctor is counting on the Rexall Showcase International business to pave the way for his return to the reason he became a doctor in the first place. "Right now we're on target to bring in about 150 doctors in our organization," Dr. Beasley says. "So it looks like I'm back to Honduras! I've already spent time down there doing mission work. Caring for people in need is what I became a doctor for. What this business is providing me with is a chance to provide well for my wife and children and still retire and head back to the jungle!"

Practicing While They Preach

Not all doctors are getting into Rexall Showcase International so they can get out of their practices. Some, like Dr. David Ennis, a forty-one-year-old doctor from Westchester County, New York, who is board-certified in internal medicine, are doing both side-by-side to diversify their income and update their skills in preventative medicine.

"My initial attraction to the Rexall Showcase International opportunity was not the opportunity at all," he says. "I am married with three small children and spend sixty to seventy hours per week working in my medical practice. I didn't see any way this could fit into my life."

Dr. Ennis's interest started with the products. He detected a growing interest in natural remedies among his patients and started taking Bios Life for his own health. "I got tremendous results. My cholesterol level dropped and has never been as high since I started using the product. And in six weeks, those fourteen pounds I put on during my honeymoon ten years ago came right off. I was sold!"

Subsequently, Dr. Ennis has put more than 400 patients on a variety of Rexall Showcase International products, and watching the usually good results has been an eye-opening experience. "The fact is that I had very little training in nutrition. Thankfully the young students coming out of medical school today have more of it."

But soon this doctor looked to Rexall Showcase International for more than just effective products. "The dramatic changes in the health care industry over the past few years have made it clear to me that I needed to change my plans for the future as well. Otherwise I'd be working just as hard ten years from now with nothing additional to show for it except more stress and maybe less money," he says. "Managed care has taken a tremendous toll on my practice.

As patients change employers and employers change insurance companies, people are shifting from doctor to doctor. They have no choice. A lot of the loyalty has been squeezed from the system."

Accepting the alternative offered by Rexall Showcase International was not easy. "While I really struggled with the concept of network marketing, the more I learned about the industry and about Rexall Showcase International the more open I became to it. Now, I carve out some time each day, each week, each month, to build the business."

Spurring Dr. Ennis along is his wife, Laurie, a nurse who now works at the business full-time. Over the last three and a half years, the Ennis team, following a consistent game plan, has reached the coveted Century Club level, building a distributor organization that stretches from coast to coast and internationally as well.

"Just over three years ago this business was a luxury in my life, but now it plays a vital role in our family finances," Dr. Ennis relates. "But it's not just the income. The ability to get up in the morning and see our children get off to school, finding the time to exercise, and having breakfast with my wife—all of this has opened my eyes to a life that is available to me outside of a hectic medical career."

Dr. Ennis still practices medicine full-time but puts whatever energy he can into the Rexall Showcase International business. "It's a great way of hedging the future given what's happening to health care," he says, adding that "I know for a fact that many doctors have the same foreboding about the future that I have—but not all are willing to step out of their comfort zone."

Dr. George Watson of Wichita, Kansas, has been in some uncomfortable zones in his life—war zones! He served as an Air Force navigator in Vietnam; and as a flight surgeon in the Air National Guard, he was activated during Desert Storm.

Now with a full-time family medical practice and a still-active Air National Guard schedule, "I thought I didn't have time for another business," Dr. Watson says. "When Dr. Neal Secrist introduced me to Rexall Showcase International back in 1994, I didn't immediately see how the business and the products could fit into my life."

But the more he reflected on the idea and the more he studied it, the more Dr. Watson's view began to change. After all, unlike many physicians of his age (he's fifty-two now), Dr. Watson is certified in the practice of preventative health. From the standpoint of the Rexall Showcase International products, the fit was perfect. Then he took a close look at his financial situation and the lack of free time that had come to define his lifestyle.

"I asked myself what income level I could achieve if I spent the next four and a half years building a distributorship, and I laid that alongside what I'd make if I continued my full-time medical practice and Air National Guard service. I knew one thing for sure— the Guard would pay me $1,000 a month and I would be at risk of another call-up." Dr. Watson hadn't forgotten that when he was activated during Desert Storm, he had to sell his medical practice. All that uncertainty for what he figured would be a $1,500 per month pension when he retired from the Guard.

Then there were the changes in health care that we have seen so many other doctors comment upon. "More and more doctors are realizing that the rules have changed in medicine," he explains. "We have less control over the direction of our patients' care and less control over our own lives."

Armed with his analysis and his misgivings about the future of his medical practice, the doctor journeyed to a Rexall Showcase International training session in Dallas. He was impressed with the caliber of professionals involved in the business. "And then I knew: I can do this and I will do this!" A few days later he placed a product order and became a distributor. One day after that he resigned from the military. Dr. Watson is now steadily building his business with an eye toward replacing his entire medical income and scaling back his practice in 1999.

"When I started, I wondered if I would ever be in a financial position to retire no matter how old I was or how hard I worked. Now I can already! I have that option thanks to this business."

With his training in preventative medicine, Dr. Watson is uniquely qualified to discuss the products with patient and nonpatients alike. "I ask patients which prescription medicines they take and whether they buy anything from health food stores. Some tell me they buy as many as twelve different natural products. So I offer all my patients the option of prescription drugs or natural remedies," he explains.

"We have had patients reduce their cholesterol more than 300 points and reduce triglycerides several thousand points in a month using Bios Life 2. I lowered my own cholesterol from 212 to 160.

"My worst allergy patient was taking weekly shots until he tried Defend-OL. Now he heads up the largest leg in our group! And Cellular Essentials has improved some of my practice's worst cardiovascular cases, even restoring circulation to the hands and feet of a ninety-three-year-old patient."

A Question of Ethics

Dr. Watson's expertise in preventative care, his enthusiasm for nutritional supplements and natural remedies, and his no-apologies practice of offering the products to his patients while being in the business of selling those products has prompted a careful ethical examination in his own mind and that of many other doctors building Rexall Showcase International distributorships.

Is it proper for doctors to steer patients to the products, knowing that they may personally benefit? Does it create a conflict of interest that can be addressed only if these doctors refuse to inform patients about natural-remedy options?

Some in the medical profession have raised these questions about the "Rexall Showcase International doctors," but they might consider saving their breath. Leading doctors in Rexall Showcase International have put the question thoughtfully and directly to themselves.

Dr. Watson believes some of the outside concern stems from the high level of skepticism with which many in the medical profession view network marketing. And he points with incredulity to the fact that in his region "the two doctors who are making the biggest stink are plastic surgeons, whose incomes stem from recommending the cosmetic procedures they perform that aren't medically necessary!"

Dr. Watson points out that every time physicians not in network marketing recommend a procedure they will perform or a follow-up visit they'll charge for, the same ethical question could be hurled at them. After all, their income will be boosted as a result.

Since all of us in occupations high and low and in and out of network marketing are motivated to some degree by self-interest and the income motive, the real issue is this: Given the growing body of evidence regarding the health benefits of Rexall Showcase International and similar products, is it not a breach of ethics for doctors not to apprise their patients of those products? Dr. George Watson, Dr. Daria Davidson, Dr. Neal Secrist, and many others believe the answer is clear. If doctors, using their best professional judgment and personal scrutiny and experience, believe these products might provide a safer and more effective alternative to prescription drugs and perhaps forestall more drastic treatments down the road, such as open heart surgery, it is their moral and ethical obligation to so advise their patients.

A Chorus of Medical Voices

The views of Doctors Watson, Ennis, Secrist, and others are shared by many well-established, board-certified professionals spanning the country and medical disciplines:

- Dr. Bill Coddle of Somersett, Kentucky, practices pediatric dentistry and has been a Rexall Showcase International distributor for just over a year. "There are so many changes going on in medical care, especially with the intrusion of insurance companies, that physicians and other professionals are looking for additional sources of income," he says. "This business is well-positioned and well-timed, and the products are superb.

"I do a lot of orthodontic work on patients with gum problems. But the OraRex® product is very effective and tremendously successful with kids."

- Dr. Richard North is a family physician from Encinitas, California. He found out about the Rexall Showcase International products from his wife. "With Bios Life I've seen my own cholesterol drop 50 points and my father's has gone down 80 points," he reports. "A colleague of mine was treating an obese diabetic patient. After my colleague put him on Bios Life, this patient dropped 50 pounds and no longer has to take insulin!"

- Dr. Ann Hyman is a board-certified emergency physician from Tacoma, Washington. "I thought the products might benefit my husband," she says. "He had a heart attack when he was just 40 and after that tried two different medications to lower his cholesterol. They didn't work."
But after six weeks on Bios Life, Dr. Hyman's husband saw his cholesterol drop more than 100 points. "From then on I was sold on the products and wanted to do the business," she explains. "But I thought how could I? It's a conflict of interest. Then I came to understand that it would be a conflict of interest *not* to introduce people to this because I'm here to improve their health."

- Dr. Robert Green, who has practiced internal medicine in Westchester County, New York, for twenty years, acknowledges that, because he graduated from medical school back in 1971, his training didn't expose him to the role and possibilities of nutrition and prevention in overall heath. "I was very skeptical about Rexall Showcase International," he reports. "But after being badgered by a friend for six weeks, I relented; and when I saw the drops in cholesterol that

Bios Life was producing in patients, I was just stunned! Then I looked at the business opportunity and thought it was a home run."

- Dr. Caroline Rieser of Kansas City, Missouri, practices in a mental health clinic and finds that many of her patients respond particularly well to Rexall Showcase International's products designed to combat fatigue. "And, I reduced my own cholesterol and lost 30 pounds using the Rexall Showcase International products!" she adds.

- Dr. Terry Brown, a dentist from Memphis, achieved similar personal results. "I have been on Rexall Showcase International's Prescription for Life weight management program for two years and the results have been phenomenal," he says. "I lowered my cholesterol level 68 points, took off 29 pounds, and kept it off!"

- Dr. Gary Pitts, a urologist from Boone, North Carolina, played by all the normal rules to combat a serious high cholesterol problem, but nothing seemed to work. "I had been fighting it for eight years with a low-fat diet and lots of exercise. I very much wanted to get it under control because my family has a history of heart disease."

  But with Bios Life and Cellular Essentials, he has now successfully driven his cholesterol from 279 down to 199. "I also see a lot of patients with compromised bladders, enlarged prostates, and allergies," Dr. Pitts explains. "The Defend-OL product works particularly well. It just may represent a tremendous breakthrough in getting patients off antihistamines."

- Patients have long looked to Dr. Tom Entwistle, a chiropractor from Bristol, Connecticut, for natural approaches to their health problems. He finds the homeopathic products designed to fight insomnia very effective. "In my practice, I only have two hands, but through my Rexall Showcase International business, I can help improve the health of a huge number of people, give them a chance to improve themselves financially, and improve their lives in general," he says.

- Both the products and the changes in health care led Dr. Steven Brooks, an optometrist from Orlando, Florida, to Rexall Showcase International. "I was pretty depressed with all the changes in managed care and with health care reform, so I started looking for alternatives," he admits. "I wanted to leverage myself and get away from the daily stresses and aggravations of my practice."

  A close friend who was a dentist introduced Dr. Brooks to Rexall Showcase International, and the first impact was substantial improvement in his own health. "Taking the Bios Life product, I have lowered my cholesterol from 223 to 157 in three months and lost 20 pounds. I feel better than I have since I played football in college!"

- Dr. Richard Hill, a physician from Blackfoot, Idaho, has been in the Rexall Showcase International business for two years and, when appropriate, recommends the products to his patients. "They have seen dramatic results, especially addressing problems like high cholesterol, high blood pressure, and diabetes. Another patient whose pregnancy left her skin disfigured got great results from Aestivál. The problem cleared up within two months."

- Dr. Win Witlow, a dentist from Houston, went all the way once he was introduced to Rexall Showcase International. "I sold my practice when I saw this business," he reports. "It's the best thing I've ever done next to marrying my wife!"

  Three years to the day Dr. Witlow started in Rexall Showcase International, the business had grown to the point where his wife, an attorney, could quit *her* practice. The couple raise their two children together at home.

  "My father is a walking testimonial to the strength of the Rexall Showcase International products," he adds. "He was seeing a cardiologist for thirteen years, but it took Bios Life and Cellular Essentials to get him off all of the drugs and achieve some real improvements in his health. I remember when he couldn't even walk up the stairs to my office—and now he plays golf a couple of times a week!"

- Rather than leave his practice, Dr. Michael Brenvie, a family practitioner from Hendersonville, Tennessee, found that some Rexall Showcase International products were actually helping him *grow* his practice! "There was a lady who came to my office seeking a prescription medication to ease her anxiety and help her sleep," he explains. Instead, Dr. Brenvie directed her to try Rexall Showcase International's homeopathic insomnia remedy called Calmplex-2000. "The next week she sent me three new patients. Rexall Showcase International was actually growing my practice."

  Dr. Brenvie acknowledges that he was skeptical when first exposed to the products. He chalks that up to a bit of professional arrogance. "I was supposed to be an authority on these things, but I really didn't know anything about it." His personal turning point came when he tried treating his own allergies with Defend-OL. "I have always had to take decongestants for my problem," he says. "But after three weeks of using that product, I didn't have to take them anymore.

  "The products really do work. There are more and more clinical studies establishing the benefits of fiber, vitamins, and antioxidants for the heart. Learning to appreciate that and then finding out there was a business opportunity behind it, it just hit me. 'Wow!' I said—this is going to be explosive!"

- Dr. Steven Hearst, an orthopedic surgeon from Northern California, feels he has a strong personal reason to rely on the Rexall Showcase International products. "I'm the first male member of my family to make it to age fifty-five without a heart attack." He'd like to keep it that way. In addition to better health, Dr. Hearst is counting on the business to make up for lost income in medicine. "Developments in health care have terribly impacted our remuneration, especially here in California. I was looking for some other vehicle because I found myself working harder and harder for less money."

- Dr. Tom Glass is a professor of pathology at the University of Oklahoma who also has thirty years of experience as a medical examiner. He'll never forget the story of a forty-year-old referee at a local football game who suddenly collapsed on the field three minutes before half-time. "Despite all the resuscitation efforts, he died right there of a massive heart attack," Dr. Glass relates. "Afterward the family called to find out what had led to such a tragically premature death. "Here was a man who had nothing in his history, had regular exams, and was in good shape—but he had a disease he never knew he had."

  Dr. Glass is reminded of that story when he considers the preventative philosophy behind the Bios Life product and underscores that people should not wait for problems to arise before caring for their health. "Bios protects you from what you don't know you have," he says.

  "I would like to tell people in *advance* of death how they could have prevented death!"

- Dr. Ellie Bloomfield from Los Angeles needed no convincing about the positive role dietary fiber plays in health maintenance. "Fiber was well respected by the time I was in medical school," she says. "But I just couldn't see myself in the business of selling it!"

  That attitude began to change as she watched what was happening to her medical colleagues. "I practice 60 percent of my time for HMOs and 40 percent on a fee-for-service basis," she explains. "Over the last five years I have seen three groups lay off doctors. I left one group for another right before it got bought out and pay was cut 30 percent.

"I thought I had gotten out just in time, but then I was laid of from my group!"

Dr. Bloomfield is in the Rexall Showcase International business now and strongly urges other doctors to "take a good hard look at what's coming down the line.

"Do you want an income that is going to grow in the coming years or one that will shrink in the coming years?" she asks.

It's not a question of giving up the mission of caring for others that inspired most doctors to medicine in the first place. "If I work my hardest, I'll see maybe 125–150 patients a week in practice," says Dr. Bloomfield. "But in my Rexall Showcase International business I know I have 10,000 people on preventative health products and programs."

- Dr. Diane Thompson, a nurse and hospital administrator from Kansas City, echoes Dr. Bloomfield's sentiments. "Many of the ways we deliver health care are illness-related," she says. "But over the last five years we've begun to realize that we can't sustain that kind of system, especially as the baby boomers retire.

This doctor believes society and medicine can do better. "I for one am not satisfied with just getting by. I don't want to simply mask the disease process. Medical schools are finally coming up with courses on nutrition, and it's about time. Prevention is the name of the game."

Even so, Dr. Thompson predicts real change will be slow in coming. "Don't forget that the medical field today is still reimbursed on the basis of people being sick, not being well," she explains. "At the hospital we used to joke in a lighthearted way when it snowed because a snowstorm meant more people shoveling, more heart attacks, and more business."

Some may say that doctors are like economists in the sense that you can always find one with another point of view. But prevailing thought in the medical establishment has in modern times been far more monolithic than that of other professions. The fact that so many health care professionals, cutting across so many disciplines and levels of experience, are breaking out of that monolithic thinking by joining the Rexall Showcase International business and advocating the use of Rexall Showcase International products is highly significant.

I trust some readers may find it hard to sympathize with doctors' complaints about shrinking incomes, when as a profession they make far more than the national average. This skepticism overlooks the immense cost of and commitment to education and training, and it ignores a larger concern we must address—it is certainly in our health interests as a people to foster a system where the caregivers are professionally fulfilled and challenged rather than disheartened and disgruntled.

For doctors who feel that changes in the health care delivery system have turned them into employees punching a time clock, Rexall Showcase International gives them an opportunity to diversify their income streams. Many others are finding that Rexall Showcase International gives them a venue to explore new frontiers in preventative medicine, frontiers some of them never learned about in medical school.

Perhaps most importantly, this business has provided for many doctor-distributors a chance to return in a gratifying way to their core mission—which is to be caregivers. It is the restoration of the tradition of caregiving in medicine that could ultimately be the greatest contribution a company like Rexall Showcase International makes to health and society. That's why you can count so many doctors "in"!

CHAPTER NINE

Winners Welcome Here

In Chapter 3, I cited Direct Selling Association research that showed that the overwhelming majority of participants in this industry did it part-time to reach modest financial goals—to buy a new car, pay off some bills, get some desired products at a discount, or earn some extra money for Christmas presents.

My own review of practitioners reveals that most of them come from humble beginnings and many of them have suffered a number of personal and financial setbacks before finding success through network marketing. Given these circumstances, they are understandably fervent true believers in their business and want to share their passion with others. So what you commonly find in many network marketing businesses is a common story pushed to the forefront and told and retold: people who were down on their luck, with limited education and financial resources, and who perhaps suffered severe strains in family life and personal relations. But thanks to the business opportunity, all that has changed.

This is an inspiring story. No matter where you come from or how low you have sunk, you can change your life, stage a comeback, and achieve your dreams. The most successful network marketing companies have built their legends around these kinds of stories in their effort to appeal to the broadest swath of average citizens. There is nothing wrong with this approach—in fact, it has high appeal. And we will see in Chapter 10 that Rexall Showcase International as well has as some of its top leaders those whom have in the past felt the sting of failure and fought against long odds to succeed.

But this drumbeat message has come at a price to the direct selling industry. By basing the appeal of the business on emotion rather than economics and by emphasizing its low cost, ease of entry, and simplicity of execution, those who advocate network marketing cause many successful, higher caliber professionals to feel it is not for them. And emphasis on only the "rags-to-riches" stories and insistence that the business becomes one's all-consuming passion—a kind of substitute religion—turns off those who take a more studied dispassionate approach to life's activities.

Rexall Showcase International does it differently. The approach and appeal is more businesslike and professional. The methods advanced for building the business are geared more for busy professionals, who are likely to say in so many words, "Save the sermons and pep rallies, just give me the facts." As a result, the demographics of the Rexall Showcase International distributor force are like nothing the industry has seen before:

- They have an average income of $66,000, nearly triple the national average.
- 20 percent earn over $100,000 a year.
- 30 percent come out of the health care field.
- 85 percent own their own home.
- 60 percent have college degrees.
- 85 percent allocate 10 hours or less to the business each week, reinforcing that this is truly a part-time business.

Those who have already succeeded in life, as well as those still struggling to find their place, are invited in. Winners are welcome here.

Finding Crusade Material

There's nothing like a plane crash to focus your thinking on your approach to life and its priorities—especially when you were the one piloting and crashing the plane!

Stewart Hughes, along with Randy Schroeder and Todd Smith, represents the very highest tier of the Rexall Showcase International distributor leadership. Recently, with his business growing and propelled by its own momentum, the forty-three-year-old Utah native decided he wanted to be a pilot. So he took the requisite training and logged ten hours in the air with his flight instructor by his side.

Soon it was time to go solo. "Nobody's really ready for that," Stewart explains. "It's mainly to build your confidence. Instructors often spring it on their trainees. If they sense the time is right, they land the plane, hop out and tell you to give it a try. I guess that's so you can't spend too much time thinking about it and getting all worked up."

Stewart's maiden solo voyage went fine. But then business commitments kept him out of class and the cockpit for more than a month. When he was finally able to make it to the airstrip for another session, there was a mix-up. His flight-instructor was nowhere to be seen. Stewart looked up at the clear, expansive Western skies and thought, "Boy it sure is a nice day for flying. I've come all the way out here. I've soloed before. I'm going to go for it."

Getting up was the easy part. Soaring around the sky was joyful. But then there's the landing. First approach—missed. Second approach—missed again. On the third try, Stewart finally landed the plane. Except instead of landing on the airstrip, he put it down in a marsh! As the aircraft sank deeper into the muck, he realized he was unhurt and scrambled out to safety, expecting the plane to explode at any second. "That's what always happens on TV and in the movies," Stewart says. "The hero rushes out just as the plane erupts into a fireball. I was actually kind of disappointed when it didn't happen."

The media, the police, and the curious spectators thought it was interesting nonetheless and quickly gathered around to see how some guy could put a plane down nose first in a marsh. "The irony is that I went on to become a pretty good pilot," Stewart reports. What I learned is you can't expect to be good at something just because you do it once. You have to pay attention, follow the rules, practice, assemble a good team, and constantly improve your skills. Some people will tell you they have twenty years of experience in their job, but what they really have is one year of experience which they've repeated twenty times."

The lessons Stewart Hughes drew from his close call as a pilot reflect his serious and methodical approach to business. After growing up in small towns around Utah, he settled in Bountiful, outside of Salt Lake City, where he and his wife, Bonita, have eight children ranging in age from one to twenty. (Family responsibilities have obviously been a strong factor in Hughes's choice of career path. The first time I spoke with him, his seven-year-old son was home sick with the chicken pox, and Stewart took great satisfaction in the fact that he had found a business that allowed him to be home caring for the sick child.)

By the early 1980s, Stewart had settled into a successful career as a resident vice president, based in Utah, for a major New York–based investment firm. The state had by then become a fertile ground for the development of direct selling companies such as Nu Skin and Nature's Sunshine. So Stewart was afforded considerable exposure to this business approach, and when Nu Skin became a firm client in 1987, it was his job to thoroughly learn, scrutinize, and analyze the company.

"I was very impressed," Stewart reports. "I got to know all the principals at Nu Skin and had a chance to study the company inside and out. As a result, unlike many other professionals, I developed an extremely positive view of network marketing from the very beginning. Done right and with integrity, it is the most exciting and impressive way to do business."

In 1990, Stewart decided to put his opinions into action. "Nobody ever pitched me to do the business, I pitched myself on them. That's kind of an interesting twist!" At first, he worked the business part-time while continuing to manage thirty people for his investment firm. But after five months, he was ready to take the full-time plunge.

Yet although he was very successful and still maintains great respect for and close friendships with leaders in the Nu Skin business, the range of products left Stewart unsatisfied. "They are good, but not dramatic enough for me—simply not crusade material for Stewart Hughes," he says.

So he began looking around again—and, for the second time, "recruited myself" into a network marketing company. This time it was Rexall Showcase International. "I met with Damon DeSantis and was very impressed by the company and the quality of the leadership," Stewart reports. "Remember, I knew how to examine these things from my prior career and found Rexall Showcase International very solid.

"Just as important, I thought that if the Bios Life product worked, it was something I could get really excited about. This could be crusade material."

Stewart Hughes signed on as an Rexall Showcase International distributor on August 15, 1991. He remembers the date precisely because at that moment his cholesterol level stood at 206. Forty-five days later, it was 144—thanks to the Bios Life product. And while the cholesterol went down, the Hughes's income started going up and up and up! "I brought home $300,000 the first year, doubled it the next year, and reached $800,000 the third year," Stewart relates. "Last year I made $1.5 million doing this business, and I'll exceed $2 million in 1998.

"But even more important than the financial success is the tremendous flexibility you achieve in your life. This is the only business in the world where you can be at this level and not be totally stressed out when you're not in the office or when other commitments or projects keep you from being on the job," Stewart emphasizes.

"In my former career, I found that the more successful I became, the less freedom I had and less attention I was able to pay to my quality of life. Isn't it supposed to be the other way around?"

Today, Stewart works out of his home and has time for family and other pursuits—such as trying to fly planes and taking care of the unfinished business of getting his college degree! Once he attained his initial financial success in this business, he decided to take time off to pursue a degree in philosophy at Brigham Young University. While Stewart did not complete that program, he did do the necessary coursework to obtain the bachelor's degree he had begun chasing after years earlier. "So it took me fourteen years to get it done!" Stewart jokes.

And he's particularly impressed by the fact that his business keeps functioning even when he cannot. In the fall of 1998, Stewart had the only two surgeries of his life within two weeks of each other. The first was a minor procedure, but it caused him to miss out on a major trip to Asia where the Rexall Showcase International business has started to blast off. "I was disappointed, but impressed at how others immediately picked up the slack. It's a teamwork business here. You're in business for yourself but not by yourself."

Shortly after the first surgery, Stewart seriously injured his hand and had to have surgery to close up the wound and repair nerve damage. "As the anesthesiologist was about to put me under, he asked what I did for a living. I told him I sold vitamins, and his curious, positive reaction underscored how much the medical profession has changed its attitude toward vitamins, preventative care, and natural approaches to health. You can see that in how many health professionals have started Rexall Showcase International businesses."

To Stewart Hughes, the success Rexall Showcase International has had in attracting highly trained and successful professionals from the medical world reflects the serious, disciplined, and factual approach to business. While careful not to criticize other companies, he crisply defines the features that make Rexall Showcase International different:

"We tell people we're a serious business and want to run it like one. We don't run it like a church; we run it like a business. Others try to superimpose a crusade on the business. That's understandable because their products, while necessary and high in quality, aren't suggestive of a broader or bigger health or lifestyle movement. They're simply products people need and want to use in their everyday lives."

Furthermore, Stewart has observed—as have I—the tendency of other network marketing companies to "dumb down" their business, emphasizing its simplicity. They discourage participants from learning much about the products or services because they need to sign people up in a competitive workforce environment as quickly as possible. This approach is less than satisfying for today's "knowledge workers," who enjoy the intellectual challenge of understanding their products and industries and the broader economic context in which they operate.

"At Rexall Showcase International, we want our distributors to be knowledge workers," Stewart explains. "There are things you need to know and need to understand. We probably could have had a bigger spurt of people signing up at the beginning had we launched a more purely emotional appeal. But we're building it solidly instead. With Rexall Showcase International the crusade comes from the products. We don't superimpose it on the business. We present serious professionals with a solid opportunity they can pursue while maintaining their current careers.

"But please understand, you can be factual and thorough and still be passionate about what you're doing. We are very passionate about this company and where it's going in the future."

Taking Stock

Like Stewart Hughes, Jim Moyles has known mostly success in his professional life. After growing up in the Chicago area, Jim worked for some of the nation's finest companies, such as IBM and Lehman Brothers. Resettling on the west coast of Florida, he started his own merger and acquisition firm, often earning commissions of over $100,000 per transaction. But after eighteen years in this field, Jim found himself looking for something different. Something he learned from the merger and acquisition business was that even more valuable than earning large fees is building value in a business that can be sold or given to your children.

One day a friend of his son's called to ask Jim for his advice about a business he was getting started. It turned out to be a network marketing business, and the product was a "buyer's club" style membership. Jim was intrigued by the idea and decided to get involved. "We quickly built a team and it was fun," Jim recalls.

There was just one problem. They soon found out that in Florida membership sales are off limits for network marketing companies. "I had so much fun doing this business and I could see the potential was enormous. So I decided to learn from this experience and find the right company with the right product line. I found that the only companies in this industry that went on to long term success had one thing in common—*consumable products!*

What added to my determination to find the right company is that I came to realize that multilevel marketing is a brilliant method of doing business. The challenge is to find one of those few companies that have integrity and are destined to go on to long term success. I discovered that if you can find such a company and you put together a team of quality people some marvelous things can happen. First, it can create more income than anything else that you can do. This is because of the tremendous leverage. Second, it's also a better kind of income. It's residual! It becomes independent of our day to day activities. I now have a business that generates a seven figure income, a business that I can give to my children or sell. There's never been a company in this industry that does it better than Rexall Showcase International."

He reviewed the range of products and companies in a methodical, businesslike fashion that has become his hallmark in the Rexall Showcase International community. After about a year of looking he found Rexall Showcase International. "This company with its name brand recognition seemed like 'an unfair advantage.'"

Jim decided to build an organization in Clearwater, Florida. During his first month, he invited ten people to meet with him regarding a "new business venture" and five decided to join him. "We didn't know if we were going to make a lot of money but there was no downside. We all felt it would be fun to work together as a team. We were all impressed that Rexall Showcase International was behind it and we all could see the value in getting the products at wholesale."

It didn't take long for Jim Moyles to recognize he was on to something big. Although his first Rexall Showcase International check in September 1991 was $160, the next check was for $2,100. After one year, he was earning $13,000 a month. Today Jim is one of the highest earners in the company—his group moves $1.6 million in product monthly, bringing him a check of over $100,000. That's not per year, that's every month.

As noteworthy as Jim Moyles' success in Rexall Showcase International is, it is important to understand that like so many others in this distributor force, it is not his first taste of success. He came to the business of his own volition, out of his own sense of curiosity and business acumen. He was not down and out, but rather doing just fine before he ever heard of Rexall Showcase International.

So why did he do it? "It was an easy decision. It's designed to be done on a part-time basis. Why wouldn't anyone want to diversify and develop a second source of income? As for doing this as your primary focus, you have to do a little soul searching." Jim suggests that prospective distributors look at their career or business and, income aside, ask some basic questions. "Are you truly enjoying your business or career? Is it more fun than it was a few years ago? Is it allowing you to live the lifestyle you want? Are you in a field that is taking advantage of the trends? Only by putting your foot in the water can you decide if you'd like to make Rexall Showcase International your primary focus."

Jim's suggestion is based on simple logic and common sense. Perhaps that's why so many bright people are joining Rexall Showcase International. They may have achieved success as the professional world defines it, with salary, status, title, staff, promotions, responsibilities, travel, busy-ness, but isn't there more to life? Public opinion polls show that 80% of Americans are dissatisfied with their businesses and careers.

By the same token, it is a huge admission to tell an anonymous pollster or anyone else that we hate our jobs. Since work is such a central part of life, to do so is basically an admission that we hate our lives. Few are willing to entertain such thoughts. So instead, we whine and complain around the edges. "I'm on the road too much." "I don't have enough time to see my kids." "My company management doesn't know what it's doing."

Having held executive positions in government and business, which by any definition add up to a "successful" career, I often find myself caught on the horns of the same dilemma. One day I love my job. The next day I hate it. I come close to the edge of leaving it, then inevitably pull back. I'm pleased with myself for what I have achieved—the financial success and peer approval—but I'm continually looking for escape.

Many successful professionals harboring similar thoughts will play those mind games on themselves for their entire careers. They'll never act on the many "coulda, woulda, shoulda" plans they concocted while counting off the years in their company or organization. By the time they reach the minimum retirement age—or are offered an early retirement package—they're ready to get out and retreat. This helps explain why demographers who are rightfully concerned about the growing shortage of workers in the United States, Japan, and Western Europe should not count on longer life expectancies to therefore produce legions of people who want to extend their working lives beyond the bare minimum. Only if financially desperate will most consider doing so. Polls regarding job satisfaction aside, most employees in traditional careers will vote with their feet by getting out the moment they can.

What Rexall Showcase International and leaders like Jim Moyles present to successful but dissatisfied people is this: an opportunity to diversify and make other choices from a position of security and strength, not weakness and despair. If after you assess your own level of happiness and financial security, you find them wanting, why wait until you are forced to act or are too old to act? Why not do it now, alongside your current career or business and put yourself on a path that gradually but steadily addresses the changes you want to make and build a second income and perhaps the life you really want to lead?

"This business is designed to be started part-time, ten to fifteen hours a week," Jim explains. "In fact, you wouldn't have enough to do if you put in more time than that.

"The secret of my success is building a team. What we tell someone who is open to joining our team is that we'll help them sponsor their first five to ten people, if they'll agree to help the people they bring on board do the same with our help. It's very much a team approach. That's how we help people get three or four levels deep, where they generate significant sales volume and start to see the income potential.

167

"And don't check your experience at the door. What I did was bring my business experience to compliment a great opportunity," Jim emphasizes, "We're now attracting the best and the brightest to Rexall Showcase International. Busy people who would like to diversify but who don't have a lot of time. What these people are coming to realize is that the traditional business is changing. Rexall Showcase International is time effective. Look at what's happened to those in the insurance, medicine, banking, and travel industries. What do you think will happen to CPAs if we move to a flat tax?

"The bottom line is that relationship marketing will be the distribution method of the twenty-first century. Add to this Rexall Showcase International's financial strength and the fact they are the #1 preventative healthcare company in the U.S. There's no better field to be in and no better company to capitalize on these trends.

"Rexall is one of the most recognized brand names in the U.S. and the Rexall Showcase International division has unique, exclusive products that are major breakthroughs in preventative health care. And the timing is impeccable. Our sales jumped from $105,000,000 to $158,000,000 in 1998. This division will soon be doing $1 billion in annual sales and there will be hundreds of thousands of distributors. The potential is absolutely incredible."

To Jim Moyles, it is the successful bright people who will propel Rexall Showcase International forward because "never before have so many high-quality people been so unhappy with their careers and businesses. They want to take control of their lives and we have the best vehicle."

Jim understands what a rich reward this is in a most personal way. His two older children are now grown. His oldest son, Sean, is an attorney and his daughter is a schoolteacher. Jim and his wife now have a two-year-old boy and one on the way. "I love being a father and it's so much fun the second time around," he marvels. This is a business that is so compatible with family life. "I can get to play with my two year old all day if I want."

A Business Calculation

Gordan Oswald didn't pursue his initial career for very long—he majored in psychology at the University of Utah and worked briefly for the state as a counselor. But perhaps it helps explain why he has been so persuasive and successful in ventures as varied as show business production, commercial real estate, and network marketing. An "army brat," Gordon grew up all over the world before settling in the Salt Lake City area. Once he had left counseling behind, his first real entrepreneurial adventure came when he teamed up with a friend to launch a company that designed laser optics applications for various uses—including laser light shows for flashy Las Vegas productions.

Gordon sold that company in 1977 when opportunities in commercial real estate prompted a move to Southern California. He then entered an exciting world of big deals and high finance—and he loved every minute of it.

"I was on top of the world," he recalls. I helped a major company open an office in Beverly Hills. I flew around the country in corporate jets. I was given $40 million by my clients to find them $300 million worth of good acquisitions. Everywhere I went I was wined and dined, by people who wanted me to give the thumbs up to their project or property."

But when the real estate bubble burst—again—in 1986, that particular part was over for Gordon Oswald. "I found out I was a legend in my own mind," he quips. He had learned an important lesson—that in many fields people may make a lot of money, but they lose a lot of money too. Gordon began to wonder if there was a way to generate a steadier stream of income that was not so tied to the boom and bust cycles that came to define so many businesses in the 1980s and 1990s.

But for now, real estate was Gordon's only game, and he successful weathered the 1986 downturn and got ready to ride another wave. He was recruited to start an independent real estate sub-sidiary of another bank in Southern California. And he began his own asset management services company, focusing on apartments and other commercial properties.

"1987 to 1990 was the second wave of fun," he remembers. "I did $500 million in transactions, mostly with the Canadians and Japanese." This experience would later give Gordon solid insights into markets of vast potential for Rexall Showcase International.

But in 1990 business once again came to a screeching halt, and Gordon's only income came out of his property management company.

"It was then that I got a call from a friend in Florida who asked me to take a look at a business opportunity. It was Rexall Showcase International. Given what was happening in Southern California real estate then, he caught me at just the right time!" Gordon says.

"After looking at some materials, I was interested enough to go to Florida. I wanted to see the company's headquarters and its manufacturing facilities. I spoke to the executives. Their openness impressed me. I had known people in network marketing busi-nesses who made a lot of money, but had never considered doing it myself and didn't know much about how to do it," he explains.

Nonetheless, Gordon's visit to Florida convinced him to do it. "Everything seemed to click," he says. The significance of his judg-ment should not be missed. For here was a man who once made a living advising mega-rich clients on which properties and compa-nies to acquire. No superficial pitch or platitude-laden pep talk would charm Gordon Oswald. "I made a purely business calcula-tion," he confirms.

His wife, Megan, however, did not share Gordon's calculation. "I didn't really know what it was at that point," she told *Upline* magazine. "Still I didn't like it at all. . . . I told Gordon, 'Oh, you don't want to do that! Those are those pyramid people.'"

Despite Megan's protests, Gordon gave the business a try and started having people over to the house to explain it. "I went up-stairs to get away from it all," Megan recalls.

"But then one night I eavesdropped, and I began to see network marketing in a whole different light. It sounded really intriguing. I started trying the products and I loved them! My whole attitude changed."

It was a good thing, too, because Gordon found the early days tough going. "I didn't have any upline in California," he recalls. "My upline was in Florida! So I was basically all by myself out here doing the business without any hands-on assistance.

"The people who were helping me did the best they could through conference calls. And they flew out about once a month and gave us some very good support," Gordon told *Upline.* "Sometimes people get into network marketing because they think it's going to be easy. But it takes time and it takes work. Some people just want to get rich quick, and when they find out they're actually going to have to do some work, they drop out before they really give it a chance."

Being on the frontier wasn't the only hurdle the Oswalds faced. "I did have to have a self-identity talk with myself," Gordon explains. After all, as good as the Rexall Showcase International opportunity appeared to be, selling little packets of a fiber-based health supplement seemed like quite a leap from those high-flying days of private jets and multimillion-dollar real estate transactions! But Gordon made that leap because in his words, "I care about what other people think, but I've never been one to run with the pack. I quickly came to the conclusion that the only way this business could hurt me was if I tried it and failed.

"But I was convinced that properly worked, this would be a superior kind of business compared to all the ups and downs of other businesses."

The Oswalds worked together out of the family home. Unlike other leaders in the business, who had meteoric rises, they started relatively slowly. "I was putting about fifteen hours a week into it the first few months. By the eleventh month, we got a monthly check for $5,000. That's nice but our house payment was $10,000 a month!"

But six months later, with about the same level of effort, the check doubled to $10,000 a month. "There's the house payment!" Jim recalls exclaiming. "I felt I could double it again with some more effort, and I did in another six months," says Jim, who began to scale back his real estate activities. Today he spends 90 percent of his professional time building the Rexall Showcase International business, accounting for much of the Californian as well as Taiwanese and Korean distributor networks. Nice "territories"! The Oswalds are among the top seven earners in the company, and Jim is a member of the prestigious Presidential Board of Advisors.

Given his prior business experience dealing in many of the Asian business cultures as well as the presence of many Asian Americans in his California organization who have lucrative links to their home countries, count on Gordon Oswald to be a driving force behind Rexall Showcase International's expansion in the Pacific. While acknowledging the role electronic communications and technology can play in the network marketing duplication process (tapes, voice mail, and the Internet), Gordon still places a high premium on face-to-face, personal contact. He attributes his success in California in large part to the technique of scheduling distributor and prospect meetings up and down Southern California's infamous freeways, about thirty minutes' drive-time apart. Gordon and the key members of his team would kick off one meeting, jump in the car, and "crawl" up the freeway to the next meeting.

"The audiotapes are excellent tools, as are meetings," Jim says, explaining his approach. "But I have found that the tapes alone won't close the deal and, more importantly, there's a need for personal contact between the time someone signs up and the time they start earning significant income. The weekly handshake, the smile, the recognition, the sharing of a business idea—you have to look them in the eye to keep them going."

Megan Oswald underscores this point: "A lot of people quit because they give up too quickly. Let them know right away that this is going to be a little work, so don't quit your day job. Start out on a part-time basis, because it's going to take some time to replace your current income," she advises.

"Think of it as a business. If you were to start your own small company, you wouldn't expect to make a profit right off the bat. You'd expect to have to put some time, work, and effort into it. Network marketing is no different."

Don't Forget Fun

Fifty-year-old John Berta likes to say that he semi-retired at age forty—semi-retired from his first career building and running a successful multi-office accounting, real estate, mortgage brokerage, and property development firm in the Tampa Bay area. John moved there from New Jersey more than twenty years ago after methodically picking the community in which he wanted to live and do business. "I hand-selected Tampa Bay," he says coolly.

But then John Berta is, to use his own words, a "logical" guy. He doesn't jump at things. He checks them out. He prefers facts to hype, long-term potential over a short-term quick strike. So when he found himself growing bored with his business and "semi-retiring" when barely into middle age, he began to look for something new. "I basically stumbled onto network marketing," he says. "Like many professionals I didn't see myself in it. But I did the due diligence and really checked it out, and I came to the conclusion that it is absolutely the best way for companies to efficiently distribute their products. Word-of-mouth is and always will be the strongest way to market. Network marketing takes advantage of that fact even in a technological age."

In November 1991, John began his Rexall Showcase International business. Soon thereafter he met a woman named Julie Berry, another successful distributor who in a very personal way had come to appreciate the power of the products and the business opportunity. She had a severe asthmatic condition that had made

173

her dependent from birth on prescription medications. The Rexall Showcase International products freed her from that dependency. "Today Julie and I have an organization that spans all fifty states, Mexico, Korea, Hong Kong, and Taiwan," John reports. Four years ago, while speaking before 3,500 people in Atlanta, John proposed to Julie and to the delight of the crowd and John, she accepted.

"I can't promise this to everyone who joins Rexall Showcase International," he cautions. "All I can do is tell you that Rexall Showcase International changed my life in wonderful ways. Julie and I work the business predominantly from our home. We spend anywhere from twenty-eight to forty hours a week, forty weeks a year." The couple is today among Rexall Showcase International's top earners, and John sits on the company's ten-member Presidential Board of Advisors.

John Berta is convinced that network marketing generally and Rexall Showcase International in particular are poised for remarkable growth. Unlike many that poke fun at the baby-boomer generation, John has a different assessment. "I believe with the boomer generation you have people who are leaders, who are questioning kind of people. They're going to look at the trend-lines, examine what's going on around them and make smart decisions based on the facts. They are less willing to be tied to the old ways of doing things simply because that's the way they've always been done," he explains.

"The baby boomers who are in their forties today are beginning to take stock. They know they have a good chance of living longer than generations before them. They understand that they aren't really prepared to retire in a way that allows them to maintain a good lifestyle. And they have seen more changes in business and professions in the last five years than have been seen in decades.

"They aren't stupid; they see what's going on around them," John continues. "Boomers go into the grocery store and instead of the teenager who used to bag their groceries, there's a seventy-year-old man doing it because he needs the money. And they're wondering, 'Is this what's in store for me when I'm seventy?'"

John sees the convergence of several strong factors that will drive Rexall Showcase International forward. "Take the combination of all these factors—the boom in preventative health care, the reemergence of the home-based economy even as we globalize, and the desire of the boomers for a business that makes them financially secure, makes room for family life and makes room for fun—and that's why Rexall Showcase International will grow in the future."

And he strongly believes that as network marketing goes mainstream and comes increasingly to define the primary mode of marketing and distributing products in the twenty-first century, it will be those companies that adopt a more professional, businesslike face that will earn the greatest following. "We're basically a conservative, middle-of-the-road, professional company. That's the foundation we're building on," John says. "I for one only ask people to make a decision on the facts. We've never been a company of hype, a pep-rally company, and I hope we never will be."

The Price of Success

"If you are in network marketing there are two statements you never want to hear," says fifty-three-year-old James Oznick of Gilbert, Arizona.

"From your spouse: 'You know honey, your check doesn't have a comma in it yet.'

"And from your upline: 'I wonder why he's still around.'"

We have seen that—breaking the pattern of many network marketing companies—Rexall Showcase International has attracted an unusually high number of successful professionals with high education and considerable assets and experience. Because strong self-confidence is a mark of distinction in most successful people, it is not surprising that some would arrive on Rexall Showcase International's doorstep thinking that success there would be a snap—or that they knew everything there was to know about building a profitable operation and didn't need anyone telling them how to do it.

James Oznick was one of them. He was so convinced that he would excel at Rexall Showcase International that, unlike most others, he went into the business full-time from the very beginning. He even sold a successful cellular phone business to do it.

It was more than supreme self-confidence that drove James to this decision. He wanted out of the small business grind he found himself in. "I had worked hard all my life and thought I got to know business inside and out," James explains. His dad owned a small candy factory in Dallas and James helped him out. He trained as an accountant at Southern Methodist University and became a CPA. In the early 1970s he built a successful chain of car stereo and accessories stores. Later, as the cellular phone craze caught fire, he began a business that included seven stores and 200 employees.

"I made a lot of money. I also lost a lot of money—especially in real estate. But whatever success I enjoyed, I found there was something missing—a sense of serenity. Eventually I just got tired of all the headaches that came with my business," James explains. When I asked him what those headaches were, he replied "One word—employees!"

By the early 1990s James set out on a search for a different opportunity. He researched more than a hundred companies and business opportunities before concluding, "for a business to provide a sense of fulfillment, you not only have to make money, but also need to develop some emotion, some passion, about the products."

That was easy to do when James looked at Rexall Showcase International. "My younger brother suffered two heart attacks in his early forties," he explains. "I'm ten years older and you have to wonder." He started taking Bios Life and within six weeks it lowered his cholesterol by seventy points. Surprisingly, when his brother had his first heart attack, "his heart specialists told him not to take the Rexall Showcase International products—and when you've just had a heart attack, you tend to listen to your doctor," James says. Then when his brother had the second heart attack, "you can be sure he started using the products then."

In the spring of 1992, James Oznick started his Rexall Showcase International business. Brimming with confidence, he figured, "I had worked for myself for over twenty years, and I just knew Rexall Showcase International would not be a challenge. After a few months, I was sure I'd be making a six-figure income. My wife and my best friends thought I was totally out of control."

James attacked the business with a vengeance. "I worked it hard, sometimes eighty, ninety hours a week. I did it all. I ran ads, talked to people I knew and people I had just met. I sent out flyers and made all the phone calls.

"I lived Rexall, I breathed Rexall, I ate Rexall, and I drank Rexall. I just flat-out did the deal."

And at first blush he had much to show for his frenetic efforts. He signed up so many new distributors that during the company's April 1994 convention, James Oznick was recognized with a top achievement award. But as he was basking in the applause of the crowd, he received an ominous message.

"As I came off the stage," James recalls, "my sponsor met me in the aisle to congratulate me, and he leaned over and whispered in my ear, 'Now that you got this recognition, let's try to actually make some money!' I thought that was worth listening to, considering that this guy was making $70,000 from Rexall Showcase International."

The next month James came to understand his upline's message. His first check arrived, and it was the whopping sum of $161! "Working full-time, trying my heart out, getting up early, staying up late—all that and my check totaled all of $161." He still hears the words of his wife Reta echoing in his ears: "You know honey, your check has no comma yet." One of his colleagues overheard one of the top company earners wondering why James "was still hanging around."

What had happened to James Oznick's "sure bet" was simple: Everyone he had sponsored had quit. Figuring out why it happened and what to do about it was far more complicated.

James' sponsor brought him to Florida for a visit and confronted him with some important questions. Do you really want to be a leader in this business? Are you prepared to listen and learn from those who have devised successful approaches to the business and who are prepared to help you? Are you ready to be more disciplined, not just engaging in activity, but the right kind of activity? James answered each of those questions with an emphatic "yes" and, with the help of successful mentors in Rexall Showcase International, set out to develop a new game plan.

He more clearly defined his goals and better identified key prospects, targeting his recruiting efforts at them. He followed the team-building strategy devised by the company's top performers, which features the distribution of compelling audiotapes, follow-up contacts, and three-way phone conferences featuring a Rexall Showcase International "star" to help close the sale. Equally important is the strategy's focus on helping new distributors after they have signed up rather than simply picking up your marbles and moving on.

Renée Stewart Chittick of Clearwater, Florida—Rexall Showcase International's top female earner—is particularly emphatic in emphasizing this point. "People think you have to go out and recruit the world," she explains. "That's not it at all. It's a sifting-out process. What you really should be doing is asking yourself how many people you need to build the kind of business you want. Building depth, six levels down, which is as far as you can go, is what it's all about."

As evidence, Renée cites the fact that even a wildly successful distributor like Todd Smith "only generates about 2 percent of his income from that first group of people he personally sponsored. Almost all of his wealth comes from levels two through six.

"That means your key to success is to be a teacher and a team builder. Help people all the way down in your organization become successful—that's how you fully access the Rexall Showcase International compensation plan."

James Oznick followed this advice the second time around. "I stopped wasting time," he says. "If someone did not want to take a look, I moved on. If they did, I got Rexall Showcase International leaders on the phone on three-way calls to close the deal. And once they joined the business, I did the same for them."

Steadily, the results became apparent. "By May 1995 my monthly check was over $7,000," James says proudly. "It kept growing, but more importantly, I was growing.

"Today Reta and I work the business together. She no longer thinks I'm crazy. We earn a strong six-figure income that is becoming a residual income because we have so many dedicated customers who believe in the products. And we have a handful of distributors who work the business with us in a synergistic, passionate way that attracts other professionals."

You don't have to be down and out to be up and coming in the Rexall Showcase International business. Winners are indeed welcome here, and those who keep on winning are those who arrive as open-minded students and then become great teachers.

CHAPTER TEN

Always a Beginning

"You've probably observed that Rexall Showcase International attracts a lot of distributors who have very high levels of education. I'm not one of them."

So began my first conversation with forty-one-year-old Randy Schroeder, the company's top money earner, and, along with Todd Smith and Stewart Hughes, one of the driving forces behind the rapid growth of Rexall Showcase International.

Indeed this native of the small mountain town of Rexburg, Idaho, has but eighteen college credits to his name. "What I am, always have been, is an entrepreneur," Randy says. "From the time I was a kid, I sold everything—seeds, greeting cards, you name it."

And he was almost always successful. While other twenty-year-olds were partying and maybe studying the hours away in college, Randy at age twenty-one sold weight loss franchises and made $260,000 in income that year. Not bad for the son of a hard-working father who nonetheless never made more than $40,000 a year his entire life!

Full of the self-confidence that motivates him to this day, Randy learned early on that in America making money was really pretty easy. But he also learned two other lessons that would eventually steer him to network marketing and Rexall Showcase International.

First, he learned that if making money was easy, so was spending it. As Randy's success grew, so did the needs and demands of his lifestyle.

More importantly, he realized that in most businesses and professions, at a certain point "it didn't matter any more how good you were—if the opportunity wasn't good."

Randy explains: "Take those weight loss franchises. Once we put a franchise in every town in our market, there wasn't much left to do. I came to understand that it wasn't enough for me to be good—and I was good—the opportunity had to be good."

Randy responded by starting his own weight loss franchise company. Still young at just twenty-four, he was again successful. The company launched fifty-six franchises around the country and caught the eye of the Minneapolis-based Watkins company, which bought Randy's company for a good price and made him president of its new wholly-owned subsidiary.

But Randy's tenure in the executive suite didn't last long. "I knew in about ninety days that I didn't want to remain in that corporate structure, so I quit after slightly more than a year and left for California," he explains. Still, with Watkins engaged in direct selling, he gained some important insights into that alternative marketing method that would serve him well later. But in California, in the high-flying mid-1980s, the financial services arena was the place to be for a young aggressive salesman and entrepreneur. It wasn't long before Randy was raking in big money selling "junk" bonds for Drexel Burnham Lambert, the now-defunct firm headed by Michael Milken. Yet when the 1980s crashed and burned financially, so did Randy Schroeder. "I was heavily leveraged in Southern California real estate. Once again I found out that when the opportunity was gone, so was my income, no matter how good I was."

Randy realized something else too. "In most types of business you only get paid once. All those franchises I sold, all those stocks and bonds I sold—I didn't get paid anything ever again for all that effort."

Faced with a personal financial situation so bleak that his friends urged him to declare bankruptcy, Randy set out to find the right opportunity that would allow him to dig out of the hole he was in and create the lifestyle he desired. "I wanted a business in which I would get paid again and again and again. It was that simple."

Remembering what he saw and learned at Watkins, Randy now concluded that the answer was network marketing.

"No one ever recruited me. I was never prospected. I made my own conscious decision that network marketing was the place where I could get paid over and over again," he explains.

Randy signed on with Nu Skin in February 1990; and even though he left the company for Rexall Showcase International nineteen months later, he remembers the experience fondly. "Almost right away I made $7,000–$8,000 a month, but when Nu Skin ran into all that bad publicity, I realized it would be some time before my business would really take off," he explains. "The problem was I still had a $10,000 a month mortgage! I just couldn't weather the storm."

So in August 1991, when Randy started at Rexall Showcase International, he did so with a strong bank of knowledge but absolutely no money. He didn't even have his own telephone to make his sales calls.

Despite this handicap, he was from the very beginning successful again. By the end of his third month, he was the company's top earner. In the ensuing seven years Randy has collected more than $10 million from Rexall Showcase International. His monthly earnings today? I talked to Randy in late 1998 as a monthly income check arrived in the mail. It was for $252,000!

Randy says he's trying hard to slow down now, especially so he can spend more time with his children. Divorced but on good terms with his ex-wife, he looks forward to motorcycle rides, snowboarding trips, and other adventures with the children—secure in the knowledge that his business will keep growing and the income will keep on rolling in even when he is taking time off.

"I still have what I call a refugee attitude," Randy says. "The experience of being broke was so powerful that I want to put as much distance between it and me as possible." So he keeps on traveling, working, speaking, and building, dividing time between homes in California, Utah, and Florida—not to mention frequent trips to Asia, which he predicts "is going to be unbelievable for Rexall Showcase International."

Reflecting on his success despite limited options, long odds, and many ups and downs—and the prospects for others in similar situations to duplicate that success—Randy Schroeder makes an astute observation. He reminds us that one of the strengths of network marketing is that there is virtually no barrier to entry. If you're an adult with fifty bucks for a distributor kit and a few hundred more for training, materials, and a product order, you're in.

But no barrier to entry means there's also no barrier to exit. "It's not like sinking $100,000 into a franchise. You can't just decide one day not to show up. And if you suddenly want to sell out, suppose no one's buying? You say to yourself, 'I can't quit. I've got my whole life sunk into this,'" Randy observes.

Thus one of network marketing's greatest strengths—its openness to those with limited means—can also be a weakness. The distributor pool constantly churns because in terms of dollars and cents, there's virtually nothing to lose by quitting.

And therein lies what Randy considers the key to his success—and that of others: "You have to create a barrier to exit that is so high that you can't and won't quit. That's what I did. I put my entire future on the line."

Day of Reckoning

The day a flat-broke Jeff Mack walked into the local bank with his father so that his dad could co-sign a credit card application for him was the day the then twenty-seven-year-old decided that failure was simply no longer an option.

"God bless my dad," Jeff says. "I was the youngest of five children and pretty much the disappointment of the family." Growing up in the small town of Moorsville, North Carolina, where his folks owned a retail clothing store, "I was always an erector-set kind of kid," Jeff recalls. He got an engineering degree and plunged into the roller-coaster world of construction and real estate in the fast-growing Raleigh and Charlotte markets.

Early in his career, Jeff observed his superiors closely and started questioning whether climbing the ladder in his field would bring with it all his expectations of wealth and happiness. "I looked at my bosses and I saw them making a lot of money, but they didn't have a decent lifestyle. They were totally stressed out," Jeff recalls.

"Then you had the economy going bad and banks stopped lending to developers. There were all the regulations and subcontractors that didn't show up. I thought, 'There's got to be a better way.'"

Jeff also considered the example of his own parents. "They worked six days a week, twelve hours a day in their clothing store. But despite all that it didn't generate a lot of income, they couldn't sell it, and they couldn't afford to retire."

Jeff found that "better way" when he ran into a friend from college, Eddie Stone, who was involved with Nu Skin. "I looked at network marketing and almost immediately I got the fever," he recalls. Jeff signed on as a Nu Skin distributor but came to realize that "while it was a good company, it was not the right opportunity for me." Meanwhile, Jeff was digging himself ever deeper into financial difficulty. He lost his job and took a downgraded position as an estimator. He overspent and made bad financial decisions. "By the time I was ready to join Rexall Showcase International in

184

August 1991, I was so broke I couldn't afford the rent. I had accumulated $40,000 in high-interest credit card debt." He soon had no choice but to move into the dark basement of the Mack family home. Jeff had to wear a hat and sweatshirts to keep warm and will never forget the smell of antifreeze and the rusted old refrigerator that competed with Jeff and his Rexall Showcase International business for space.

At the same time he was courting a young woman named Lisa. Dating was a little complicated with no money, Jeff recalls. "I was trying to impress the young lady, so I'd take her out to Burger King and she'd have to pay," he jokes.

But he believed the Rexall Showcase International opportunity offered him his best and perhaps only way up from the basement. So he took out a second loan on his car at 31 percent interest so that he could pay down a credit card with 18 percent interest to get started and place his first product orders. And as we have seen, his father stepped in at this critical moment as well. "I had something big to prove," Jeff says. "I simply wasn't going to fail. That was not an option." Remember Randy Schroeder's advice about erecting a barrier to exit so high that you just couldn't quit? That's precisely what Jeff Mack did the day he walked into that bank with his dad.

Flash forward to November 1998. Jeff is thirty-four years old and in the first eleven months of the year, has earned $774,000 from his Rexall Showcase International business. "I went from being an idiot to a genius in six years," he says.

The basement, the antifreeze, the rusted old refrigerator have been left far behind. The "erector-set kid" is building a 6,000-square-foot home with 200 feet of private beach on the shores of North Carolina's Lake Norman. The home will include a four-car garage, a private gym, and a movie theater.

And it will include Lisa. The couple married three years ago after Jeff concluded a motivational speech before 3,000 Rexall Showcase International distributors and prospects with a very public marriage proposal right from the stage. I asked him how he could be sure Lisa would say yes. "I figured if she was treating me to dinner at Burger King in the bad old days, she must have seen something she liked!" Jeff replied.

To a great degree, Jeff Mack credits his delayed success to "finding the right vehicle." For a network marketing company to be successful, it "has to have strong products that people can relate to, a fair compensation plan, and a system that is simple to follow and simple to teach."

Jeff believes Rexall Showcase International has all these strengths, but quickly points out they are not enough. "People have to bring to a business like this their own personal drive. You see everyone has wants, but not everyone has desires. Those people don't succeed. I think the reason I did was that I had a very clear picture of why I wanted to do this business. I had a lot to prove. Every time a person turned me down, that just made me more determined to succeed."

As we have seen, Rexall Showcase International is altering the demographic profile of network marketing—bringing in a high representation of well-educated, white-collar professionals, steeped more in business fundamentals than in religious fundamentalism.

Yet the paradox of network marketing is that while it nurtures an upbeat, optimistic culture, it has an easier time attracting practitioners during periods of economic hardship. Just as fear ultimately outsells hope in the world of politics, poverty outsells prosperity as a motivating force for many in network marketing. As much as companies like Rexall Showcase International are starting to attract those who have graduated from business or medical school, those who graduated from the school of hard knocks continue to be a major force.

This is not a judgment, but rather an observation. No one enjoys good old-fashioned American rags-to-riches stories better than I do. They are part of our history as a country and our folklore as a culture. What's intriguing about Rexall Showcase International's distributor force is that those who achieved success and status prior to joining the company seem to work smoothly and cooperatively with those who turned to Rexall Showcase International under tough circumstances or with few options or resources. It's a level playing field, but one that exists on a plateau, not in a valley. Rexall Showcase International embodies a form of entrepreneurship that makes room for those like Jeff Mack who, for various reasons, find themselves desperate for a new beginning.

Still Running to the Bank

Even with six years of tremendous success to her name as Rexall Showcase International's top female earner, Renée Stewart Chittick still considers each arrival of her monthly income check nothing short of a miracle. "There's never a time when I don't cry, pray, or run to the bank—because it might all be just a dream!"

Fifty-one years old now, Renée was forty-five when she started her Rexall Showcase International business. She and her husband were supporting their two daughters "by selling T-shirts and rubber alligators to tourists who visited our souvenir shop in Clearwater, Florida." She was struck by how tough and expensive it was to be in the retail business—the long hours, the big bank loans, the merciless ups and downs of the economy, the weather, and the flow of tourists.

Even so it was the products, not the business opportunity, that first led Renée to Rexall Showcase International. "My husband was a recovering cancer patient who lost 30 pounds and lowered his cholesterol 90 points thanks to the Rexall Showcase International products," she recalls. Defend-OL helped Renée manage a serious allergy problem; and by taking Bios Life, she lost 13 pounds. "That didn't turn me into Twiggy, but it did prompt me to take a serious look at the business opportunity behind these products."

When she investigated and understood that it wasn't door-to-door selling, "but a chance to teach a small number of people to do the same thing you were doing and building an organization out of that," Renée was excited. By now divorced from her husband, she wanted to provide her daughters with both a comfortable upbringing and a strong example that "there is hope for women who want to be both successful in business and good mothers."

Active in the Clearwater community for years through volunteer work and involvement in the PTA, Renée put her network of friends and contacts to good use. With her daughters as her partners, Renée built a Rexall Showcase International business that today, after six years, earns her a million dollars a year. Pointing out that just six-tenths of one percent of working women in America make over $100,000 a year, Renée is both proud and grateful.

Yet as much as she enjoys her financial success, Renée also values what she calls the "perks" of her business—the opportunity to help people and "being able to work in a positive environment. It's great to be around upbeat, optimistic people all the time," she says.

"You can't underestimate the power of the products," she continues. "People have an emotional attachment to the Rexall Showcase International products because it concerns their personal health. Even people who drop out of the business continue to buy and use the products."

Consider the long, tortuous forty-year journey, from college graduation to retirement, that many of us move along in our professional endeavors—all in the hopes of attaining a modicum of prosperity, security, recognition, and personal fulfillment. Consider also how reluctant we are to start something new or begin again, perhaps reasoning that it's too late or that the years we have invested will be squandered. Then think about Renée Stewart Chittick, who did not, until age 45, begin, train for, or even really understand the business that just six years later would earn her a million dollars a year. Think about a woman who has the opportunity to spend her life with positive people and gets the opportunity to mentor others to success.

It is no wonder that she still does all that crying, all that praying, and all that running to the bank!

A Second Chance

"I'm just an average Joe, a regular guy from middle America," says thirty-five-year-old Eddie Stone, a triple diamond Rexall Showcase International distributor from Cary, North Carolina. But for a guy who likes to stress what he has in common with the average American, Eddie has had some pretty uncommon experiences and remarkable highs and lows.

Growing up in North Carolina, Eddie seemed destined to follow in his father's and grandfather's footsteps, working in the family-owned construction business. He gave it a shot after attending North Carolina University, but working in a family business was not always easy. "I realized there was only room for one chief in the teepee," Eddie says. He decided to break out on his own.

It was tough. "Being a professional builder and real estate developer can be a good business," Eddie explains. "But it's so unpredictable. It has so many ups and downs, and it's so sensitive to changing interest rates, the local economy, the national economy, and even the weather. You can make a lot of money, but you can also lose a lot of money."

And lose money he did. Financially, Eddie and his wife Maria headed into a downward spiral they couldn't stop. In 1991 the couple declared bankruptcy and lost everything—even their home.

It was a dark and depressing time, and the loudest of wake-up calls! Eddie realized he had to leave construction and look for an opportunity that required limited resources but that would help his climb out of the bankruptcy hole. "We bounced around for a while but then suddenly came upon the concept of network marketing and Rexall Showcase International. Unlike many others who were predisposed against it, I had no preconception one way or another. I guess in our financial condition, I couldn't afford to rule anything out," he remembers.

"I treated it like any other business opportunity—which is how I think everyone should approach it—evaluating the requirements for entry, the company behind it, the products, and the compensation plan. I was struck by the mainstream credibility of Rexall Showcase International, a company with a great name, a billion dollars' worth of market capitalization, a company with some of the most modern manufacturing facilities in the country, and the best research scientists on board.

"The bottom line is that for a very limited investment, even if you're an ordinary person like myself, you can suddenly put yourself in an environment where you are benefiting from all those assets as you build your own business."

Eddie put those assets and his own perseverance to good use. In seven years, the Stones have gone from bankruptcy to nearly a seven-figure income. Because of that bankruptcy, for much of that period they were unable to own a home. But now financially flush, they have built a beautiful new home near their old college town of Raleigh, North Carolina, where Eddie and Maria met and where Maria's parents live. "I had a lot to prove to my mom and to Maria's parents," Eddie reflects. "They and Maria really kept believing in me during the difficult years, and it's great to be able to move back to the Raleigh area with our two kids."

Although Eddie Stone appreciates the "rags-to-riches" quality of his experience with Rexall Showcase International and still openly marvels at how far he has come from the days of bankruptcy, he sees significance in the opportunity he found with Rexall Showcase International lying elsewhere. "There's a new trend in the kind of people who get involved with Rexall Showcase International, and I think I'm representative of that trend," he says. "More and more top-notch professionals—physicians, nurses, lawyers, and business executives are participating. Network marketing has a new found respectability.

"As a professional builder and real estate developer prior to joining Rexall Showcase International, I understood what it took to make money—and to lose it! I think I understood what organization structures had to be in place in a corporation that would give me the framework to succeed. What I needed was a second chance financially. Rexall Showcase International gave me the foundation for success, but I'm the one responsible for building on it."

Insane Money

Michael Kaplowitz worked for a company that he never wanted his three sons to work for, in a profession—sales—that he never wanted his sons to be in. Michael's dream for his boys was that they would become professionals.

The three brothers, David, Jan, and Jeff fulfilled their father's dream. They did well in school, excelled in college sports, and all three entered what was in the 1970s the very lucrative chiropractic field. "Jeff went out on his own, but Jan and I teamed up and opened a practice in Stamford, Connecticut, in 1977," David explains. "It was a great practice. We were making good money and, at one point, seeing 700 patients a week."

But as the 1980s progressed and the economics of health care shifted, things began to go south for the Kaplowitz brothers. "Cutbacks in insurance reimbursements and the rise of the HMOs completely changed the climate for us," David says. "My patient load fell from 700 to less than 350 in eighteen months."

It wasn't just the big changes in health care that caused the Kaplowitzes to reevaluate their position. The nature of their profession, which allowed very little time for freedom, began to wear on them.

"As a chiropractor, if you go on vacation or take time off, you lose patients. If these repeat patients stop coming in because you're away you stand to lose many of them. Therefore, you have to rebuild your practice base over and over again," David explains.

Things began slipping away. "As the practice continued to shrink, we started running through our life savings just to maintain our current lifestyle," David says. Soon he and his wife Jodi had to make a wrenching decision—with three children and the prospect of paying for expensive education looming before them, they sold their dream house and moved into a smaller house. "We were going down, not up, and I knew unless things changed it would get even worse. I remember telling Jodi that if we didn't do something we'd end up living out of a shoebox," David says.

It wasn't a question of work. "David and I are incredibly hard workers," his brother Jan says. "We like to work, and we'll do it from early in the morning until late at night. When the money was rolling in from our practice we didn't mind the hard work at all. But when the income slowed, we found ourselves working twice as hard for half as much. It was like beating your head against the wall. And all you can say for that is when you stop, it feels good!"

In 1996, David heard about Rexall Showcase International. He didn't waste any time checking it out. "I got on a plane in August 1996 and flew to San Diego, where the company was having its national conference. When I got there, I was fascinated to hear the stories of people who on a part-time basis made $3,000 a month. Rexall Showcase International is a great business for part-timers," David explains.

"Because my goals were large, I focused on the successful distributors like Randy Schroeder who were making an insane amount of money—and I said to myself, 'If I'm going to do this, I'm going to do it all the way. I'm after the insane money!'"

David signed up in San Diego and returning to Connecticut, convened a family meeting. He told his wife, Jodi, his brother, Jan, and his wife, Roni, that Rexall Showcase International was the opportunity that would turn things around for them if they "attacked it aggressively."

They did just that. Working out of a 12- by 12-foot office with three desks and a fax machine, the Kaplowitz brothers and their longtime loyal assistant, Ester Iannotta, soon ranked number one in the company for new business growth. Their first check was for $13,599—David, of course, remembers the precise amount. Today, between them, the Kaplowitzes move about three million dollars of Rexall Showcase International products through their small operation per year. And within nineteen months from the time they started, they sold their practice. Chiropractic was a thing of the past.

But David emphasizes that "this is not a get-rich-quick scheme. It's hard work. But the beauty is once you do it you can get paid over and over again because you've leveraged your time and effort." He recalls how he signed up his very first distributor back in 1996: "It was 11 o'clock at night and I was getting dressed to go meet my prospect, who was getting off work. Just as Jodi, my wife, was taking off her makeup and getting ready for bed, she asked me where I was going. When I told her out to meet a prospect, Jodi said, 'It's almost midnight! Are you crazy?'

"I told her it might seem that way but if she could give me carte blanche for twenty-four to thirty-six months, and understand that I needed to free up my time, I could create a lifestyle for us that would forever answer all our dreams and the needs of our family. And she said 'I believe in you—go for it!'"

David and Jan feel theirs is a message that will particularly resonate with other chiropractors and medical professionals. "Every chiropractor knows what I'm talking about when I say what a good feeling it is not to have to fight with insurance companies, worry about bad weather keeping patients away, or going on vacation and having to rebuild your practice when you come back," Jan explains.

They take pride in the fact that they have personally sponsored a great number of medical health professionals. "Knowing that chiropractors have had their challenges with the medical establishment, when I speak before a group of medical doctors who have joined the business, I often joke with them that ten years ago, I would be sitting in your place listening to you. Did you ever imagine you'd be sitting there listening to me?"

Although the line gets a laugh, everyone in Rexall Showcase International understands that "this business is a level playing field. Everyone has an equal chance. If you make it, you deserve it!"

Michael Kaplowitz, the father who didn't want his sons to be salesman but to seek a better life, is eighty-five years old now. I asked Jan what his dad thinks of the turn of events that has taken the family from the professional world to network marketing. "He's a very intelligent and well-read man, and while there was no knee-jerk reaction against what we were doing, he felt bad about what had happened to our practice. But Michael said 'Let me hear more about Rexall Showcase International,'" Jan reports. "And when we told him more, he said, 'I wish I was thirty years younger so I could join you.'"

A Better Vehicle

Thirty-four-year-old Doug Overold calls himself "a pretty average guy." Growing up in Fargo, North Dakota, he was but a "C" student in high school and went on to get an associate degree in marketing at a local technical college. Realizing his educational performance would open up few career paths, he inevitably gravitated to the family business.

"For forty years, my family operated a medium-sized Oldsmobile and Cadillac dealership," Doug explains. "I thought maybe if I worked long enough I could gain some equity to buy out my father's ownership and create the kind of lifestyle that we all hope for."

But it wasn't long before Doug got a quick education in retail business and found it left much to be desired. Bank loans, inventory, receivables, employees, attorneys, upset customers—they all governed Doug's daily life on the job, and he struggled to imagine himself doing it his whole life. "I guess my heart just wasn't in it," he concludes.

"On top of all that, Oldsmobile had lost 40 percent of its market in the previous six years. I therefore learned a vital lesson about how important timing is in any business."

One day, an entrepreneur walked into the business and made Doug's father a cash offer for the business. Since his son was in line to take it over, the elder Overold asked him what he should do. "I told my Dad to take the money and run. I didn't tell him at the time that I was actually quite relieved that I would be able to stop chasing the wrong dream," Doug confesses.

Soon after that, with his future up in the air, a friend convinced Doug to attend a meeting and hear about "an opportunity of a lifetime." It was business presentation for a network marketing company that sold water-filtration systems for the home. Making the presentation was "a twenty-six-year-old with no education who had a background as a maintenance manager at a potato chip factory. He was now making $10,000 a month, working out of his house, and had the lifestyle I always dreamed of."

That young man's name was John Haremza—and if Doug Overold had known at the time what he knows now about John's arduous climb up the ladder of success, he would have been even more impressed and more motivated than he was leaving that first meeting.

John, who is now thirty-four, grew up in the small town of Perham, Minnesota, about 60 miles east of Fargo. His father was a janitor at the high school; his mother worked in a dog food factory. While it was not diagnosed until adulthood, John suffered from a learning disability, a severe form of dyslexia that to this day has prevented him from learning to read or write with any facility. "I've still never read a book in my life," he says.

In school, neither teachers nor his fellow students understood the problem. They made fun of John, calling him stupid and slow.

The most humiliating moments came when he was called upon to read aloud. He couldn't do it. Before long he was placed in special classes, with teachers confining their efforts to teaching him the most rudimentary of skills such as balancing a checkbook.

"I went through school trying to be invisible. I had no self-esteem," he continues. "When I graduated and landed a job at the potato chip factory, I was ecstatic. With a $24,000 annual salary, I thought I had the world in my hands!"

In 1989, John attended his first network marketing meeting. He was impressed and thought he could make some extra money. "But I didn't really understand the concept of networking at all. I treated it like a door-to-door sales job, banging on people's doors trying to sell them water filters." But he listened and learned and most importantly, watched who else was making it in network marketing. "At one meeting I saw a guy walk across the stage in overalls and boots, looking like he had just come out of the barn. He proceeded to tell the audience how he was making $10,000 a month in network marketing. I thought if he could do it, I could do it."

John bought his first suit and started to make some serious money. Later, when he decided to leave his job at the potato chip factory, his co-workers teased him unmercifully. "Look, the worst thing that can happen to me is that I have to come back and get a job like you have," John coolly replied. Today he wants to thank his cynical co-workers for piling on the abuse. "When you run into naysayers, you can have two reactions," John says. "You can curl up into the fetal position and not do anything—or you can go all out to prove yourself just to spite them. That's what I did!"

By the time Doug Overold attended his first business opportunity meeting run by John Haremza, John had become a leading distributor in the water-filter company. Inspired by John's example, Doug signed up on the spot. "The thought of signing up a few customers and sponsoring a few distributors—then receiving lifelong residual income was very attractive.

"I poured my heart and soul into that company for two solid years. I built a good organization of several hundred distributors and started to see some financial success. I was hooked on the independence of being my own boss." The venture soon became a family affair as Doug's father, Cliff, joined the business as well.

But while John Haremza and the Overolds were sold on networking marketing, they had doubts about the long-term prospects of their company. "There are five key elements to a successful and long-term opportunity," John believes. "Company, products, compensation, timing and training, and support. We were weak in several of those areas and I could sense that my organization was unraveling. I had found the dream, but I had the wrong vehicle."

Undertaking a search for the right vehicle, Doug answered an ad Todd Smith had placed in *USA Today*. Together with his father and John, they met Todd and carefully evaluated the company according to the five criteria they had devised. "We looked long and hard at Rexall Showcase International's new network marketing division and found that not only were all the elements in place but they were compelling—a company that carried a reputable name with the capital, the management, and the integrity to stand the test of time. A product line that was unique, consumable, affordable, backed by clear medical research, and actually did what it claimed to do.

"The compensation plan had provisions for the part-time distributor to make money and yet looked compelling and obtainable for the person who wanted to go for it full-time. The timing was great because Rexall Showcase International was just starting to take off and so was preventative health. And finally, the upline support and training were world-class. They have created a culture of teamwork, integrity, and professionalism."

In October 1992, John and the Overolds made the jump to Rexall Showcase International. In John's first year, he made $76,000—three times what he made as the maintenance manager at the potato chip plant. In 1998, he wound up his sixth year in the business with an income of just under $400,000. "I calculated that it would have taken sixty-six years at the potato chip factory to make the same money I've made in the last six years in Rexall Showcase International," John explains. Thinking back to the $174-a-month trailer he used to call home (with the thick frost forming on the inside walls during the frigid Minnesota winters), John, wife Jana, and their two young daughters today divide their time between two homes, one in Fargo and one on the shores of Minnesota's upscale Pelican Lake.

"In just sixteen months from my entry into this business, my life was completely transformed," John concludes. "I became one of the top income earners in our company and began speaking before thousands of people. My self-esteem soared. Although the money has been great, what I have become as a person and the personal growth I have experienced have been worth much, much more."

His friend Doug Overold echoes these sentiments. "Everything I had imagined happening in my life and a lot more has been made possible by this opportunity—and all by the age of thirty-four," he says.

"My group has exploded around the world with thousands and thousands of distributors that span the United States, Mexico, and Hong Kong—with more soon to follow in Taiwan, Japan, and Canada. I have earned over one million dollars and have a monthly residual income in the mid-five-figure range. More importantly, I have been able to help several people in my organization to reach six-figure incomes, many more to achieve their goals and their dreams, and thousands of people to benefit from improved health by using the products."

And the time freedom Doug has earned has helped him become a better father and husband. "I get to spend a lot of quality time with my wife, Sue, and our son, Logan. I got my pilot's license and bought my own plane. We have traveled all over the United States and made three trips to Asia," Doug says.

"But the most important gift I have received from this business is what I have become as a person. Eight years ago I was immature, lacked self-confidence, and had no direction in my life. The satisfaction and recognition you receive from building an organization in this business is priceless. This business can truly change your life in the most positive way imaginable."

Ready, Fire, Aim!

Sometimes when you see your second shot at success, you go for it too soon. Instead of "ready, aim, fire," you "ready, fire, aim"!

That's what happened to thirty-eight-year-old Mickey Dillon, today considered one of Rexall Showcase International's energetic, up-and-coming leaders.

"I quit my job too soon," Mickey explains. But that big step was triggered by a strong desire to escape the corporate world. During his career in pharmaceutical sales and management, Mickey found he was continually being shifted from assignment to assignment and from territory to territory. When his company wanted to move this Huntsville, Alabama, native to the Northeast, Mickey balked.

"Thirteen months earlier, Eddie Stone called me about a great opportunity with Rexall Showcase International," he recalls. "Since I've always had what you'd consider an entrepreneur streak in me, I signed on, part-time at first, putting in my fifteen hours a week just like they said."

But with another company transfer looming ahead, Mickey quit his job and started to work the business full-time—even though he had yet to build his business to the level necessary to replace his income.

"The problem was my income changed but my lifestyle didn't," Mickey says. "Soon I started running through my savings, my 401K, everything. I found myself flying in all directions, working out of desperation."

Todd Smith helped him come to his senses. "He told me to go look at myself in the mirror—and to start looking and acting like the successful person I wanted to be. From then on, when I engaged in a particular activity to build my business I applied a simple test: Is this something a successful person like Todd Smith would spend his time on or was it a waste of time?"

With his efforts refocused and his professionalism improved, Mickey soon began seeing results. He has been in the Rexall Showcase International business nearly seven years, is earning far more than he was in his corporate career, and "is living the perfect network marketing lifestyle."

"I travel, I make great friendships all over the country, and I'm living where I want—in Nashville. It's just a blast!" Mickey says.

"The most important bottom line for me is the personal growth I have experienced in this business. I just didn't get that in the corporate world. There it seemed like my goal was to just get through the day.

"In network marketing you're forced to grow."

The opportunity to start over, to try something different, to fail and get another chance, to close one chapter in life and create a completely new one—this idea has always had a powerful grasp on the American psyche. And it is part of our culture that has sparked the imagination of other cultures from Europe to Asia. A network marketing company like Rexall Showcase International offers a welcoming avenue for those new beginnings so many dream of or feel compelled to seek. Success is not promised or guaranteed—but the chance to take the first step is open to all.

CHAPTER 11

Life in
the Balance

W hat does it mean to be bankrupt? It depends on your definition.

Is it possible to make a good, mid-six-figure income, pay all your bills on time, be sought after for your consulting services by the biggest companies in America—and still be in a state of bankruptcy? Tom Bissmeyer knows from personal experience that it is.

"I was taught the old school method of success," he explains. "Get a good education, work hard, and keep your record clean and everything will work out fine. So that's what I set out to do."

After getting both bachelor's and master's degrees in business and finance, Tom went to work for an international accounting and consulting firm. "This was my first exposure to the fact that hard work wasn't the only thing that would get you promoted. It also depended on who you knew." After being recruited away to be part of a capital acquisition team for a large real estate development company, Tom seemed poised for success. It was the mid-1980s, the economy was booming, and Tom and his team raised over $100 million in financing in one year. The reward for their efforts, however, was a very small bonus.

"This taught me another valuable lesson about the business world," he explains. "If you truly want to be paid what you're worth, then you had better be the one writing the check!"

With such lessons learned, Tom decided to go into business for himself and, through strong effort and some lucky breaks, built a successful speaking, training, and consulting business. He advised some of the top companies in America and became a sought-after lecturer on financial planning.

There was just one problem. "I soon found myself working seven days a week," Tom explains. "Often I would do corporate consulting during the week and contract speaking on the weekends. This went on for several years. I found myself traveling in excess of 250 days a year."

From a financial perspective, Tom could not complain. His earnings were well into the six-figure range. "But from a family and life perspective, I was bankrupt," he admits. "Even though I was providing for my family economically, I sure wasn't being the kind of husband and father I wanted to be to my family."

A collision was coming. Tom remembers hearing his daughter's first words over the telephone and learning about her first steps during a call from his wife, Lynne. When the couple's second child was born in 1992, Tom was determined to take part. He took three weeks off. "My family needed me and I wanted to be there, but I lost over $40,000 in income because I wasn't working."

He felt trapped. "I realized I had built a monster that was eating me alive. I didn't have any idea how to achieve a balance between work and the other parts of my life. If I slowed down even for just a second, income slowed right down behind me," Tom said.

At least becoming a consultant was a choice Tom made himself. In today's economy, many companies are making that choice for you. As discussed in Chapter Five, the new corporate ethic is to shed as much long-term cost and obligation as possible to meet both the test of global competition and the test of Wall Street, which habitually celebrates company downsizing and layoffs with a rise in the stock price. Outsourcing and turning employees into consultants is, from the company's point of view, an effective way to get services without all of the overhead and obligations that a regular full-time employee can bring.

Some professionals greet this development favorably. More flexibility, a greater feeling of independence, the ability to take on more than one project and diversify work and income can indeed be some of the benefits. But Tom Bissmeyer has a warning for all those who choose or are forced to enter the consulting world:

"I realized that there is something out there that is worse than a boss; it's called clients. They drove my schedule and my travel. They didn't care if it was my children's birthday, my anniversary, or something else important in our lives. They basically said if you want to continue to be our consultant, you must be available when we need you and where we need you. If not, we can easily find someone else."

By 1992, Tom had had enough. "I always considered myself a student of success. I became convinced there was a perfect business out there that would allow me to continue to work for myself, generate above-average income, control my own travel schedule, and build a leveraged income. I was determined to find it!" he explains.

But you don't find mid-six figure incomes like the one the Bissmeyers enjoyed just like that. Through a process of analysis and elimination, Tom began to sort out the possibilities. "I looked at other types of consulting that wouldn't require as much travel, but I would still have had all the client issues to deal with. I looked at franchising, but I just couldn't get excited about putting half a million dollars on the line and managing a bunch of teenagers for a living."

As he winnowed out less attractive options, Tom took his first serious look at network marketing. He had been exposed to the business before, but like many upscale professionals, accumulated a good deal of mental baggage about it. Nonetheless, he decided to keep an open mind and for the first time really study the industry and its track record.

"The more I began to read and learn about the industry, the more excited I became," Tom reports. "I really began to dig. I looked at several companies and studied the compensation plans closely.

"Network marketing seemed to offer everything I was looking for: something I could begin part-time and then move into full-time; a leveraged income as opposed to one dependent solely on my own efforts; an unlimited income potential if I were willing to work really hard at it; and a flexible schedule that would allow me to spend time with my family and keep those parts of my current career I really enjoyed, such as public speaking.

"I could choose whom I would work with. The capital needed to enter the business was extremely low. I could not only work out of my home, but because this kind of business is a portable business, Lynne and I could also choose where we wanted that home to be!"

Many of us have been in the position of trying to convince ourselves to make an important decision about our lives and careers where the evidence and logic are so compelling that the necessity to act just screams out at us. But still we hesitate and resist and often fail to take that first step. Tom felt those same pressures and anxieties. The analysis he had created was so overwhelming, but he still worried, "What are my friends going to think? What are my colleagues going to say? What if I fail?"

His resolve to act was made all the more difficult by the fact that this was a person on whom society had already hung a great big "success" sign—a mid-six figure income, prestigious clients, notoriety as a sought-after speaker, a loving wife and two children, one girl and one boy. Perfect.

But Tom overcame his doubts and complacency and he stopped living by others' definition of success. He entered network marketing in the spring of 1993. "I believe one of the biggest keys to early success in network marketing for successful professionals is to develop a strong WHY. My WHY was so big that I was able to look right past the naysayers."

Once he crossed that bridge into the industry, it was easy for Tom to settle on Rexall Showcase International as the destination. "I wanted a company that was servicing a growing segment of the population, the aging baby boomers," he reasoned. "I wanted to have a name behind me that people would recognize and trust, Rexall Showcase International. I wanted a company that was publicly traded so I could verify the financial situation. And I wanted an upline that could teach me the industry and was willing to put the time in to train me and help me succeed."

Success came to Tom Bissmeyer—again. But he wouldn't want anyone to think it was easy. "It took a lot of hard work to get it going and I had plenty of setbacks along the way. There were many times I felt like quitting during the first couple of years. By having a strong WHY, I was able to stay focused during the tough times."

Tom's toughest decision after starting the business was to go full-time after nine months, even though he had yet to rise to the level of his consulting and speaking income. "I just took a leap of faith," he says.

It paid off. Today Tom is one of the most successful Rexall Showcase International distributors, earning an income approaching seven figures. "And I fully anticipate it will double within the next couple of years."

But more important is the balance Tom has restored to his life. "I have complete control of my schedule now," he explains. "I take my children's school calendar and plan my business activities around that—what a reversal!"

Recently the Bissmeyers fulfilled another dream by relocating to the foothills of the Rocky Mountains. "One of the greatest joys of this business is that I can work out of my home," Tom says. One of those seemingly very ordinary but special moments occurred recently that keeps coming back to Tom as a reminder of how his life has changed for the better: "I was in my home office doing a three-way phone call with a distributor. The entire family was in the office with me. My wife was on the computer e-mailing some friends. My daughter was at my desk doing her homework. My son was drawing a picture. Our dog was lying in front of the fireplace.

"I thought I had to sacrifice those important family moments in order to be successful and provide for my family. I was wrong. Boy, was I wrong!"

Tom Bissmeyer knows that the trap he was in has snared many other successful professionals. "I am amazed by the number of well-educated, well-paid professionals who tell me that they are unhappy with their careers and their lives," he says. "When they tell me their goals, they are remarkably similar to the ones I had been chasing but found elusive.

"I can sincerely relate to their frustrations because I had them too. I really believe I have found a better way to live and work and that's why one of my missions is to tell the professional world that there is a better way."

A Balanced Life

Tom Bissmeyer articulates well a growing disquiet in the still male-dominated professional world—a tough world where deals are struck, fortunes are made, power is accumulated—and where it can all disappear overnight! These men worry about missing their children's growing up and are earnestly seeking a better way. But many are at least comforted by the knowledge that at home, a nurturing mother will do her best to make up for their absence.

But what about the single mothers who must do it all—earn the money, run the household, and minister to their children's everyday problems and crises?

Janie Fischer, a forty-year-old single mother of two, fully understood how important her Rexall Showcase International business was to her during the two weeks last year when she had to push it aside. Janie's thirteen-year-old son fractured his skull in a swimming pool accident: "For two weeks, I didn't work, I didn't make any calls, I didn't do anything except stay by his side," Janie recalls. "And you know what? My Rexall Showcase International income actually went up 10 percent that month!"

Janie credits her strong organization for the fact that she could be AWOL from her business and still generate a significant flow of income. "I introduced the Rexall Showcase International business to seventy people, and eighteen have chosen to work with me. From these eighteen people, we have developed an organization of thousands of distributors in all fifty states and several countries."

But for Janie it all comes back to family. "As a single mother, parenting has to be the principal focus of my life," she explains. Reared in Oceanside, New York, Janie relocated to Florida when she was twenty to study counseling at the University of South Florida. After five years as a practicing counselor, she left the practice because of her desire to be with her family. Her focus on parenting her son and daughter has always been her priority.

Yet, even if she had been financially able to be a full-time, stay-at-home mom, that would not have been enough for Janie Fischer. Like most professional women, she did not want to have to make a choice between being professionally fulfilled and a good parent. Wasn't there an approach, she wondered, that would permit her to excel simultaneously on both fronts?

Six years ago when she first heard about Rexall Showcase International, she thought that maybe this was a company that offered both a lucrative career and the time flexibility to raise two children. But first, there was a big barrier of suspicion to overcome.

"Network marketing was brand-new to me, and I was highly skeptical," Janie recalls. "If it were not for the Rexall name, which I remembered fondly from my childhood, I would not have taken a second look." She put both the company and the products through sharp analysis. "I gave the products to a doctor to run a complete check. Then I got on a plane and flew down to visit the company headquarters."

What Janie saw and learned impressed her sufficiently to give the business a try. In August 1992 she began to work the business just five hours a week. There just wasn't the time to do anything more.

But Janie learned that the power behind the Rexall Showcase International business model was that it could be harnessed very effectively even with a part-time commitment. "There's a simple two-step process to this business that works wonderfully for extremely busy people," she explains. "You hand out the tapes, which explain the business, and you follow up to determine interest. You don't have to do house parties or attend a bunch of rallies. You don't have to sneak around and not tell people what kind of business you're in. The successful people in Rexall Showcase International are direct, factual, and professional. I never twist people's arms."

Within three months, Janie scaled back her other endeavors and stepped up her involvement in Rexall Showcase International to twenty-five hours a week. And that's where she has stayed—twenty-five hours a week—a part-time business so she can be a full-time mother. Even so, Janie has succeeded in rising to the highest level, triple diamond, and has been named to the company's prestigious ten-member Presidential Board of Advisors.

Most remarkable in Janie's eyes was finding out that "with just a few hours of effort a week, I could earn more in one month working Rexall Showcase International part-time than working in my former career full-time, all year!"

Moreover, she's finding that the values that led her to her initial career as a counselor are better fulfilled in her new business life. "I went into counseling because of a desire to help people, and it was particularly meaningful to me to counsel the children of divorced parents," she reflects. "But I've found I am helping more people in Rexall Showcase International than I ever could in counseling. These are not only life-changing products. This is a life-changing business."

It has certainly changed Janie Fischer's life. "The greatest thing I've been able to achieve is to create a healthy balance in my life—a life where I'm really in control." She's proud of the fact that she's able to drop her children off at school and pick them up everyday. "And I never work between the hours of three and seven. That time is reserved for activities with my children."

Today her six-figure income and multimillion-dollar sales volume are generated with a business infrastructure that consists of little more than a home office phone line and a fax machine.

As a single, working mother, Janie has reflected a great deal on the significance of this kind of business for women. "There is no glass ceiling here," she insists, and finds it particularly rewarding when she brings harried professional women into Rexall Showcase International. "Before Rexall Showcase International, they were driving their kids to day care, working forty hours or more a week, picking up their kids from day care, cooking dinner, cleaning the house—and collapsing!

"It's very rewarding to help someone in that kind of position take control of her life."

Back to Ohio

It was a phone call from Janie Fischer six years ago that convinced Joy and Sam Hillman, who were then living in Clearwater, to become Rexall Showcase International distributors. "When Janie called and invited us to look at a business she had just joined, we weren't looking for a new opportunity because our lives were already so full," Joy relates. "But it was our respect for Janie that convinced us to look anyway."

Both the products and the business immediately intrigued Joy. "I had two babies and a small retail store to run," she explains.

"Sam was busy with his law practice. I thought there had to be a way out of this rat race." Joy was further motivated by the fact that her shop, which sold gift baskets, was an uneven business, ringing up most of its sales around the holidays. With a background in accounting and knowledge of business, Joy thought there had to be a better way.

Sam was less convinced. There might be something to this Rexall Showcase International idea, he thought. But how would they ever find the time to add anything new to their already incredibly busy lives?

Sam's misgivings aside, the couple gave it a try, devoting at first about six hours a week to Rexall Showcase International while continuing their full-time occupations and raising two boys who were at the time two years old and three months.

They were soon spurred on by an important personal experience with the Rexall Showcase International products. "Sam comes from a family with a high risk of heart disease," Joy reports. "His brother had triple bypass surgery at age 40 and his father died at 53 from heart disease.

"Sam's own cholesterol was at 224, and his triglycerides stood at 406. Sixty days after starting on Bios Life, his cholesterol dropped 49 points and the triglycerides dropped 200 points."

Joy had her own health problem—severe allergies. "I used Defend-OL, which soon allowed me to stop taking three allergy prescription medicines as well as an asthma inhaler.

"With our belief in the products growing, we did everything we could to find a few extra hours per week to build our business."

The Hillmans' business results soon became as impressive as their health results. "Six months after joining Rexall Showcase International, I closed my shop," says Joy. "Sam and I spent the next three years devoting twelve to fifteen hours a week to the business. On the strength of that effort alone, we replaced Sam's income as a lawyer even though he had been practicing for twenty years."

Two years ago, Sam closed his law practice so he could work by Joy's side building their Rexall Showcase International business and caring for their sons. Since that time, the Hillmans' income has doubled. In 1996 the family made a journey many more Americans in recent decades have been making the other way around. The Hillmans moved from Florida back to the Cleveland, Ohio, area where Joy grew up. "It's where we want to raise our kids," Joy says with a laugh.

Most important to Joy is how the business has strengthened their family and set them free from the professional trap so many others are locked into. "Many people would like to start a business with their spouses but cannot afford to because that would usually require their giving up their household income," Joy explains.

"Sam and I are now building a business together, raising our children together, and have an incredible amount of flexibility in our lives—which is a dream many couples have but think they cannot accomplish."

And they have found an extended family in Rexall Showcase International. "We have built friendships with people throughout Rexall Showcase International that will last a lifetime," Joy believes. "We have shared good times as well as helped these friends weather personal tragedies, experiences that have added invaluable meaning to our lives."

Three Great Things

Julie Berry of Yankeetown, Florida, likes to recount the "three great things" her Rexall Showcase International business has brought to her life.

We were introduced to one of them in Chapter Nine—her husband and fellow Rexall Showcase International distributor, John Berta. They met through their mutual involvement in Rexall

Showcase International and four years ago, John concluded a business presentation to thousands by extending a very public marriage proposal to Julie right from the stage.

John and Julie both enjoy telling that story, but what we don't hear from him and had to learn from Julie is that he wouldn't let her near a microphone to reply. "I guess he wasn't sure what my answer would be," she says.

But unlike John Berta, who joined Rexall Showcase International on the basis of a cool-headed business decision, Julie was first motivated by serious health problems.

"I was a severe asthmatic," she explains, having moved from her native Maine to Florida to find some relief in the climate. Even so she was used to being rushed to the hospital after unusually desperate attacks and had to take ever-increasing levels of medications, including steroids, which brought with them many toxic side effects.

"It seemed like my whole life was built around my sprayer, my steroids, and adrenaline shots for the really rough attacks." Then a single mother with two teenaged children, her physical health was thus further challenged by the mental anguish of worrying about their welfare.

One day, while she was working at her $40,000 a year job as an administrator at an OB-GYN clinic, a physician encouraged her to take a look at Rexall Showcase International. Julie was consumed by doubts. "I resisted it for almost four months. I felt very dependent on my medicines, and I knew nothing about business. I didn't know that many people, and I just didn't think I'd be good at selling."

In October 1992, she attended a meeting on the Rexall Showcase International products and business that changed her mind. "I came to realize that it was more about communicating some exciting information about a subject everyone cares about—their health—than it was about selling."

Within a year, the other two "great" things Julie credits the business with started to happen. Thanks to products like Defend-

OL, her health began to improve dramatically. She no longer had to take steroids and gradually withdrew from other medications as well. "The Rexall Showcase International products helped my body heal itself," she says. "For someone who has constantly been sick ever since I can remember, you can't imagine what a great feeling and change that was."

As Julie's physical health strengthened, so did her financial health.

She replaced her salaried income in just one year and left her job to work at her Rexall Showcase International distributorship full-time. Today the woman who was sure she didn't know anything about business, didn't know enough people, and couldn't sell anything earns over $300,000 a year!

Better health, solid finances, and true love—you can't ask much more from any endeavor. Yet for Julie Berry there is something more. With her business and income continuing to grow, mentoring others has become her top priority. "I'm mostly in the support mode now," she explains. "I promised a number of people I brought into this business that I would personally help them reach a certain level so that they could achieve their dreams. I'm going to keep those promises." She is particularly proud of recently helping an optometrist reach the level where he could sell his two practices and thus enjoy the time, freedom, and income security offered by Rexall Showcase International.

"And I have made a point to talk to a lot of working women and single mothers who may wonder if they can really make it here. I tell them, 'Look at me!'"

Today Julie Berry and John Berta live in a small settlement of 750 houses, a couple of hours up the Florida coast from the Tampa Bay area. Down the street live Julie's eighty-year-old parents whom she was able to relocate from Maine thanks to her thriving business.

"Last year marked their sixtieth wedding anniversary," Julie relates. "To celebrate I booked four generations of our family on a

Caribbean cruise—and my parents renewed their vows in a new wedding ceremony. None of this would ever have been possible without this business."

The Network Marketing Lifestyle— Is It Right for You?

Janie Fischer and Julie Berry—single mothers starting with zero knowledge about business or network marketing, then working their way to the highest levels of a relatively new business, collecting healthy six-figure incomes, living where they want, and spending all the time they need with their families. Yes, it's for real!

But we all recognize that lightning does strike. The real question is, Can this success be reasonably duplicated? Is it within the realm of possibility for you? Is it too late to get in? Is the market saturated? What's the best formula for success? These are questions that face all network marketing companies and their current and prospective distributors. A company like Rexall Showcase International, which can argue that it is a solid company bringing desirable products to a growing market, must face the bottom-line issue: Is there a reasonably good chance of success for the typical distributor?

Network marketing's standard way of addressing that issue is to lay most of the burden of success or failure on the distributor: "You 'hire yourself' in our business," they say. "You 'fire yourself' by walking away. Anyone can succeed if they follow the plan," many companies insist. "If you are one of those who doesn't succeed, there's no one to blame but yourself!"

There is an element of truth in those concepts. We have seen from our discussion in Chapter Three that income levels industry-wide in direct selling are highly influenced by the level of time and effort put into the business, and even more importantly, how you define your goals. Those making it their principal and full-time

214

endeavor, a notable portion—approximately 10 percent—earn more than $100,000 a year. That may not sound high on a percentage basis, but it is significant when you consider that the average household income in the United States is approximately $35,000 and that the capital and educational requirements for entering direct selling are virtually nil.

Yet statistics can be totally accurate but still not describe the real world. Can success stories like Janie Fischer's, Julie Berry's, or the many others recounted in this book be readily duplicated, or are they really the exceptions to the rule?

And here's another important issue to consider: As idealistic as the lives of successful network marketers like Tom and Lynne Bissmeyer and Sam and Joy Hillman seem to be, will every professional react as positively to the independent, home-based business environment as they have? Entrants should consider that they might find the culture of work fostered in both network marketing and home-based businesses a radical departure from the pattern of their current lives. Some may not even like it.

Before considering the issue of duplication and how Rexall Showcase International addresses it, let's consider the possibility that some may actually find the lifestyle of prosperous network marketers one they don't really want.

Let me explain by drawing an example from the transportation world.

For years an effort has been underway in major metropolitan areas to convince more Americans to scrap their one-person-per-car commutes in favor of carpools or mass transit. Some anecdotal evidence uncovered as to why this "sell" is so difficult may surprise you: Many commuters actually like the time they have to themselves in the isolated confines of their vehicle! For many it is the only time of the day when they can be alone, be somewhat anonymous, listen to music, or daydream without interruption. Others use the time to listen to books on tape, hear self-improvement messages, or even learn foreign languages.

Few want to admit that they enjoy escaping their hectic household or harried workplace. Fewer still would say doing so is actually worth the price of sitting in traffic! But those tempted by the undeniable lure of working out of their home should consider the other side to the benefits of "commuting down the hall."

I have worked for considerable periods out of my home and find a lot of distractions alongside the enviable convenience. By interchanging periods of work with periods of domestic duties, chores, errands, and the like, I find that the day's work never seems to be finished. Technology that allows you to stay in touch with customers, bosses, and partners is invaluable, but if you're like me you find yourself checking and responding to e-mail messages at all hours of the day (or night) seven days a week.

Those accustomed to compartmentalizing their lives, drawing sharp lines between work life, home life, and leisure time may find these distinctions uncomfortably blurred when working out of the home in network marketing or any other business. Some people may find life more orderly and balanced by keeping the home sacrosanct, physically leaving their place of residence in the morning, working hard and working well for the day, and then leaving it all behind when quitting time comes.

While I don't doubt the network marketers in Rexall Showcase International and other companies who have talked about the relatively few hours they put in to make sizable leveraged incomes, I have not yet met a successful leader in the industry who isn't on the phone at all hours of the day or evening. There are conferences to attend on weekends and meetings to conduct in the evening when most Americans are curled up on a comfortable sofa reading or watching television with their loved ones. The leaders in these businesses appear every bit as consumed with what they are doing as executives running large companies. They just seem to be having more fun doing it! Indeed maybe that's why a lot of it doesn't really seem like work to them.

216

The lifestyle put within your reach by associating with a company like Rexall Showcase International has undeniable appeal. But only you can assess whether it offers the right life for you. You should go into it with open eyes.

The successful network marketing companies of the future will not be those who rely on simplistic jingles to spur involvement or content themselves with laying the blame on the distributor for quitting or failing to make it big. The winners will be those who provide an effective system for the new distributor to follow, are up-front about the level of commitment required to reach the top levels of the business, and offer an option for those who want to work in the business without making it the centerpiece of their lives or even their careers.

By devising an opportunity and support system for the part-time distributor, Rexall Showcase International has embraced a strategy that will minimize turnover and serve as a "feeder system" for the development of its future business leaders. Distributors who simply want to diversify their income stream and improve their health and finances—without altering their entire lives—are welcome alongside those with grander dreams.

"When the Student Is Ready, the Teacher Appears"

Successful companies in and out of network marketing are coming to realize that the presence in their organizations of teachers, mentors, and trainers will be every bit as important to long-term success as the researchers who develop the products and the executives who devise business strategies and deploy company assets. We live in a knowledge-based society, but a society whose economy and professions are changing so fast that a classroom-based education system—from preschools to universities—that is essentially isolated from the workplace can't possibly keep up with those changes. So our companies and workplaces must become our classrooms, and our learning must be a lifelong experience. The workers of the future will increasingly rely on the workplace for education and find among superiors and peers some of the best teachers they will ever have.

This is particularly true in network marketing companies. You can go to school to learn about business. You can even find university courses in network marketing. But can there be any question that the best place to learn is from the inside looking out, not the other way around? Especially when the price of admission is so low?

The long-term success of companies like Rexall Showcase International depends on their ability to develop an adequate training and support system that allows the business opportunity to be workably duplicated for a wide range of people: from busy professionals to homemakers, from surgeons to retirees, from those who want an additional source of income to those virtually without income who need a new career and perhaps even a new life.

And there's another important reason why a Rexall Showcase International-style company should elevate the mentoring process to the highest level of concern—to provide the most successful leaders with a higher calling than simply adding to their own organizations and wealth.

Speaking for myself, one of the most rewarding aspects of my own career as a writer and a communications executive has been the opportunity to mentor those coming up the ranks behind me. It's the psychic reward that comes with coaching others, helping them learn from your own triumphs and disasters, and watching them grow and succeed. Likewise, I have met many successful network leaders in Rexall Showcase International and other companies who have scaled all the heights of income and personal recognition—and now consider their more valued compensation to be the chance to help others succeed and achieve their dreams. We saw that in the case of a woman like Julie Berry and, earlier, with Bob Crosetto—whose parents were teachers and who wanted to be one himself, but who ended up selling insurance. Just like the doctors who found in this business a second chance to fulfill the mission that originally led them to medicine—that is, to be caregivers— many others like Bob have found a new opportunity to be teachers and mentors, finding new rewards that extend beyond money. That's why he and other top Rexall Showcase International distributors stand at the ready to help others move up the ladder, assuring them that "when the student is ready, the teacher appears."

Rexall Showcase International's Team-Building Approach

But configuring an effective duplication system in network marketing is easier said than done. Rexall Showcase International leaders believe they have found the way to do it.

John Hargett, whom we met earlier in Chapter Five, has thought long and hard about the ingredients and strategies that make a network marketing business an achievable and realistic dream for average people. His enthusiasm for the Rexall Showcase International products is unmatched, but several years ago, as he was feeling his own way in the business, he and a partner learned that excellent products weren't enough.

"Back in 1994, I fell in love with these products," John remembers, "and I went to Portland from Seattle to launch the business for the first time there. A friend I was working with agreed that the products were so strong we didn't really want to talk about network marketing—we took the approach of just trying to sell the products.

"We put an ad costing $1,200 in the paper announcing a meeting, called everyone we knew, and rented a big room at the hotel. The big night arrived and we waited for the folks to stream in."

Eighteen people showed up. To add insult to injury, John remembers that another network marketing company selling long-distance phone service had a meeting on the same night, in the same hotel, just across the hall. "Their room was jam-packed and soon they were stealing extra chairs from my room!" he painfully recalls.

John professes to be flabbergasted that "people would jam a room to save $5 on their phone bill," but wouldn't even show up to learn about products that would improve their health and lifestyle.

"Then it dawned on me. Network marketing is about opportunity—dream building—not about products," he says.

Others were learning similar lessons and they prompted Rexall Showcase International to develop an easily duplicated system. The company and its leaders looked carefully at the entire network marketing industry, drawing the best lessons for others' success and failures.

"That industry has changed dramatically since the 1960s," John explains. "The fact is that most companies that go into network marketing don't make it. What we did was develop an audiotape system that makes the business easy to do. You let the tapes sell it. I've found that when you send them out, about one out of three will want to learn more, and you follow up.

"The other thing Rexall Showcase International did was after much study develop a compensation plan that doesn't require you to bring in huge numbers of people. And it is designed to support teamwork. I can earn as much by helping people as by finding people."

Todd Smith echoes this point: "You don't find the fiefdoms developing here that you see in other companies. The culture is different. When you go to our conferences, you'll see people in my downline socializing with people from other organizations. And you won't find separate meetings going on in different parts of the hotel with different systems and different materials," he explains.

What happens is that each new distributor works from the same playbook—which the company calls its Team Building system:

- The budding entrepreneur is prompted to methodically define monetary and nonmonetary objectives and then list prospects for both product sales and sponsorships.
- Sales pitches are reviewed. Tips for handling rejection are offered.
- Distributors are then advised to make their approaches in a step-by-step manner that begins with sending out company-approved audiotapes featuring Rexall Showcase International distributor leaders as well as doctor and patient testimonials. Many distributors say these tapes not only prove to be compelling for many prospects, but also act as a sorting-out process. Precious time is therefore not wasted on those who simply aren't interested.
- Follow-up calls are next to determine interest. These calls often include an upline distributor on the phone to help get the prospect off the dime.
- Distributors are also encouraged to conduct small meetings of prospects and distributors or bring them to scheduled events around the country to reinforce the Team Building exercises and help their downlines build strong organizations. Yet, unlike the strong emphasis placed on meetings and rallies in other network marketing companies, Rexall Showcase International believes distributors should first go through the sorting-out process and make full use of technologies such as three-way calling (conference calls) and its Virtual Voice messaging system through which organization leaders distribute tips, messages, and news.

And as James Oznick reminded us, using his own "false start" in the Rexall Showcase International business as a vivid example, tremendous attention has to be paid to new distributors after they sign up. Don't just paste another star on your wall and move on!

Century Club members Rick and Camille Peterson offer a few tips on what Renée Stewart Chittick calls the "nurturing" process in Rexall Showcase International:

- **Get new distributors started right.** Make sure they come into the business the right way for the right reasons. Help them match their activities with their goals and expectations.
- **Explain the business.** Make sure they understand the ProfitPlus program, Rexall Showcase International's multi-faceted compensation system, so they can chart a systematic plan for making the kind of money that's consistent with their goals and time commitment.
- **Take it easy!** New distributors have to become familiar with preventative health care, a whole new product vocabulary, a prospecting process, a presentation process, and a follow-up process. Feeling they have to know everything right away is overwhelming, so help them take it in stages.
- **Explain the support structure.** Make sure they're familiar with the audiocassettes, three-way calling process, business meetings, Virtual Voice, and other technical supports. Then make sure they know how to use people support, especially their upline's expertise and enhanced credibility.
- **Build the belief.** Help them have confidence in the company, products, and opportunity by showing them how you are successful. Applaud success and coach through problems.
- **Work side by side.** Spend the first couple of months working side by side to ensure they're comfortable with the simplicity of the system and are using it correctly.

It should go without saying that in a network marketing company, should you not be inspired by the desire to help others, then let self-interest be your guide. The better those you have sponsored do, the more money *you* make. In this fashion, network marketing puts a more human face on capitalism. By recognizing the power of profit motive, but then reconfiguring it so that your profits become dependent on the success of others, a new and refreshing business ethic is created. The dog-eat-dog mentality seen in today's merger-mad corporate sector is overpowered in these businesses by the ethic of people helping people.

Helping yourself by helping others. Pursuing a profitable and rewarding career that makes room for and strengthens the family. Finding opportunities to teach, mentor, nurture, and guide others to success. Regaining control over your own time and schedule. Living where you want and traveling when you want. Building retirement security for yourself and others while helping ensure that you and they will make it to retirement through exciting products that enhance personal health. These are the ingredients of a balanced life that so many seek but so few find. Tens of thousands of Rexall Showcase International entrepreneurs are convinced their personal searches are over. And they're ready to meet the world.

CHAPTER TWELVE

New Frontiers

On a clear, brisk Saturday morning in Las Vegas in December 1998, more than 1,000 well-dressed men and women weaved their way around the banks of slot machines and past the rows of card tables and entered the Jubilee Theater at 9:00 A.M. sharp. They were greeted by the mellow music of a saxophonist on a stage that was simply adorned with displays of Rexall Showcase International products. Shortly thereafter, Rexall Showcase International President Dave Schofield kicked off this daylong series of briefings, testimonials, and training sessions with a financial and strategic overview of the company's progress and future plans.

Having been to other network marketing meetings sponsored by different companies, I was struck by the seriousness of purpose on display at this one. It was a business meeting, not a rally. Virtually everyone was professionally attired. There were no chants, cheers, whoops, or hollers. No one rushed the stage after the speeches to get autographs from their favorite company or distributor "celebrities."

The presentations were heavy on factual information, business developments, and social trends, relying very little on what I call the "you gotta believe!" sloganeering. The greatest moment of enthusiasm among this group came when word leaked out about new products to be introduced—and when Dave Schofield revealed that in response to an industry-wide drop in stock prices, including Rexall Sundown's, the company would be revaluing stock options at a lower level, making them far more attractive.

Clearly this atmosphere marks a departure from the one normally associated with network marketing. As the industry moves more into the mainstream, Rexall Showcase International's meeting style will likely become the model for the future. Motivation, excitement, and even fun are all critical components to building a successful team, be it made up of employees in a traditional company or independent distributors in a network marketing concern. Yet increasingly, new entrants, particularly those from the professional world, are saying, like Sergeant Joe Friday used to do on *Dragnet,* "Just the facts, ma'am."

As it seeks to build its distributor force beyond today's, Rexall Showcase International's challenge is to retain its professional, upscale, serious demeanor while opening itself to potential recruits from other walks of life. Indeed, while the Las Vegas attendees appeared evenly split along gender lines with a broad cross-section of ages, little ethnic or income diversity was readily apparent—at least at this meeting. The children and babies I have seen disrupting other network marketing conferences with their cries and antics were nowhere to be seen here.

Still, the maturing process underway among network marketing sales forces will likely pay off for Rexall Showcase International and the industry in the long run, even if in the short run greater numbers of less serious recruits could be signed up faster using the more inspirational, take-it-on-faith approaches of the past.

It's happening overseas as well. The annals of direct selling's move into Asia and Latin America, particularly in developing countries, are filled with dramatic stories of thousands of poor but hopeful recruits standing in the rain and beating down doors to sign up for a small sliver of the American dream. But now a more cool-headed approach is taking hold. Dave Schofield reports, for example, that during a meeting with new and potential Hong Kong distributors last year, they peppered him with detailed questions about Rexall Showcase International's market capitalization and future business strategies.

Making the transition to a more businesslike approach should also pay dividends as network marketing companies confront government regulators in the United States and abroad. Unfair as it may be, a company whose management and finances are hidden from public scrutiny, which operates under a veil of secrecy while at the same time whipping thousands of citizens into a frenzy over its business opportunity, is sure to trigger the suspicions and paranoia of many governments, particularly the more authoritarian regimes of Asia.

It is against this backdrop of change in the industry and with the cementing of its own distinct identity, that Rexall Showcase International looks to the future. As Rexall Showcase International prepares to move into its second decade, as Rexall prepares to move into its second century, and as we all ready ourselves for the new millenium. Where does a small company that has already made a big mark on business, on health, and on the lives of many go from here to keep the momentum going? A big part of the answer rests in new markets, new products, and new technologies.

New Markets

Ninety-four percent of the world's population does *not* live in the United States of America. Most of the markets, consumers, and distributors of the future exist outside our borders.

Industries across the board have been recognizing this new global economic reality. Exports now account for between one-fourth and one-third of the entire U.S. economy, a dramatic increase in just twenty years. These international opportunities are not simply confined to the largest corporations. More and more medium- and smaller-sized businesses are getting into the act—and statistics show that, on the whole, firms that are engaged in international business pay higher wages, are more profitable, and are less likely to go out of business than those who do not participate.

Many Americans are uncomfortable with this changing economic landscape. Of course, they don't mind seeing our products sold overseas. That part is okay! But international trade is a two-way street. In order to be the world's number one exporting country and the world's largest investor in other countries, we must accept foreign goods and capital in our country. Some people are dissatisfied with this bargain. Furthermore, by linking our future so closely to markets elsewhere, when there is a downturn in those markets—as has been the case in Asia—we feel the impact here at home. People lose their jobs and livelihoods because of events in a far-away place and feel a loss of economic control. Finally, still others are troubled by our economic participation in countries that don't honor human rights or adhere to the same level of environmental and labor standards that we do in this country.

All of these concerns have recently prompted a growing number of citizens, politicians, and interest groups, ranging from labor unions to the religious right, to try to slam the door shut on the global economy. But such a course is doomed to fail. Other trading countries will be happy to sell the products and make the investments if we don't. Even more important are the tremendous opportunities we would be missing out on—not only to enhance our own prosperity but also to help other societies lift themselves up economically as well.

For network marketers—who take pride in a business ethic whereby you build your prosperity by helping others build theirs—the opportunities to apply that ethic on a global scale are tremendous. Today some 36 million people participate in direct selling businesses all around the world. Direct Selling Association President, Neil Offen, estimates that number could soar as high as 200 million over the next ten years. Think of the potential for a company like Rexall Showcase International to share its business opportunity and preventative health care products with the world's budding entrepreneurs.

The company and its leaders have already opened the business in Hong Kong, Korea, Mexico, and Taiwan. The Japanese business will debut in the spring of 1999. Rexall Showcase International has set as a further goal the establishment of operations in one to two countries each year for the next ten years. "What we do for health and for opportunity is needed all around the world," says Dave Schofield.

Reigniting the Asian Miracle

Asia is the first focus of this aggressive international expansion strategy. What has prompted Rexall Showcase International to head straight for the epicenter of the global economic meltdown to seek new sales, distributors, and growth? It's simple. Even in the face of the current crisis, Asia is where the people, profits, and markets of the future reside.

In his recent book *Megatrends Asia,* futurist John Naisbitt writes: "The Asian continent now accounts for half the world's population. Within five years or less, more than half of these Asian households will be able to buy an array of consumer goods—refrigerators, television sets, washing machines, computers, and cosmetics. And as many as a half billion people will be what the West understands as middle class.

"That market is roughly the size of the United States and Europe combined."

Naisbitt identifies other developments that make Asia a natural prospect market for a company offering products that focus on a healthy, modern lifestyle:

- The number of Asians in poverty has decreased from 400 million to 180 million since the end of World War II, even while the population has increased another 400 million.
- The growing middle class, not including Japan's, will have amassed $8 to $10 trillion in annual spending power shortly after the turn of the century.
- Currently, more than 80 million mainland Chinese earn between $10,000 and $40,000 a year. In South Korea, 60 percent of those who describe themselves as middle class make over $60,000 a year. One million families in greater Bangkok, Thailand, earn over $10,000 annually.

Naisbitt's analysis was completed before the financial crisis slammed many Asian economies. No doubt some of his projections have been slowed and skewed by that crisis. But as we assess Asia's prospects for recovery and its viability as a market for Rexall Showcase International, it is important that we keep several factors in perspective:

- Even in the face of global financial turmoil, economies like those of Taiwan, Singapore, and China are still growing, albeit at reduced rates of growth.
- Many analysts believe the worst is likely over in Thailand, Korea, and Hong Kong. They are on their way back.
- Asian cultures have long traditions of both entrepreneurship and interest in natural health remedies that make even weakened economies choice targets for a company like Rexall Showcase International.
- Economic insecurity traditionally spurs rather than dampens interest in network marketing opportunities. This is

particularly true in Asia, where the social safety net is far less developed than in Western economies. A modern economy like Hong Kong's, for example, does not even have a government-sponsored unemployment insurance program. If you're out of work, you're out of luck.

A recent article in the *Far Eastern Economic Review* focusing on the example of Thailand underscores this last point: "Decades of rapid economic growth have left officials unprepared to deal with the swelling numbers of unemployed created by Thailand's recession. Averse to expensive Western-style welfare systems, the government faces growing anger over its perceived indifference to unemployment."

Even in the face of such criticism, don't look for fiscally strapped governments in the region to try to play catch-up now. "Thailand, like the rest of Asia, has been reluctant to cast the sort of costly social safety net often provided by the West," the magazine continues. An economic advisor to the Thai Prime Minister quoted by the *Review* then discusses an interesting alternative approach: "Thailand does not aspire to emulate the Western unemployment insurance scheme. . . . Rather than handouts, the present administration prefers soft loans toward the establishment of small-scale businesses."

The magazine is quick to point out that the standard "soft loan" envisioned by the Prime Minister's office is just $235, which it says won't go far toward the creation of small businesses. We know from our discussion that there is only one kind of small business you can get off the ground with that kind of money—a network marketing business!

In a later article, the *Review* confirms that elsewhere in Asia "necessity is the mother of invention for . . . laid off workers as they flock to become their own bosses."

For example, China's economic reform program—which centers on the closing or restructuring of inefficient, money-losing state-owned firms—could generate an astounding 17 million layoffs of urban workers throughout the country. The government is actively encouraging affected workers to start small enterprises and gives great prominence to those who have succeeded in the hope that others will follow their lead.

Several years ago, one Shanghai couple lost their jobs at a manufacturing facility. With a young son to support, they made ends meet by cleaning restaurants and office buildings at night. As soon as they were able to save enough money, they started their own cleaning business, securing several contracts at prime Shanghai office towers. The company now employs thirty-five people, nearly all laid-off workers, and the couple clears $2,500 in profits a month. "I only wish I'd been laid off earlier," says the husband.

Another couple, Zhuang Hongwei and her husband Chen Junming, both lost their jobs in state-owned facilities in the early 1990s. In 1996, the *Review* reports, "they set up a food preparation and delivery business.

"Zhuang's idea was quite clever. She reckoned there was an opportunity to create ready-to-cook meals for the growing number of two-income families that are too busy to shop and cook for themselves."

Today the couple's company employs 100 laid-off workers who prepare and pack the meals and then deliver them on bicycles to clients all over Shanghai. The government eagerly promotes their success story. "The couple, in their early 30s, have been lionized in the Shanghai press, interviewed on local radio shows, lavished with national awards, and even introduced to U.S. President Bill Clinton on his swing through the city in July 1998," the magazine reports. Zhuang believes that "if you have talent you can excel. In the past you were assigned a job from the time you left school. Now society is becoming more equal and there's fair competition."

The fact that many Asians are responding to adversity by becoming entrepreneurs is one more reason why the Asian miracle, chronicled so frequently through the 1980s, will be rekindled.

Hundreds of millions of aspiring middle-class Asians, seeking both new opportunities and products to match their new, more upscale lifestyles, make this region a prime target for Rexall Showcase International.

The company has already begun to lay down a marker in this giant market, with operations established in Korea, Hong Kong, and Taiwan. Rexall Showcase International President, Dave Schofield, reports that 2,000 distributors attended the company's one-year anniversary celebration in Hong Kong in November 1998. "After just a year in business there, we went from nowhere to the fourth largest network marketing company in Hong Kong," he reports.

November 1998 also marked the opening of Rexall Showcase International in Taiwan. Three thousand aspiring distributors attended the opening ceremonies. This prosperous island economy of 21.5 million people is already home to well over two million people engaged in direct selling, who collectively generate nearly $2 billion in annual sales. That's an astoundingly high percentage of the population that has embraced this business model, a population that has become increasingly focused on health, fitness, and a modern lifestyle.

The Promise of Japan

Japan, the second largest economy in the world and the most important country in Asia, is today suffering its worst national crisis since the end of World War II:

- The economy has not only stopped growing, but in 1998 it also actually shrunk.
- The banking and financial systems, burdened with more than $1 trillion in bad debts, are in need of serious reform.
- The political system, heavily reliant on consensus and back-room deals among interest groups, seems incapable of decisive action.

- A nation that revolutionized the auto and consumer-electronics industries has dropped far behind international competitors in its embrace of information technology.
- The implicit lifetime-employment compact, under which Japanese professionals would remain with one company their entire working lives in exchange for income and retirement security, has fallen victim to American style layoffs.
- The distribution system contains multiple layers of inter-mediaries, causing Japanese consumers to pay exorbitant prices for the basic staples of life.
- Inefficient land-use policies, which this crowded country can ill-afford, have forced most families into residences that are exceedingly small by Western standards and typically located up to two hours away by train from their places of work.

It is perhaps no wonder that many leading observers have found a crisis of confidence and spirit among the Japanese. But as one who has spent considerable time in Japan, who once opened an office there, who haltingly speaks some Japanese, and who has met many top leaders and average Japanese citizens alike, I am confident that the nation will soon pull out of the current crisis and lead the world in many respects once again.

Consider the achievements of this remarkable people. Approximately 127 million Japanese inhabit an island country smaller than California—a state we consider crowded with its 36 million residents. These crowded yet isolated conditions have given rise to a strong emphasis on social organization rather than individual initiative. Japan is a beautiful but mountainous country and home to virtually no natural resources. Its entire oil supply and many other essentials of an industrial economy must be imported.

The ravages of fire, earthquake, and war have on a number of occasions during this century forced Japanese society to almost completely rebuild itself. Just over fifty years ago, the major urban centers of the country were reduced to rubble (largely due, of course, to its own complicity in the tragedy of World War II). Within a generation, the Japanese had rebuilt their country and within two generations had become a world economic powerhouse.

I have no doubt that the same perseverance and determination to triumph over adversity will be marshaled again as Japan confronts its current challenges. But the Japan that reemerges will be a different Japan, one that combines the best qualities of its hardworking, consensus- and team-oriented culture with new approaches to career, business, lifestyle, and commerce.

And that's where network marketing and Rexall Showcase International come in. All the trends driving this industry and this company forward in the United States are even more pronounced in today's Japan:

- The aging of the Japanese demands different approaches to health and retirement security.
- Economic dislocation and the lack of fulfillment in the corporate and professional worlds find many looking for alternative incomes and more satisfying entrepreneurial careers.
- An overregulated, overpriced economy is squandering national and consumer wealth, prompting the Japanese to seek more efficient ways to buy and sell and do business.

A society steeped in tradition and slow to change is today readier than it has ever been to try a different path. The groundwork has already been laid for firms like Rexall Showcase International, thanks to pioneering companies like Amway, which understood nearly twenty years ago that certain aspects of Japanese culture are very much in sync with their kind of business—selling based on relationships, families, and an intricate series of networks. Today, Japan is home to an estimated 2.5 million direct sellers, who account for more than $30 billion in annual sales, nearly 40 percent of the world's total. With companies like Rexall Showcase International on the verge of entering this market, those numbers are going to go way up. Let's look more closely at how and why.

For years, experts have tried to reconcile the fact that while Japan's overt trade barriers—tariffs and quotas—were low by global standards, trade deficits remained stubbornly high. In my own trade development work on behalf of the State of California, the number one complaint I heard from frustrated exporters and marketers was that the rigid Japanese distribution system simply froze them out. They could get their products past the *shores* of Japan, but not into the *stores* of Japan.

What these U.S. companies may not have realized is that many domestic Japanese companies, particularly smaller start-up products and services firms, faced similar barriers. For Japanese consumers, the result has been artificially high consumer prices—the highest in the world. As *Fortune* magazine once described it, "Even when the economy was booming, Japan had one glaring problem: a distribution system as labyrinth as a shogun's palace. Everything a consumer bought—made in Japan or imported—had to weed through the books of as many as half a dozen middlemen. Some of them never took possession of the products, but all extracted a toll, creating the world's most exorbitant prices. A bottle of 96 aspirin tablets cost $20, and not just because of the strong yen."

Richard Johnson, who heads Amway's operations in Japan, explained the challenge this way in a recent interview: "It's not so much that the government or society has said foreign products can't be distributed. It's rather that the major manufacturers have created a very disciplined distribution channel that doesn't permit any outsiders in, be they foreign or domestic."

He then goes on to cite the beer industry as an illustration of the kind of "discipline" he was talking about: "Up until a short time ago, Kirin Brewery Co. basically dominated the wholesale network. It was very hard to introduce a new product, regardless of all the advertising a company did, because then bars could only order what their wholesalers would provide. And the wholesaler might say, 'If you want a case of Sapporo or Suntory [other brands of Japanese beer], you've got to take 10 cases of Kirin."

Given that direct selling is based on the notion of bypassing the normal distribution chain, this form of business represents nothing less than a direct, frontal assault on the Japanese business establishment. In the case of Amway, Richard Johnson recalls, "Our start-up was very difficult. We did very little business in the first five years."

Yet with increasing fervency, the supposedly complacent and organization-minded Japanese have embraced direct selling and the entrepreneurial business opportunities it carries with it. "All the ferment, and the new willingness of Japanese consumers to give American innovations a chance, are creating opportunities for U.S. companies to transplant to Japan successful business strategies from back home," explains *Fortune*.

But economic insecurity and dislocation also help explain the motives of Japanese network marketers. "Many of the distributors are refugees from the stultifying, hierarchical world of Japanese big business," observed Yumiko Ono in the *Wall Street Journal*. "They want to work for themselves and be paid according to their performance, not according to their seniority. The growing number of people who do marks a big change in Japanese society."

For many Japanese, the current economic crisis has ruptured the traditional compact between employers and employees. University graduates struggle to find the jobs they were all but promised when they entered school. Middle-aged men find themselves laid off with few prospects for being rehired. Again, these are familiar circumstances for Americans during times of economic slowdown, but for the Japanese they are unheard of in the post–World War II era.

Yet other employees are not pushed out; they want to jump out to a bigger, more interesting challenge in their professional lives rather than simply don the company uniform and work one job at one firm every single day from age twenty-five to sixty.

The yearning for more satisfying career options has grown especially strong among Japanese women. Japanese homemakers have long held sway over their country's consumer economy—controlling the household purse and purchasing decisions, carefully parceling out allowances to their "salaryman" husbands for their bowls of noodles at lunch and after-work beers and snacks with colleagues.

However, for all the immense collective spending power enjoyed and exercised by Japanese women, it has proved to be a boring dead-end existence for many. For a brief period in early adulthood, Japanese women experience some measure of freedom: higher education away from home, perhaps an international trip to Hawaii or California with classmates, a job in a nice office in Tokyo. Then, for most women, comes marriage. One or both spouses leave home in the predawn darkness for the ninety-minute train ride to work and return exhausted long after dark. If the wife works, she will likely return first to care for children and take care of the house. While conditions are changing for working women in Japan, the glass ceiling in the corporate world remains a formidable and foreboding barrier. Meanwhile, her husband will typically arrive home much later, long after the children are asleep, after an evening of fraternizing with co-workers, which is deemed an important and almost obligatory part of a man's career.

Economic insecurity and vigorous questioning about the quality of life received in exchange for all those hours of commuting, working, and socializing have sparked great interest in alternatives like network marketing. Explains one Japanese Amway distributor to the *Wall Street Journal:* "People are starting to wonder what they could do as a single gear in a company. They want to have fun. They want to do something. But they have nothing. When they join Amway, there's something that clicks."

Forbes magazine recently assessed network marketing's appeal here as follows: "[The] be-your-own-boss pitch may be greeted cynically in the United States, but in regimented Japan it finds a willing audience, especially among housewives and frustrated salarymen."

The stage is clearly set for a boom in network marketing in Japan. Rexall Showcase International has an opportunity to lead that boom because in addition to offering the Japanese a practical alternative to the lack of financial security and professional fulfillment, the company's products address the needs of a health-conscious population that is aging even faster than America's.

Consider these dramatic developments and projections:

- Japan boasts the world's longest life expectancy, but the number of births continues to drop.
- In other words, the population is not only aging, but also shrinking. The country is home to 127 million citizens today; by 2020 it will drop to approximately 124 million.
- Today 15 percent of Japan's population is sixty-five years of age or older, up from just 8 percent in 1975. By 2020, 27 percent will fall into that age group.
- By 2005, Japan will have one retiree receiving public health care for every two workers supporting the system.

With the number of workers available to support Japan's health and retirement systems shrinking and the number of elderly depending on those systems growing dramatically, the nation is caught in a demographic squeeze. How are the medical establishment and health insurance and delivery systems responding to this ticking time bomb? Not very well, according to Professor Iwano Nakatani of Hitostubashi University. "The ills of Japanese health care are well known: Doctors, providers, researchers, and pharmaceutical manufacturers are overregulated, and patients underserved," he writes.

"Special favors are available for the few who have the money or the personal connections to skip the long waiting lines. There is little room for initiative, and all attempts at reform are thwarted by those who oversee it. Government policymakers, for their part, seem trapped in the postwar mindset of rationing and regulation.

"The current government health insurance system simply cannot expand to meet the coming demand," Professor Nakatani concludes.

Most Japanese are already highly responsive to traditional Asian health remedies using food-based and other natural ingredients. The aging of Japanese society and the burdens that will place on the current health care system will surely accelerate their embrace of preventative health care products.

Anticipating an enthusiastic response to the Rexall Showcase International products and business opportunity, the company formally announced its entry into the Japanese market effective in spring 1999. The speculation leading up to this announcement and the announcement itself created a buzz of excitement on both sides of the Pacific. I indicated in the introduction that it was a Japanese American friend working in Tokyo who first alerted me to the Rexall Showcase International story, based on all he was hearing and reading about the company in Japan. At least one Japanese American distributor has moved back to Tokyo in anticipation of building an organization there in 1999, once Rexall Showcase International formally begins operations.

U.S. distributors will find a rich vein of sales and recruiting opportunities to tap once the Japan market opens. Residents of Japan should now be getting ready to answer these questions:

- Would you like to use and share with your family and friends natural, nontoxic, food-based health products that promote a healthier lifestyle and can forestall expensive emergency medical procedures later in life?
- Do you wish to start a business of your own for a very low cost and an initial time investment of just ten to fifteen hours a week, while maintaining your current profession?
- Would you like to create a separate and secure stream of income to protect against the possible loss of other income as Japan weathers a severe recession?

- Do you want to create the possibility, after a reasonable period, that you can free yourself from the tremendous time demands and pressures of the corporate world and other professions and thus spend more time with your family and in leisure activities?

If residents of Japan respond positively to any one of these questions, then they should take a serious look at Rexall Showcase International as it prepares to enter Japan.

While Asia has been the initial launching pad for RSI's global expansion, other key markets are being researched and seriously considered. Following the Japan opening, expect to see the company focus on Australia, Canada and then to Europe. The Mexico business is now in an expansion mode. Latin America (especially Brazil) is prime Rexall Showcase International target as well.

New Products

As Rexall Showcase International expands its reach around the globe, new products targeting the unique needs and wants of global customers are being developed and introduced.

Rules governing product requirements vary in the overseas markets Rexall Showcase International has entered. As a result, most of the company's U.S. products require modifications before they can comply with a country's specific regulatory requirements and be offered for distribution. For example, Rexall Showcase International offers an Oyster Calcium product and an herbal tea that are exclusive to Korea, because oyster shells offer the only type of calcium that meets Korean regulatory requirements.

Rexall Showcase International Hong Kong recently introduced three especially designed herbal products featuring formulas designed for that market (including Omega-3 Fish Oil Softgels). In Mexico, Rexall Showcase International has introduced Essential

Fish Pill Concentrate 3000/300, which provides active protective nutrients that can impact cholesterol levels, vital organs, and the cardiovascular circulatory system.

Weaving one's way through the international maze of varying regulations, standards, and business practices is a complicated and expensive undertaking. It's one more reason network marketers need to evaluate the strength of the parent company that will back them up in their business when choosing an organization to join.

Long-term success also requires a flexible company that responds to changing markets, consumer needs, and challenges from competitors. To stand still in any sector in today's economy is to fall backward. New products, improved products, fresh packaging, and participation in innovative research must all be undertaken to keep consumers and distributors motivated and competitors at bay.

At the February, 1999 annual conference, this year being held in Albuquerque, New Mexico, Rexall Showcase International will announce a breakthrough product in the area of weight loss: BodySynergy. Conceptually a different approach to the stubborn problem of weight reduction, BodySynergy is expected to revolutionize the $50 billion weight loss industry. At the heart of this project is the recognition that the brain is the fundamental site of appetite and cravings. While traditional methods of weight control have always focused on the stomach, this state-of-the-art technology points to the existence of a "Reward Cascade" in the brain: a complicated neural pathway that relies on specific neurotransmitters to maintain feelings of well-being and satiety. The theory: keep the brain satisfied and in turn the dieter will feel contented and satisfied. Clinically tested and proven, the product helps you resist food cravings and thus limits caloric intake.

BodySynergy is available as a complete weight loss system which includes: Enzygen, a product designed to support the digestive system; Diet Essentials, packed with key vitamins, minerals and nutrients critical for proper metabolism and good health; and Bios Life 2, a nutrient-rich mix that supports healthy cholesterol levels and creates a "full" feeling in the stomach by adding fiber to the diet. The total weight loss system, marketed as BodySynergy, is Rexall Showcase International's four-pronged approach to weight reduction and offers real hope to dieters looking for new solutions to an old problem.

But weight loss isn't the only arena that Rexall Showcase International is entering; it's exploring the new frontier of herbals. Traditionally used for centuries by cultures around the world, herbals have recently dominated the health picture here in the United States. A recent article in *The Los Angeles Times* estimates that 40% of Americans regularly use herbal products. Baby boomers, especially, are looking for natural ways to live longer and healthier.

In response to this spiraling market demand, Rexall Showcase International has formulated five new proprietary blends that offer significant health benefits in the areas of mood enhancement, stress relief, healthy immune function, heightened sexual performance, and sharpened mental function. The products—BalanceBlend, CognoBlend, ImmunoBlend, PassionBlend, and CalmingBlend—are blends of exotic botanicals cultivated in remote locations around the globe. Rexall Showcase International's global search yielded herbs backed by years of well-documented research that has made its way into peer-reviewed scientific journals.

BalanceBlend is designed to lighten and lift your mood, this product features St. John's wort in a proprietary blend of mood-balancing and adaptogenic herbs to promote a feeling of well-being.

CognoBlend is designed to promote mental clarity and alertness, this product features the proprietary ingredient PTI-00703. This breakthrough in neuroscience is believed to have amyloid-inhibitory actions and thus may be a powerful ally in supporting brain function.

ImmunoBlend promotes healthy immune function with a proprietary blend of herbs. This product features Echinacea as the primary ingredient which studies have shown helps support the body's natural defenses especially during the cold winter season.

PassionBlend was created to help support sexual function and libido, this unique mix of herbs features Swissoats A111®, a patented combination of green oats extract, nettle extract, and sea buckthorn fruit to help maintain vitality and endurance.

CalmingBlend is for those stressful times, reach for this all-natural combination of herbs that helps your body soothe away everyday stress and strain. Features Valerian, Kava Kava, and Ashwagandha among others.

All herbal products are free of excipients and meet pharmaceutical standards for purity and quality. In short, Rexall Showcase does everything *scientifically* possible to bring you products you can rely on.

Another product debuting at the February 1999 conference is aimed at supporting healthy joint function. Shifting demographics that point to an aging population have made scientists increasingly aware of the effects of aging on our bodies. Millions of Americans leading active, energetic lifestyles don't want to be restricted by the wear-and-tear of aging joints and their limiting effects on mobility.

Approaching this concern from a nutritional as well as a homeopathic perspective, Rexall Showcase International has developed a kit that: 1) nourishes both bone and cartilage while it 2) relieves symptomatic pain and discomfort. Total joint support is accomplished through a complementary strategy—combining the latest breakthroughs in nutrition with the time-honored traditions of homeopathy. For those baby boomers who want to maintain flexibility and healthy joint tissue, the Osteo-Basics Kit can extend their years of activity with its two components: Osteo-Essentials (nutritional) and Osteo-Blend (homeopathic). In addition, Rexall Showcase International is sponsoring independently conducted clinical research that in the words of Dave Schofield, "could prove to the world the important role our patented fiber products like Bios Life can play in lowering cholesterol and maintaining cardiovascular health."

NEW TECHNOLOGIES

How does the individual distributor attract new people in new markets to proven products and a proven business opportunity? Or bring new products to new markets around the globe? The answer lies in technology. Rexall Showcase International has fully embraced the concept defined and described by Richard Poe in his groundbreaking book called *Wave 3: The New Era for Network Marketing*.

"The most advanced network marketing companies today stress simplicity above all. They use computers, management systems, and cutting-edge telecommunications to make life as easy as possible for the average distributor," he writes. In Poe's conception, "Wave 3" represents a new phase of individual entrepreneurship that marries old-fashioned relationship selling with cheap, easy-to-use information and communications technologies.

Rexall Showcase International and companies like it have thus made it easier than ever for individuals to start and run their own business—right from their home in the community of their choice—and gather customers and downline distributors from all over the world. For a relatively few dollars of initial investment, you can operate what in many respects is a "virtual business"—a company without walls, a warehouse without inventory, a workplace without a workforce, a backroom without a billing or accounting department, an appreciating asset without capital or risk.

A senior executive at IBM recently observed that it is possible today to build and run a profitable multinational business from a home office equipped with a phone, a computer, a fax machine,

and a modem—and we've been introduced to many Rexall Showcase International distributors who have done just that! The biggest
bookstore in the world, she further observed, is not really a store
at all. It's a "virtual" bookstore on an Internet Web site called
Amazon.com.

What has empowered today's entrepreneurs and puts so much
business potential within their grasp is the speed at which new
communications technologies are made available and accessible to
the average person. While technology is becoming ever more complex in what it can do, it is at the same time becoming simpler to
use and cheaper to buy.

Consider that the capacity of the microprocessor is doubling
every fifteen to eighteen months and will continue to do so for
the foreseeable future. The IBM executive I spoke to illustrates
the impact of this development by recalling that just ten years ago
she attempted to perform a particularly complex function on the
largest mainframe computer her company had to offer—the kind
of computer that used to fill an entire room—and "brought it to
its knees." Today, she does the same function with ease on a
"think pad" at her desk!

A recent article in *Success* magazine sums up the marriage of
network marketing and entrepreneurship and technology this way:
"[Multilevel marketing] is creating a whole new marketplace outside the box of TV advertising, storefronts, inventory, and middlemen, and has the power to render the conventional retail world
obsolete. That power arises from the union of modern technology—computerized record keeping and telecommunications—
with the ancient art of schmoozing."

And John Fogg, editor of *Upline,* pinpoints the role technology
can and should play in building a network marketing business
when he observes, "All of the tools and technology free you up to
focus on that one most intangible part of this business, which is relationships with your people. Your job is to develop your people
and support them in building your business."

Rexall Showcase International has embraced this vision of technology and is pushing it to new frontiers. Rexall Showcase International Online features a "distributors only" site where they can place product orders, check sales volume, and process new distributor applications on a twenty-four-hours-a-day, seven-days-a-week basis. The information is encrypted to safeguard privacy. A second system, the REX automated voice response system, takes orders by phone for those distributors away from their computers or not yet online. Customers may also place online and telephone orders, with his or her distributor receiving full credit automatically for the sale.

Alongside these capabilities is Rexall Showcase International's Virtual Voice messaging system, which not only allows busy entrepreneurs to send and receive messages, but also serves as a motivational tool that lets distributor leaders send announcements and business-building tips to their downlines. The Autoship program, whereby a customer's order is refilled regularly on a routine basis not only enhances product sales, but also eliminates unnecessary paperwork and order processing. And of course, the audiocassettes featuring pitches from top distributor leaders eliminate the need for many in-person business presentations so that the businessperson can direct his or her focus to only the most serious prospects.

With the company assuming much of the burden for order taking, processing, and shipping, the distributor is, as John Fogg indicates, freed to build his or her organization. In addition, these technologies give the business a more modern feel, helping it break away from the image direct selling companies have had in the past—where being in the business meant your garage, den, and car trunk would be filled with boxes of product and precious hours would be spent delivering them. Technology has thus become a critical component in the industry's ability to attract more upscale, better-educated, busy professionals.

In these ways technology—from the simple to the sublime—has been put to work at Rexall Showcase International. Already, 20 percent of the company's business is coming in electronically. But the most important future development as the company expands overseas will be a global seamless computer system and compensation plan. As Dave Schofield explains, "Most competitors, when they open in a new country, essentially make you start all over again in the sponsoring process. What our technology will enable distributors to do is build a global organization and receive one commission check for worldwide sales volume.

"This means, for example, that you can be based in Las Vegas, sponsor someone in Los Angeles, who sponsors someone in Taiwan, who sponsors someone in Mexico, who sponsors someone in Dallas—and it's all part of one organization," Dave says.

"With our global seamless computer system and our international expansion plan, distributors will make money and grow their businesses even while they sleep—because [they will] be "open" for business in all time zones, twenty-four hours a day, seven days a week."

CHAPTER THIRTEEN

A Time
for Choosing

Preventative health care is and will be one of the fastest-growing industries on earth as populations around the globe live longer, grow more prosperous, and sharpen their personal focus on fitness and the quality of life.

Network marketing is already reshaping the marketing and sales strategies of major industries. Going forward, it has the potential to fundamentally alter how we work, where we work, how long we work, and how we get paid. This in turn will re-shape our relationships with family and friends, as balance is restored between work and leisure, between professional life and home life.

Put these two dynamic forces against the backdrop of growing economic insecurity and dissatisfaction with established health care practices, and you have defined the conditions that could make Rexall Showcase International one of the most significant companies of the next decade and beyond.

The question facing those who share this assessment, who are attracted by this industry, and who are excited by the possibility of making a positive difference in people's lives while enhancing their own physical and financial health is, Do you choose to be a part of this vision?

Only you can answer that question, and as you attempt to do so, let me anticipate a few practical doubts and concerns. Only after pushing through this underbrush will you be able to see with clarity whether Rexall Showcase International's "prescription for success" is the right prescription for you.

I'm still skeptical and confused about network marketing. So much of what I've seen and heard suggests these businesses are phony pyramid schemes set up to take advantage of people like me.

When I began my own examination of this growing but still unorthodox approach to business, some of my own friends and associates—many of them from highly skilled professions—criticized me for writing favorably about multilevel marketing and condemned the companies as pyramid schemes. Finally I challenged one to explain his remark.

"You just called this company a pyramid," I said. "Just what is that anyway?"

"Well, it's when a company, um, you see . . ." My friend stammered for a minute as he tried to explain the precise meaning of his criticism, what it means, why it was bad, and how it applied to the company in question. He didn't get very far.

Clearly both the news media and word of mouth had poisoned his attitude against companies such as Amway, Excel, and Rexall Showcase International. He had simply heard that these companies were pyramids and that pyramids were bad; therefore, the companies must be bad. Case closed.

Unfair as these judgments are, the fact is that network marketing still suffers from an image problem. Someday the image will catch up to the facts, which are these:

- Direct selling is catching on across America and around the world, drawing an estimated 36 million participants today, rising to as high as 200 million a decade from now.
- Companies and individuals who had never considered it before are now adopting it in varying degrees.
- It is changing the way we buy and sell goods and services.
- It is providing additional income, options, and opportunities to millions of people who otherwise may have had none.

What in fact constitutes an illegal pyramid? U.S. federal and state laws are subject to different interpretations. But generally it is seen as an operation that is built almost exclusively on paying people to sign up as distributors—with little or no focus on gathering actual customers to buy products and services. New recruits are required to buy large quantities of a product up-front, with no opportunity to return unsold inventory for a refund. Intense pressure is applied to get them to buy expensive tapes, instructional manuals, and tickets to meetings and rallies. Essentially, participants feed off each other, with the big fish consuming the resources and energies of the smaller fish.

The entire multilevel marketing industry faced a legal day of reckoning in 1979, when the Federal Trade Commission ruled that Amway was a legitimate business and not a pyramid. The ruling set forth many of the ground rules network marketing companies abide by today.

By all measurements, Rexall Showcase International passes muster easily. Its parent company, Rexall Sundown, has been in the consumer health products business for years, selling those products through retail sales and mail order long before it started a multilevel marketing arm. That makes it pretty simple to establish that the economic foundation of the company rests on products rather than recruits.

It is a publicly traded company subject to the full scrutiny of investors and financial regulators. It discovers, patents, develops, and manufactures its own unique products in sophisticated laboratories and other facilities and then markets and sells these products. While strong emphasis is, of course, placed on sharing the multilevel opportunity with others, the end consumer remains the core of the business. As we have seen in numerous distributor stories, particularly those coming from the medical profession, it was positive experience with the preventative health products that led them to try the business, not the other way around.

Yet as we also remember from those accounts, a great deal of skepticism about network marketing remains—in part because it is still a relatively new approach for most people. Doubts are also fueled by competitors who have sunk fortunes into hiring sales forces, buying ads on television (an industry which itself has much to lose), and developing intricate retail distribution networks. They have a vested interest in keeping suspicion alive, even though many of them are migrating toward direct selling approaches themselves.

In *Wave 3,* Richard Poe draws an interesting parallel in his discussion of network marketing's bumpy road to acceptance and legitimacy: "New ideas are always attacked and rejected at first. In its earliest days, franchising endured similar abuse from the press and from the corporate world, and for almost identical reasons. . . .

"The media attacked like hungry barracuda. Exposés featured destitute families who had lost their life savings through franchising schemes. Attorneys general in state after state condemned the new marketing method. Some congressmen actually tried to outlaw franchising entirely.

"How quickly things change! Today, franchises account for 35 percent of all retail sales in the United States."

I didn't get all this education and work this hard to rise in my profession simply to end up as a salesman. Wouldn't becoming a network marketer be a big step down?
Although it enjoys a proud tradition in many cultures, selling is inexplicably frowned upon by many in our status-seeking society.

251

You see this attitude most among people with impressive-sounding jobs but modest incomes and no control over their time. Since I work among many highly skilled and status-oriented professionals in law, politics, and the corporate world, I confront such condescension all the time.

For many from the so-called boomer and yuppie generations, building an independent business through network marketing simply doesn't jibe with their carefully cultivated image as worldly-wise, white-collar professionals. They crave title, rank, status, and most importantly, security. They seek the identity and social approval that comes from their association with a prestigious company, a big-name law firm, or an important government agency.

Yet this attitude is changing. As the security of the status jobs disappears and the frenetic, pressure-cooker lifestyles they bring lose their appeal, many upscale professionals who used to dismiss network marketing are talking a close look at companies like Rexall Showcase International. There are only so many times smart people can watch others build much happier, more rewarding lives before they conclude, "Why can't I do something like that?"

When we look at the successful people in Rexall Showcase International, we see doctors, lawyers, professors, and corporate executives as well as teachers, homemakers, real estate salespeople, and small-business owners. We see those who came to the business at a time when they were down and out and those who were sitting on top of another field but wanted something different. In short, if you're looking for someone like you who has succeeded in Rexall Showcase International, chances are you'll find that person—a person willing to coach and lead you along the same path.

I don't think I'll be very good at selling. Can I do it?

The number one roadblock to successful selling is the fear of rejection—that most natural of human frailties. I know it well. I've enjoyed great prestige and influence serving in top government political and policy positions. A few years ago, after eight years in the

California governor's office, I attempted a transition. I left my powerful position to build a communications consultancy in which I had to sell my professional services. After years of having executives knock on my door, suddenly I had to knock on theirs—without title or status. I had to rely on people I thought were my loyal friends. At least they acted that way when I was in my political office. But I quickly learned the hard truth behind President Harry S. Truman's admonition: "If you want a friend in politics, get a dog!"

Within a year I closed my consultancy and beat a retreat back to another government office at less pay and stature than I had before. I was going backward.

It was only after reflecting on this experience and meeting many people in network marketing that I realized that what held me back was not the perceived slights of friends and acquaintances, but my own fear of rejection. I did everything possible to avoid having to overtly promote my services or myself because I was afraid of being turned down. During sales calls on prospective clients, I failed to exude confidence and ability. I turned sheepish when the subject turned to money. I avoided "the close"—that most important moment of any sales effort, thinking I would follow up later in a phone call. Then I found myself ducking those calls! Meanwhile, too much time would elapse between my initial presentation and those follow-up calls. Thus, whatever interest I had been able to spark had dissipated.

One advantage a company like Rexall Showcase International offers those who fear they would have experiences similar to mine are distributor leaders like Todd Smith, Randy Schroeder, and Stewart Hughes, who came to the business in its infancy with their own strong backgrounds in sales. They helped the company devise a Team Building system that helps you to present the Rexall Showcase International opportunity effectively but through low-pressure techniques such as distributing audiocassettes. This approach serves to quickly sort out those who are likely to tell you no, so that you can focus on those likely to tell you yes. Leaders in your upline are also willing to get on the phone with you in a three-way call to assist you in making the "sale." And the compensation plan has been designed so that, in the words of Renée Stewart Chittick, "you don't have to go out and recruit the world."

Furthermore, the exclusive Rexall Showcase International products have proven to be so intriguing to people that even those not wanting to start a new business will engage you in a discussion about their health and very likely become your customer. So even when you are being rejected from a recruiting standpoint, you may still be helping your business by acquiring a new customer. This helps build confidence and it removes much of the sting of rejection.

Most importantly, all the top leaders in Rexall Showcase International can tell you about the many rejections they have had along the way—and even so they are successful and have maintained a positive attitude. Being rejected is not a barrier to success in this business. It is simply a normal and natural part of the journey to that destination.

Does anyone really get rich in this kind of business, except for the few at the top who got in early?

Turnover is high throughout network marketing. People move in and out of the business all the time. In some cases, it's because they've achieved the relatively modest set of goals they established at the outset: to earn some extra money to pay off bills, buy a new car, or take a vacation. Others join because they like people and want opportunities to socialize and broaden their network of friends, but they never focus on making the business their full-time occupation. Some are initially attracted by the low entry fee but don't enter with a serious level of commitment. As Randy Schroeder has pointed out, it is because the cost of entry is so low that the cost of exiting is low as well—and so many people head for the exit. Some who leave Rexall Showcase International or businesses like it have soured on the experience and believe the deck was stacked against them. The riches they envisioned didn't materialize, and they blame the company.

It is true that most people who join network marketing never develop incomes to a level where they can leave their full-time jobs. As with most endeavors, you get out of it what you put into it. As we have discussed, those who do work direct selling businesses full-time earn above-average incomes. More than half of the full-timers make over $50,000 a year. One in ten makes over $100,000.

Would it be possible for you to attain the levels of income, success, and happiness attained by the Rexall Showcase International distributors profiled in this book? Absolutely. Are there any guarantees? Absolutely not. Is it worth it for you to give it a try? In the final analysis, only you can answer this question. Much depends on the status of your own life and your own individual definition of what success and happiness mean to you.

The question of market saturation is a hotly debated issue in network marketing. Companies that have been around a long time and have produced large numbers of wealthy distributors go to great lengths to insist that similar success is equally possible for the new distributor who joins that company today. They point to the opening of new international markets and the introduction of new products and services as reasons why you would not be "too late to the party" if you joined now. And they underscore that experience, longevity, and a proven track record, particularly in an ever-changing industry like network marketing, offer you the stability, credibility, and support you need to get your business off the ground.

Others say that you have a superior advantage by getting in at the beginning of a network marketing venture, that there is greater teamwork and more enthusiasm because people like being part of something new and different. If you do well in a newer venture, you're more likely to be singled out for recognition and publicity by the parent company, which gives you further opportunities to lead and build your organization.

Both sets of circumstances have their strengths and weaknesses. Many people joining Rexall Showcase International today say they find a company at that ideal intersection of experience and stability on the one hand, but novelty and entrepreneurial enthusiasm on the other hand. The company has been around long enough to learn from mistakes, perfect a system, and develop a track record. But it still retains the willingness to change and be open to new people and ideas. And with both the domestic and international market for innovative health products barely scratched, most are convinced that the best opportunities for the individual distributor lie ahead.

But the fact remains that not all of the value in this business can be calculated in dollars and cents. Many Rexall Showcase International distributors argue that the personal growth and time freedom they have earned from their businesses far outweigh the money on their scale of values. The "fringe" benefits in the business can be pretty good!

- As parents, you have more time to spend with your children.
- After a lifetime of working for someone else, you get a chance to build something for yourself and your family that might be worthwhile even if you were to make less money.
- You can face the prospect of old age with financial security and improved health, so that you don't become a burden on your children and grandchildren.
- You can make lifelong friendships among highly successful, positive people, people from all walks of life, all around the country and the world, whom you would never have met otherwise.
- You can enjoy the satisfaction that comes with helping others to better health and more secure finances by becoming a teacher, mentor, and leader in your organization.

Most people do not become rich in network marketing, but many become *enriched*. Suppose you're half of a working couple, and both you and your spouse are holding down forty-hour-a-week jobs outside the home. Maybe you're earning $40,000 a year but paying thousands of dollars a year for child care you don't really trust. How much income from a business like Rexall Showcase International would it take to convince you to quit that job and stay home with your children, considering all the money you wouldn't have to spend on child care and all the other ancillary benefits you would gain by being a full-time parent *and* a business owner?

For most of us, it would take less than that $40,000—especially considering the potential of earning much more.

I'm too busy. How could I ever find the time for a business like this?

The "no time" excuse is probably the most commonly invoked reason why people turn down a friend's or associate's invitation to join a business like Rexall Showcase International. There's no question that time poverty is a serious issue for two-income families struggling with the demands of both careers and children. However, a recent book by time-study experts John Robinson and Geoffrey Godbey suggests that most of us could find the time to undertake a new activity, like starting a Rexall Showcase International business, particularly since the opportunity has been designed for part-timers with full-time occupations.

It's a question of priorities. These researchers examined the lifestyles of 10,000 survey participants and concluded that contrary to popular belief, Americans actually have more free time now than at any other period during the last thirty years—an average of forty hours a week.

If you find that difficult to believe, consider that the study found a wide gap between people's perception of how busy they are and the reality. Study participants were asked to keep detailed diaries of their activities. When the results were analyzed, it was found that on average, working men perceived that they spend 46.2 hours on their paid, professional work. In actuality they spent 40.2 hours. Women perceived 40.4 hours but actually worked just 32 hours.

What's the reason for the exaggeration? "Being busy has become a status symbol," Robinson told *Newsweek* recently. "As you say time is more important to you, you become more important yourself."

"In fact," the magazine goes on to report, "Americans are working fewer hours than they did in 1965—about five fewer hours for working women, six fewer for men."

Here's one other key finding: On average, working Americans spend fifteen of their forty free hours a week watching television. If, like me, you're one of them, perhaps it's time to reorder priorities and reexamine how readily we invoke that most common of excuses: "I don't have time."

Even if I overcome my skepticism about network marketing, how do I determine if Rexall Showcase International is the right company for me?

The fact is that there are bad apples in the barrel of network marketing companies. All you have to do is read your junk e-mail on America Online or other Internet service to find schemes built on flimsy premises with lousy or frivolous products, impossible compensation plans, and dubious ethics.

Here is a five-step checklist you can use to examine Rexall Showcase International or any other company you are considering joining.

1. **Check with the Direct Selling Association in Washington, D.C. at 202-293-5760.** This is a trade group that not only promotes this industry but also polices it and spurs the process of developing, applying, and enforcing "best practices." Ask the DSA whether the company you want to join is a member. Why is this so important? Because in order to be a member, the company must sign and adhere to a strict code of ethics. Rexall Showcase International is a leading DSA member and a signatory to the code of ethics.

2. Examine the company's track record and professionalism. Is it on a steady growth path? Does it have professional management that is accessible and open to distributors, customers, and the media? Does it present itself professionally in the community, the press, its newsletters, web site, product information, and meetings and conventions?

While nothing untoward should be seen in those network marketing companies that are privately owned, the fact that a company is publicly traded, as Rexall Sundown is, and thus open to scrutiny by investors and regulators, makes your process of "due diligence" easier and more complete.

3. Examine the marketing and compensation plan. Does the plan make sense to you? Is it simple and user-friendly? Can you secure the support and training you need (at a reasonable cost) to succeed? Network marketers like to say "You may be in business *for* yourself, but you are not in business *by* yourself." Make sure that is the case in the company you want to join. Many factors contribute to a particular company's culture. In Rexall Showcase International, the personalities of the leaders, the relative newness of the venture, and the shared passion for and personal health experiences with the products, have combined to create a culture that appears highly cooperative and supportive of the new distributor. And according to Dave Schofield, "our compensation plan generates one of the highest payouts in the industry. Sixty-three cents of every sales dollar is returned in distributor commissions. "Last year we paid a total of $80 million in distributor commissions. Just think what that means when we're a billion dollar company!"

4. Do you believe in the products? Are the products you will be selling ones you can really get excited about? If not, your potential customers will sense it and you will not be successful. Will you use the products yourself? Is demand for these products going to grow or are they part of a passing consumer fad?

Clearly, few subjects generate as much interest or passion as our health. Demand for preventative health care protocols and products with proven health benefits are already exploding and will continue to do so well into the next century. There is no scenario one can envision which suggests that our aging society's interest in products that lower cholesterol, lead to weight loss, and promote breast and prostate health without side effects will diminish in the coming years.

5. **Talk to the people who are working in the business.** You are likely to find people just like you, people from your occupation and income and education level, who recently experienced the same kind of questioning and exploration. Ask them how they succeeded and, just as important, ask them about the mistakes they made. Question them about those who failed. What did the dropouts have in common? Cross-check that information against the level of time and effort you honestly believe you would bring to the business.

Follow this five-point checklist and you'll be on your way to knowing whether Rexall Showcase International is the right company for you.

Former President George Bush, a man of great integrity and dedication, was nonetheless mistaken when he once derided "the vision thing." The "vision thing" is nothing more and nothing less than a road map to the future. It is a person's, a company's, or a country's statement of what they stand for and who they are—an articulation of goals and mission. Ideally, it gives you a plan that is hopeful and ambitious, yet flexible and realistic. And when others share your vision and vice versa, it can be powerful, exciting, and personally fulfilling. It's on that basis that most of us raise our families, make lifelong friends, join organizations, pursue our careers, and become something larger than ourselves.

Having such a vision and joining with others in its fulfillment has never been more important than it is today. That is because every one of us is adrift on an ocean of change. And as the saying goes, the more things change, the more things change.

Changes on the economic and technological fronts happen with dizzying speed. They're confusing and hard to define. The rules never stay the same. The economy is growing stronger, yet many workers are losing economic security. The stock market continues its rise into the stratosphere, with 66 million new Main Street Americans playing in it for the first time. Yet rather than better preparing us for retirement and the infirmities of age, those investments are merely hedges against a possible collapse of Social Security and our private pension plans. We see the global economic downturn and mega-mergers both triggering tens of thousands of layoffs. Almost overnight, the second largest company in any industry can simply disappear, bought up or gobbled up by the first. Meanwhile, other companies say they can't find enough qualified workers here and must import them through immigration. What is going on here?

Technology is changing so fast that even the experts who invent and produce it don't fully comprehend where it's headed. It was only fifteen years ago that one of the leading computer company executives in the world said he couldn't see any reason why the average citizen would ever need or want to have a personal computer at home! Just several years ago it was predicted that our television set would double as our computer monitor—now it appears that our computer monitors will also serve as our televisions, stereos, and telephones. In fact, the whole concept of long-distance telephony could simply cease to exist, as calls around the world become aural e-mails routed through local access numbers.

At a laboratory at the Massachusetts Institute of Technology, hundreds of experiments are underway fusing developments in media, communications, and technology in ways that could further impact daily life—some in a disturbing fashion. One project would enable historical novelists to call up on the computer screen a visual depiction of, say, a London street in the 1840s, which they would then describe in print as they "walked" down that street. Another would attach a computer chip to your person so that your where-abouts and activities could be traced inside your workplace. Still another computer device worn on your person would access a picture and information data-bank as you encountered a person on the street, at a party, or in a meeting and remind you of that person's identity and background. That invention would be great for politicians trying to act as if they were our best friends!

But with all these advances can come monumental miscues. Consider the so-called Y2K computer problem—brought about by the fact that without corrections, most computers will read the year 2000 as 1900 instead, because when they were programmed, they were taught to read only the last two digits of a given year. Despite the hundreds of billions of dollars that must be spent to fix the problem, as well as the potential for global economic disruption, there is something strangely and reassuringly human about Y2K. No matter how sophisticated technology can be, in many respects it is still only as "smart" as the mere mortals who build it are!

How are we to steer through such tumultuous change and still feel in control of our own lives and futures?

The Chinese word for crisis consists of the characters meaning danger and opportunity. Some see change as a crisis defined by only by danger. It will be those of us who see this change as opportunity rather than danger who will survive, succeed, and prosper in the new millennium. What Rexall Showcase International offers to many is a roadmap to the future—a vision for retaking control of one's health, finances, and future. Rather than surrender to economic and technology-driven change, the company believes it can make those changes work for the benefit of those who share this vision. For every downside we can find in today's economic and social climate, the company, through its products and business opportunity, has tried to define an upside.

Are you financially tied to your current profession, even though you see your income potential from that profession shrinking and maybe disappearing altogether? A Rexall Showcase International business is designed to be built alongside your existing job, starting with just a few hours a week.

Do you now have to choose between advancement at work and spending adequate time with your children at home? A successful Rexall Showcase International business can eliminate the need to have to make that choice—permitting you to have a rewarding career, run out of your home, while being there full-time for your children.

Have you always wanted to be your own boss but don't have the tens, maybe hundreds of thousands of dollars it takes to get started in most small businesses? Rexall Showcase International offers a low-cost business opportunity almost anyone can afford.

Are you grateful to medical science for tremendous breakthroughs that enable you to live longer, but concerned about remaining healthy and physically independent in your later years? Rexall Showcase International products enable you to take control of your health just as the business opportunity allows you to take control of your financial life.

Todd Smith puts it simply: "When you give this business a try, the worst thing that happens is you take some products that improve your life. The greatest risk is in failing to act."

Improve your health. Grow your wealth. Strengthen your family. Take charge of your life. Help others do the same. That's Rexall Showcase International's "Prescription for Success" and what it can mean to you.

Index

A

Achievement levels, 68–69

Advanced Exfoliating Body
     Polish, 60

Aestivál, 60–61
     Body Care System, 60–61
     Facial Care System, 60
     Hair Care Collection, 61
     Outdoor Body Protection
          Formulas, 61

Aetna, 127

Aging population, 12, 94–112

Alternative medicine, 120–125

Amazon.com, 245

American Association of Retired
     Persons (AARP), 99–100

Amway, xi–xii, 44, 249
     in Japan, 235–236

Anorexia, 144

Antioxidants, 49, 51–52

Archives of Internal Medicine, 123

Arthur Anderson, 84

Ashwagandha, 243

Asia, 75–77, 228–232

AT&T, 78, 84

Audiocassettes, 172, 246

Avon, xii

B

Baby-Boom generation, 98

BalanceBlend, 242

BankAmerica, 78

Bankruptcy, 201

Bartlett, Richard C., 34, 36

Beasley, Tim, 143–145

Berry, Julie, 173–174, 211–214,
     219

Berta, John, 173–175, 211–212,
     213, 214

Bio-C™, 53

Bios Life 2®, 10, 50–51, 118,
     123–124, 142–143, 210
     in BodySynergy, 241–242

Bissmeyer, Lynne, 202, 204, 215

Bissmeyer, Tom, 201–206, 215

Black cohosh, 125

Bloomfield, Ellie, 154–155

Body Care System, Aestivál,
     60–61

BodySynergy™, 54, 241–242

Boeing, 78

Bonuses, 64

Brand names, 10

Breast cancer, 113–114

Breast health program, 58–59

Virtual Voice messaging system,
222, 246
Vision Complete™, 59

W

Walgreens drug stores, 18
Wall Street Journal, 237
Water-filtration systems, 61062
Watkins company, 181
Watson, George, 146–149
*Wave 3: The New Era for Network
Marketing* (Poe), 244,
251
Weight loss products, 54,
241–242
Weitz, Barbara, 117

Weitz, Ron, 117–119
White, Elnor, 103
White, George, 103
Witlow, Win, 152–153
Women, 36
in Japan, 237
working women, 109
Women's Formula Plus™, 58–59
World Federation of Direct Sell-
ing Associations
(WFDSA), 32–34
World Trade Organization
(WTO), 76

X

Xerox, 78

About the Author

JAMES W. ROBINSON is a veteran author, communications executive, and strategic counselor to senior political and business leaders. His seven previous books, all published by Prima, include *The Excel Phenomenon; Empire of Freedom—The Amway Story and What It Means to You; Doing Business in Vietnam;* and *Better Speeches in Ten Simple Steps.*

Described as the "entrepreneur's advocate" by the *Washington Post,* Mr. Robinson appears frequently in the media and before business groups to discuss issues and topics affecting free enterprise. He is a member of the board of directors of the National Chamber Foundation, a public policy think tank, and a frequent panelist on the popular "Week in Review" public affairs television program in Los Angeles.

Mr. Robinson began his career researching and drafting radio scripts and newspaper columns for Ronald Reagan. He also served former California governor George Deukmejian for eight years as speechwriter, communications director, and chief international trade advisor. Other positions include communications director for former California attorney general Dan Lungren and press secretary to former Representative Jerry Solomon of New York. He is currently a senior vice president at the U.S. Chamber of Commerce, where he advises the organization's president and CEO Tom Donohue and other senior corporate executives on business, political, and communications strategies.

A native of upstate New York and a graduate of Middlebury College and the University of Maryland, Robinson now divides his time between residences in Washington, D.C., and Los Angeles, California.